Eddie Doherty

Wisdom's Fool

A biography of
St. Louis de Montfort
priest, poet,
founder of Religious Congregations,
miracle worker, preacher of the Cross
and prophet of the
Reign of Christ through Mary.

Eddie Doherty

Wisdom's

Montfort Publications
BAY SHORE, NEW YORK 11706

fool

Nihil Obstat:

> Reverend Francis X. Glimm, S.T.L.
> Censor Librorum

Imprimatur:

> Vincent J. Baldwin, D.D., S.T.L., Litt.D.
> Auxiliary Bishop of Rockville Centre

Printed in the United States of America
ISBN 0-910984-09-3

Contents

LE VENERABLE prêtre Louis-Marie GRIGNON de MONTFORT missionnaire apostolique Instituteur des Missionnaires de la Compagnie de MARIE et de la Congrégation des Filles de la Sagesse mort en odeur de Sainteté en 1716 âgé de 44 ans

Come, O Wisdom, come!
Hear this, a beggar's plea.
By Mary's womb, by every gush
Of Blood her Jesus shed for me,
Confound me not, nor bid me hush . . .

St. Louis de Montfort

How this book was written.

There are broadly speaking two ways of writing the biography of a Saint. The first is to do extensive and thorough research on the person's life, with on-location interviews with people who knew the Saint well or who were close to him in life. This, of course, is possible only if the above-mentioned witnesses are still alive and able to testify. But when your hero was born three hundred years ago, this is hardly feasible. And so an author must confine himself to repeating or rehashing what scores of others have written before him . . . unless a biographer can combine a second method with the first, namely by sitting, so to speak, at his master's feet and listening to him speak through his writings and his spiritual legacy to mankind.

And this is precisely the way Eddie Doherty wrote the biography of St. Louis de Montfort. For many years, he read and reread de Montfort's writings on Christ, Incarnate Wisdom, and on Mary, His Mother. He consecrated himself totally, as an individual, to Christ through Mary, according to de Montfort's way of spiritual life. As he endeavored to live this Montfortian ideal in his daily life, his meticulous research on the Saint's life gradually took on flesh and blood. The result is this gripping story of a man who was misunderstood by many of his contemporaries, but who reveals himself in and through his writings, and whose influence on the spiritual life of the Church can only be compared to that of the masters of the Spiritual Life.

Christ, Incarnate Wisdom, so identified Himself with His Cross, de Montfort loved to repeat, that we can say that "Wisdom is the Cross and the Cross is Wisdom." And since the Cross, as St. Paul says, is foolishness to the world, Eddie Doherty may well call de Montfort "Wisdom's Fool."

Preface

It is with joy that I see Fr. Eddie's biography of Louis de Montfort for he played such a great role in Eddie's spiritual development.

He made a pilgrimage, factually, to write this book, with a French speaking priest, Rev. Paul Bechard. He followed step by step as far as he could the places where de Montfort lived in France.

But Eddie's pilgrimage wasn't only factual or geographical, it was deeply spiritual. As he went from place to place he absorbed the spirit of the man he was writing about.

He brought back with him the heart of Louis de Montfort.

The heart of a strong man who understood that if he wanted to know God he had to go to Him through Mary his Mother. Because, as Eddie put it so very simply when he told us about it, God the Father brought forth his Son through Mary. So it was only natural that we should go to Him through Her.

Now that we are returning to the biblical sources that bring forth Mary, the life of Louis de Montfort becomes more significant, more important, more understandable. Fr. Eddie Doherty never ceased through his whole life to bring people face to face with Mary because he wanted them so passionately to love Her Son, to love the Trinity. He felt that the way to Them was Mary and he loved to explain the essence of the consecration to Mary of Louis de Montfort.

I am happy that this biography is being published in our days when men seek answers to the many spiritual problems besetting them and the life of de Montfort will be, I know, read for he is one of the mystics of the Catholic Church toward whom the face of modern youth is turning more and more.

Catherine Doherty

1 Montfort, the Man

Men, like lighted candles on an altar, shed most light on their surroundings, and reveal themselves most clearly, when they begin to burn toward the end of their wicks. So it seems fitting to begin the story in the small French village of Roussay, in the Spring of 1714, where, and when St. Louis Marie de Montfort neared the end of his life.

Roussay was in sad need of a mission, though its people didn't think so. They resented the fact that such a priest as Father de Montfort had been chosen for them. He was used only in desperate cases. He was sent only to the most hardened of sinners, the most wretched of people. He was the talk of all Brittany. Because of his ability to work all day and all night. Because of his severity to himself, and his generosity to others. Because of his love of Jesus, whom he called "Divine Wisdom." Because of his extraordinary love of Mary. (The more Wisdom he possessed, the more he loved her.) And because of his love for crosses.

Perhaps this generation would resent his coming, even more than Roussay did. We have made gods of comfort, ease, good food, choice liquors. We demand a forty-hour work week—even a 32-hour week. We have given ourselves to Science, Surgery, Space and Speed; and to more efficient ways of warfare. Therein lies such wisdom as we have acquired in how many hundreds of thousands of years! We shun crosses for ourselves, but not for others. And our devotion to Mary has grown flabby.

What would he say to us? How would he feel about our insistence on luxury, our goal to make a million and retire—then make another million—our arguments over the new liturgy and the various sections of Vatican II, the attitude of so many of our priests, and Religious who seek soul-mates rather than souls.

Suppose he spoke to all of us about living in poverty, chastity, and obedience? Or about accepting frustrations, disappointments, defeats, insults, slights, and other crosses, as gifts of God, meant to make us

11

happy? Or about going back to the practice of saying the Angelus, and the Rosary, every day? Would we believe his teaching that the folly of the Cross is the wisdom of the cross? Or would we remain snug and smug in our religious apathy?

St. Louis de Montfort is a greater challenge to us than he was to the wine-guzzling citizens of Roussay. And perhaps we need him more than they did, to return to sanity, zeal, true Wisdom, true Christianity.

He felt that his own generation was bad. "Evil floods the earth," he said, "and sweeps along with it even those who call themselves your servants. The world is desperate. Impiety reigns. Your sanctuary is profaned, and the abomination of desolation is to be found even in Your holy places. O just Lord, avenging God, will You leave us all to perish? Are we to see another Sodom and Gomorrah? . . . All, even the least sensitive, groan beneath the weight of the sins of Babylon . . . Who is on Your side? Hardly a single fighter comes to Your banners . . . Let me cry everywhere: 'Fire, fire, fire! Help, help, help! The House of God is burning . . . Help for our brothers whom they kill, for our children whom they murder, for our good father whom they stab!' "

One wonders what he would say of this generation.

Louis, though he is one of the great saints of all time, is not too popular. People believe that if they get too close to him, especially in prayer, he will obtain crosses for them which, otherwise, they would not have. Nobody likes a cross, apparently. Yet people everywhere, when they have crosses to bear, turn to St. Louis and ask his help.

Roussay had heard a few things about Louis. He was a great gaunt ox of a man. He was a stupid boor. He was a surly peasant in rags. He was a nice singer and a thundering preacher. He was a profound scholar. He was a fool. He was a dangerous heretic. He was a saint, a tremendous saint!

Seven most holy bishops had driven him out of their sees, out of their sight. Not just one, my friends, but seven! Name of a name! Of course those prelates were Jansenists. Jansenists had strange ideas about Our Lady, the mother of Jesus. They felt that devotion to her tended to weaken or destroy the devotion a man should pay to Father, Son, and Holy Ghost. They couldn't abide Father de Montfort's love of her. They couldn't tolerate him. He was Mary's knight, Mary's slave, Mary's missionary, Mary's troubadour, Mary's fool. And he had an argument they could neither stomach nor answer:

"How can they have God for their Father, if they do not have Mary for their mother?"

12

He might also have asked, "how can they obtain Wisdom unless they go to the Seat of Wisdom"? But people would never understand such talk as that. Wisdom to them, was the wisdom of the world—as it is to this generation. The wisdom of today is more sophisticated than the wisdom of Montfort's day. We know how to make a buck, how to get by, how to "gold-brick," how to "stall." We "get by."

St. Louis was filled with the wisdom of heaven; and with the love of the Queen of heaven. She was in his blood, in his breath, in his smile, and in the light that sometimes flashed from his eyes. She was in his speech. He spread devotion to her wherever he went, as the south wind spreads the healing wonder of the Spring. His message was simple.

The closer one came to Mary, the closer he drew to God. The further he went from her, the further he went from God. Mary had brought Jesus into the world. She wanted to bring the world to Him. Her Son was the Life and the Way. She was the door that opened on the Way. A beautiful wide door. A place where a man could rest at the end of a long journey, and bathe his hands and his feet, and put fresh cold water on his face. A place where he could enjoy peace and love, and angelic music, before the door swung open so that he might find the Way and the Life.

His critics and his enemies charged that he wanted every man, woman, and child to be a slave of Mary—or, as he put it, a slave of Jesus in Mary—to wear chains in token of that slavery, and to say the Rosary every day. To them, as to many of us today, the Rosary was "old-fogey," an unnecessary mumbling, a silly repetition of simple prayers—and a Roman custom, not a French one. If anything wasn't French in de Montfort's day, it wasn't really Catholic. Not in France. Today we might say it isn't American.

Louis believed that if he could put a Rosary around a sinner's neck, the fellow would never get away. He believed that "if you say the Rosary faithfully every day until your death you will receive an eternal crown of glory, in spite of your sins."

To him the Rosary was the Book of Wisdom translated into beads of wood or bone or glass, which even a blind man could read. It was a trysting place where the good Lord met His children and gave them a share in His sorrows, His joys, and His glories. It was a fence around a garden of holy mysteries. It was a long, long caravan, heavily laden with graces. A Christian should prize it as a duchess prizes her necklace of fine pearls. He usually had a Rosary around his neck, another

13

dangling at his side, and maybe a dozen more in his pockets, for some-body always needed, or wanted, one. And he wore a chain around his waist as a sign of his loving slavery to Jesus through Mary.

St. Louis was the kind of man who does everything superbly well. He was an artist, a sculptor, a singer, and a poet. He wrote hymns and set them to popular tunes, so catchy that a listener simply had to sing with him. He wrote books that will never die. He had such strength you wouldn't believe it. Once, a fellow missionary said, the priest had pulled up a tombstone two ordinary men couldn't lift. Why he did such a thing the missionary didn't say; he wasn't interested in the reason, only in the fact. Another missionary saw the priest take a full barrel onto his knees. He didn't say what was in the barrel, nor why de Mont-fort wanted to hold it. But a full barrel is heavy, no matter what it con-tains.

The priest had a very big nose, long hair, dimples in his cheeks, the stubbornest chin in France, and a pair of eyes that made you wish you had lived a better kind of life. When he smiled, he had you. You couldn't get away from him. He never wore a hat, for he realized he was always in the presence of God; so his hair was forever struggling with the wind. And when the dust was in it—the thick dust of the road —and the sun was shining on it—why, it put a great and glorious halo about him.

His cassock, or soutane, or whatever you might call it, was little more than a sack. It didn't look clerical at all. His collar was not white. It was blue. Blue for Our Lady. His shoes were never good enough for the roads he traveled, nor for the climates he encountered. Therefore he left "bloody footprints" wherever he walked. Yet always, even when he was weary, even when the dust and the flies and the glare of the sun beset him, even when the rain lashed at him from cold gray skies, he could lift up his heart and sing to the Lord. Sometimes it was one of his old hymns, but often it was one he composed as he walked:

> "What ill or evil, Lord, can harm
> This joyous heart that You alone can charm?
> I love You more with every breath,
> So how can I fear life or death?
> To love You, Father, is to live and sing
> The songs the angels sing their King.
> God alone in every cell of me!
> God alone! For all eternity!"

14

Montfort, the Man

St. Louis was the beggar of beggars, the poorest of the poor. He lived, through most of his life, on what divine Providence gave him in the way of alms. He walked farther, worked harder and longer, endured more punishment and abuse, ate less and slept less, than any other man of his time. His only luxury was the bit of straw he put into his mattress. No man can find clean straw every day while he is traveling; and sometimes a wanderer has to sleep where he can, indoors or out. But always St. Louis could find a suitable rock for a pillow. He usually walked wherever he was going. He usually carried a crucifix and a small statue of Mary, both of which he had carved.

The people in Roussay were more than curious about Father de Montfort when they heard he had worked marvels of healing, and that God had worked at least one miracle for him. In the town of Bréal, where the Jansenists had stirred up violence against him, a man had attacked him with an axe. But, just as the fellow was about to strike, his arm was paralyzed. The weapon fell to the ground, and the man fell on his knees.

And there was that man in the diocese of Luçon who gouged the poor by lending them money, then charging outrageous interest. De Montfort had touched the miser to repentance. But his wife had untouched him, with her greedy eyes and vicious voice; and he was worse than ever. The priest predicted that unless they amended their ways he and his wife would die in poverty. They wouldn't have enough money left to bury them. Their children would be poor too. Also, they would be barren. All these prophecies were fulfilled to the letter.

It would not be good to rile such a man. Still there were those in the village who must test every stranger, even as they tested their vintage wines.

St. Louis was weak when he came to Roussay, and near exhaustion. He had scarcely recovered from several terrible months in a hospital. He had suffered from an abscess. The surgeons had finally removed it —without anaesthetics, of course, since there were none then—and they had bled him many times. Louis had welcomed the pain, because it was sent by God—as all crosses are.

He had an intense love for the cross. He never sought one, for he wanted to do not his own will but God's; yet he knew there was great joy in the acceptance of all crosses. He could never be too grateful for these precious gifts of heaven. Hence he could say to someone he loved: "May God bless you and give you many little crosses."

He admitted he was a man of violent temper, which he did not manage always to control; yet he endured slights, snubs, insults, and disap-

15

pointments with great patience. Control of his temper let him evaluate everything in a spiritual light. He did use violence, sometimes, to gain souls he could not win with tenderness or charm. But neither was Christ always gentle. Once He took a whip into His divine hands that He might cleanse His Father's house of money-changers.

Many a night St. Louis shouldered his way into some dingy and quiet brothel, to turn it into a babel of noise, prayers, screams, sobs, and wicked curses. He entered the place armed with nothing but his Rosary. He knelt in some central spot, and, in a voice that could be heard for great distances, began to say the Sorrowful Mysteries.

Men always yelled at him. Some would start angrily in his direction—until they saw how powerful he was, and how menacingly holy. Then, usually, they would slink away, one by one. The women, frightened at first, then indignant and abusive, would stay near and look at him. They couldn't leave. They couldn't make him leave. They wished they could, for he was ruining their business. Sometimes one or two, or several, would drop to their knees. Sometimes one or two would weep, in shame or sorrow, remembering other days. Sometimes a woman would leave the place when he finally rose, gave his blessing, and departed.

He hadn't been in Roussay long before he discovered its besetting—or besotting—sin. The people were more interested in the fermented spirit of their grapes than in the blessing of the Holy Spirit. Their hearts were in their vineyards. Their piety was only wine-skin deep.

He decided to preach against the sin of intemperance. During his first sermon, to a handful of people, a group of men mocked him in loud and vulgar shouts and songs. They were carousing in a café close enough to the pulpit to be heard by the congregation. They were enjoying themselves. And some of the flock were snickering as they listened to the preacher and the plastered revellers. It was evident the priest was annoyed. What would he do? Would he stop talking and visit those men? Would he coax them to be quiet and respectful? Would he chide them for their language and the volume of their noise? Would he try to reason with them? That would be worth watching!

St. Louis finished his sermon, gave the people his blessing, stepped slowly out of the pulpit, then walked swiftly toward the café. This time he didn't have anything in his hands but holy anger. The drunkards greeted him with friendly derision. He stared at them for a moment. He wasn't smiling. They peered at him, a tall, emaciated death's head come to scold them! Some of the boys who had followed him from the church jeered too.

16

St. Louis said nothing, except with his fists. For the first time since he came to Roussay, men had a chance to see how big, and to feel how hard, those fists were. He struck them down and let them lie. He overturned tables and chairs. He smashed glasses. He walked over the bodies of stunned and sobered hoodlums, and went slowly back up the street.

Every time he preached, thereafter, in the awakened town of Roussay, he found a most respectful and attentive congregation. And when he left, walking away, singing in the rain, many men accompanied him for a mile or more. And many of the women cried as though they were at a funeral!

Yet, perhaps, the story should begin, not in Roussay in 1714, but in Dublin, Ireland, in 1921. For St. Louis' mission to that city, 205 years after his death, was a greater triumph than he had ever achieved in his life.

He had not yet been proclaimed a saint. He was known only as Blessed Louis. It was not until July 20th, 1947, that he was solemnly canonized. But the people who read his little book, whether they were Irish, English, German, French, or any other nationality, were certain he was a saint; for only a saint could write so clearly and so lovingly about the Virgin Mary.

Even if he never had been canonized he would, in Dublin, still be considered one of the greatest saints who ever walked this sinful earth. Ireland gave him a hundred thousand welcomes, in 1921, and took him to her heart.

2 Mary's Legion

St. Louis didn't come to Ireland directly from heaven. He visited many other countries in Europe first. He came not as a ghost, but as a book: "True Devotion to Mary." He had to wait until the book was translated into English before he could visit the land of saints and scholars. He was heartily welcomed there.

Among those most delighted with his coming was Matt Talbot, the humble workman who is now in heaven, waiting to be canonized. Matt read the book, and informed a friend that it had lifted him from earth to heaven. He loaded himself with chains, some of which cut into his flesh and rusted. And he induced at least thirty of his friends to become slaves of Mary and wear her chains. Matt dropped dead in Granby Lane, in Dublin, on a Trinity Sunday not many years ago, as he was coming home from Mass. After the Sisters in the hospital found the chains on, and in, his starved and mortified little body, Matt began to live gloriously in Ireland, and to attract more followers than ever. John A. McGuinness, one of his most devoted friends, imitated him in every way, even to the use of a wooden pillow. (Matt couldn't find a rock he could rest his head on. He substituted a block of oak, and he made his bed of planks.) There are many men and women in Dublin who believe that McGuinness too will someday be proclaimed a saint.

Another Irishman to whom de Montfort brought a glimpse of paradise was Frank Duff. When he first encountered the book, translated by Father William Faber, Duff threw it aside. It was dull, uninspired, and hard to read. The sentences were too long and involved. And there were too many Latin phrases. Duff, then concerned principally with the Society of St. Vincent de Paul, told his spiritual director his reaction to "True Devotion."

"Read it again," the priest bade him. "And, this time, read it on your knees."

Duff obeyed, and reaped such a harvest that he was able to sow the first field of a new crop of saints—the Legion of Mary!

19

The Legion was born in Myra House, headquarters of the Society of St. Vincent de Paul, on September 7, 1921, when the church was celebrating the First Vespers of the feast of Our Lady's birthday. And so, says Duff, "it came into life with the first fragrance of the feast . . . we were really born with Mary."

"One of the frequent topics of discussion at the time," he writes, "was Grignion De Montfort's *True Devotion to Mary*. The idea was very unusual then—almost unknown in fact—and not clearly grasped even by those of the group who were prominent in proposing the devotion. All, however, were so deeply interested in it that a special meeting was summoned for the purpose of discussing it and enabling all to grasp the idea. 'I have often,' said one of those concerned, 'tried to place that particular event; it must have been almost immediately before the start of the Legion, a matter of a month or so. It was just like making an electric connection and something happens. We spent the evening talking about the devotion. I do not say that even so we understood it fully, but at least we were in ardent sympathy with it. We desired to practice it. Then at once the Legion happened.' "

The Legion had fifteen members to begin with. Today it has more than ten thousand times that many. Naturally, or supernaturally, its first great miracle was the closing of Dublin's "red light" district, one of the ugliest, dirtiest, most murderous, and most infamous spots in all of Christendom. No gambler, learning that the Legion, in its white young purity, meant to attack the center of all wickedness, would have placed his money on it. But what the gamblers didn't know was that Duff's children worked with the Wisdom of God, not the wisdom of men, and that their prayers were more powerful than the might of hell. St. Louis Marie didn't have to bet on them. He knew what they could do. He had seen them, and thousands like them, (in a happy hour spent in some silent chapel), and he had written about them in his little book.

"Toward the end of the world the greatest saints will be those most zealous in praying to Mary . . . saints who will tower in holiness over other saints, even as the cedars of Lebanon tower over little bushes . . . They will be brands of fire, ministers of the Lord who scatter the fire of divine love everywhere. They will be like arrows in the hands of the mighty mother of God . . . They will be clouds flying, with great thunder, through the air, moved by the breath of the Holy Ghost . . . They will shower down the rain of the Word of God and of eternal life. They will thunder against sin . . . They will strike the devil and his legions with their lightning."

Fools rush in where angels fear to tread. Prayers also rush in, to the very throne of God, demanding miracles that make the angels gasp. The attack began quietly, with Mr. Duff and two women visiting several of the houses where street-walkers lived. The trio invited the girls to make a retreat. The girls had no intention of heeding this advice. A retreat would mean a drastic change of life. The girls would have to give up drinking and smoking as well as luring men. They would have to get married, go to work, or end their lives in some stuffy convent! Not a chance!

But the foolishness of God overcame the stubborn wisdom of the women. Thirty-one of them promised they would make the retreat and begin new lives. Duff arranged the retreat with the Sisters of Charity at Baldoyle, some miles out of Dublin. Twenty-three of the thirty-one women kept their promise. They were all drunk, or half drunk, as they got into the big bus that took them to Baldoyle. Duff wasn't surprised. He knew the girls had to fortify themselves to face this tremendous crisis.

He faced something of a crisis himself; for he had no place to house the girls after the retreat; and he could not let them go back to their old neighborhood. Overnight he succeeded in convincing a government official or two that they should give him a house for the girls. Fortunately the officials had such a house, and it was empty. They gave it to Duff—who then had to beg, borrow, or buy mattresses, beds and bedding, furniture, pots and pans, and everything else—including food—the women would need. He hung a picture of the Sacred Heart in it, called it Sancta Maria, put two Legion women in charge of it, and waited for the retreat to end.

Suppose it ended in defeat?

It ended in an amazing victory.

Not one of those twenty-three women ever went back to her old life. Two were Protestants. They asked to take instructions in the Catholic faith. They were solemnly baptized, some time later, and made their First Holy Communion as fervently as though they had lived most of their years in a convent school. They had everybody in the place "weeping buckets."

The fight continued until every "street-girl lodging house" had been visited, and most every inmate had been freed. But the real fight had not begun. Now they must attack the district itself, the organized houses of prostitution, which had been the devil's own for a hundred years or more.

21

The area seemed to have powerful protection, for the police had never seriously tried to close it. Every house sold liquor, without a license, and without paying any attention to the rules that regulated its sale. When other places shut down for the night, men who wanted a drink would go to Bently Place. The price was high; but a thirsty man didn't seem to care about that. He could get all he wanted to drink. Men went there every night. Men were robbed there every night. Some were beaten when they complained. Some simply disappeared, and nobody ever inquired too much about them. It was dangerous to do that. The place swarmed with tough-looking men who didn't like to answer questions.

The Legionaries knew what danger they were facing in their determination to rid Dublin of this patch of hell. They were afraid, but they didn't falter. Frank Duff learned the name of one of the women in a certain house. Mary Lyne. Her address was Number 9, Bently Place. He thought this knowledge providential. If anybody asked what he was doing in this district he could say he was looking for Mary Lyne. He didn't know how providential it really was.

At noon on March 22, 1923, Duff and a Legion woman went to Bently Place. They hesitated. Should they knock on the first door? They remembered the rhyme they had said so often. "Mary Lyne of Number Nine." They knocked on the door of Number 9. There were five women in the room, one in bed. The woman in bed was Mary Lyne and she was dying. She hadn't had a doctor; she didn't want a priest. But Duff carried her out of there, and took her, in a cab, to the nearest hospital.

The doctors didn't think she would live for an hour, but she lived for two months. And, says Duff, she made an "extremely fervent" preparation for death. On several occasions she told Legionary visitors she hoped she would not recover, as never again would she be "so well prepared." She died with a priest in attendance, and a Rosary in her hand.

The Legion gave her a funeral and buried her in consecrated ground. Some of her old companions came to the funeral and met the girls of the Legion. Sinners and saints mourned together. There was a strange joy in this mourning, which the sinners couldn't help noticing. Why shouldn't they know joy too, like the Legionaries? Mary Lyne had escaped not only this hell on earth, but also the hell that was to follow it. Why couldn't they escape too? Vice looked long at virtue, and was charmed.

22

Duff and his Legionaries walked through the district frequently thereafter. Nobody stopped them, nobody threatened them—yet there was always danger.

Many women came to Sancta Maria. They came in small groups. They came alone. In time, Duff figured there were only 40 women working in Bently Place. Then he went after the owners of the various houses, asking them to retire from business. One woman who owned many houses did close up. Two others promised, then reneged, then demanded money. Duff finally called on the police for help. There was an honest man at the head of the force. He raided the district, and ended its hundred horrible years.

Duff busied himself getting honest tenants for the vacant rooms—so that nobody would start another hell—then headed a Legion procession through the neighborhood. Three priests, who had just concluded a mission in the Pro-Cathedral, led the way, accompanied by a cross-bearer and acolytes with lighted candles, and followed by the Legionaries. Holy water was sprinkled everywhere, for the first time in a century. The vacated brothels were blessed, and each had a picture of the Sacred Heart nailed to the door. And, on a high wall that separated Bently Place from a housing development, Mr. Duff planted an enormous cross.

Eventually Bently Place was "demolished." New flat buildings were erected, and a big Good Shepherd convent was built. Thus, says Duff, one of the Legion's aims was achieved—"to plant the standard of Christ the King on the ruins of the empire of sin."

"Who is she that cometh forth as the morning rising, fair as the moon, bright as the sun, terrible as an army in battle array?"

Mary's army was new. But it grew amazingly in a few years. And it spread throughout the world, making her name sing in many lands, and giving the Church new martyrs and confessors. The army is still embattled—and St. Louis Marie is one of its generals.

But perhaps the story should begin, after all, where Louis was born, in Montfort-La-Cane; and on his birthday, January 31, 1673.

3   Montfort-la-Cane

Montfort-La-Cane, which is now Montfort-Sur-Meu, was, with its environs, one of those regions that are washed and ironed every night and hung out under the stars to dry, so they will be fresh and clean every morning. The village lay, like a recluse, cloistered on its hill top by thick high walls. It had privacy and serenity and a feeling of self-sufficiency. It had three gates, each with its own drawbridge and portcullis, which opened on the beautiful world around it. And a boy would go forth, if he wished, and wander wherever he willed.

One might tire of playing in the ruins of the old fortress or in the rubble of ancient bricks spangled with bright new dandelions, or of sitting on one of the walls and looking at the panorama stretched out before him. A boy could see God in the Garun and Meu rivers, leisurely meandering through patches of green and gold and brown and black; in the lake at the bottom of the hill—long since drained and turned to pasturage and profit—in the farms and fields and vineyards; in the stocky houses with their roofs of red tile or slate, and in the vines of gray-blue smoke that joined their chimneys to the gray-white clouds; and in the rows and rows of trees that blessed the gritty roads.

God was in the winds that brought the sounds and smells of the world to the hill top. He was in the creak of wooden wheels and their whining for a handful of grease. He was in the noise of the whip cracking over the back of a plodding ox or ass. He was in the music of the cows lowing in some hidden scrap of clover and the faint cocks crowing on some far-off farm. He was in the twitter of birds, the barking of dogs, the whinny of a thirsty horse. He was in the quacking of those ducks down there by the shore of the lake. (How exciting it was to see a line of ducklings walking away from the water! Could they be going to St. Nicholas' church?).

God was in the smells of dust, and wild flowers, and wood smoke, and the mounds of ripe manure. He was in the incense of the fagots weathering along the roads. He was in the cool shade and the green wonder of the forest, where a boy could hunt mushrooms, or dream, or read a book, or study Celtic monuments, or say the Rosary alone, or with Louise, his sister.

Sometimes it was good just to sit and look at God and listen to Him. Sometimes it was good to go adventuring to places where one felt closest to Him—the forest or the lake, the fascinating church of St. Nicholas with its mysterious legend of the duck, or the ruined chapel of St. Lazare.

Louis' father owned some property at la Bachelleraie—which made him "a landed gentleman." It was not far from St. Lazare. Mère Andrée, who had nursed Louis when he was a baby, ran this farm. She had cows and horses and chickens to take care of. She baked bread in a round stone oven. She kept the house clean and the barn neat. She liked to have a boy to pump water, chop wood, hunt the eggs, help feed the stock, and run an errand or two. It was only a few steps from there to the old chapel, which was in such desperate need of repair. Someday he might rebuild that place, he thought.

God was in the roads as well as in the trees that bordered them; and a boy could walk hand in hand with Him as he wandered about the trees. Unlike the forest, which had many varieties, the roads had but one kind of tree, the special oak made only for Brittany. It grew tall, and it didn't branch out right away. Its branches curved upward, like the ribs of a parasol turned inside out. They grew out thickly. When they were cut off they grew back, like the stubble a man shaves off his jaw on Sunday morning. They were the right size for fishing poles, fence posts, slats, or props for Mère Andrée's wash lines. There were two reasons for lopping them off. One was, of course to get wood. The other was to get more grass.

When the tree was in full brush it kept the sun from the grass. Grass must have sun, especially in the spring, or it will not grow. Grass was precious. It must not be wasted. The farmers had to put most of their acres into grapes, or other crops. They could afford to give the grass only a narrow strip alongside the road. But it must grow to the very edge of the road.

There was the two-fold wisdom of man—helping himself to wood in order to produce more grass for his horses and cattle. And there was the incomparable wisdom of God, who made the tree and the grass, and gave them both to man. The more the tree gave, the more it had to give. It gave not only wood. It gave grass too. And it saved grass. For, by the time the sun was hot enough to burn the grass, the branches had grown in again, and there was shade.

Some of those trees stood naked, and apparently as embarrassed or shamed as a woolly dog whose master has sheared him too closely. Some still flaunted the full beauty of their green branches. Some stood erect and dignified. Some leaned away from the wind. Some looked as though the mere sight and smell of the vineyards had made them drunk. Some rows were straight and gallant and at ease. Some wavered. Some looked like a line of fuzzy green caterpillars dancing tipsily on their tails.

The branches were piled, just so, everywhere along the roads, at decent intervals. And nothing on earth was as neat as those piles, not even the vines so carefully spaced in the vineyards.

This was a land richly endowed by Eternal Wisdom. Its soil did not contain gold or silver, or any sort of minerals, or precious gems, or natural gas or oil. It was a wine-happy country. The blessing of God came up from its depths, red, and white, and gold. It came up in the living sap, through the love and care and labor of men and women, and with the help of the wind and the rain and the sun. It came up gradually, from day to day, from night to night—like grace in the soul of a boy or a girl. And some day it might be changed, by an ordinary priest, from the blood of the vine into the blood of God Himself!

It was nice to walk through the vineyards and reflect that Jesus had said, "I am the vine; you are the branches." How wonderful to be a branch of that vine—providing your fruit was good! Some vines would be cut off and burned in the fire.

It was good to remember that Mary, who was not only the vineyard that produced the Vine, but also the gardener who tended it, would nourish all the branches that trusted themselves to her care. No branch given into her keeping would ever perish.

There were three churches in Montfort when St. Louis was born. He was baptized in the church of St. Jean the following day. He loved that church, and the church of St. Jacques. But the church of St. Nicholas had a peculiar attraction for him, because of the duck's leg that had been carved into its hoary reredos. Looking at this, a boy felt mysteriously close to heaven; for, he had been told, no ordinary man had left that mark.

The carving commemorated a miracle St. Nicholas had worked to protect a maiden in grave danger. Some said a group of rude soldiers had threatened her. Others said a nobleman was the villain. Just what sort of miracle was used nobody knows. There are no records.

Did St. Nicholas thrust a flock of ducks—or spitting, scolding, nagging, nipping, wing-beating wild geese—between the lass, and the man or men who menaced her? Did he turn the girl into a high-flying duck? Was it her enemies he put to flight? Or did the girl make a vow that if St. Nicholas saved her, she would send a duck every year to his altar?

The legend is that a duck did come to the church every year, bringing a bright chain of ducklings with her. She was not a local fowl. Where she came from nobody knew. Where she went afterwards nobody knew. She waddled through the church door, marched down to the altar, quacked a prayer or two, and left one of her family there. That done, she turned, left the church with the rest of her family, and disappeared until the next year.

What happened to the duckling on the altar? Was it brought up alone, apart from all the other ducklings in the village, and treated as a dedicated entrée, to be served—perhaps with oranges—in a special sauce, on St. Nicholas's feast day, in the parish rectory? Nobody knows today. Nobody knew then, it may be. But if anyone doubts the story, there is the duck's leg carved in the ancient wood to prove its authenticity.

The boy's father, Jean Baptiste Grignion—or Grignon—the Sieur de la Bachelleraie, was a crown lawyer, and a member of a distinguished family. He was not rich, but he certainly was not poor. Louis' mother was also of "gentle lineage." She was Jeanne de la Vizeule-Robert de Launay, daughter of a sheriff of the city of Rennes. Her brother, Alain, a priest, was one of the boy's first teachers. Louis was the second of eighteen children. The first died in infancy, hence Louis was the oldest in the family.

The Grignions had the right to wear swords when they were going anywhere. But Louis didn't want to wear a sword. Nor did he want to wear a distinguished name. He wanted to be a nobody; hence, eventually, he decided to call himself not Louis Grignion but Louis of Montfort. He had precedents for this, naturally; since there was a time when nobody had a family name. John of Matha, Joseph of Cupertino, Joan of Arc, Frances of Rome were examples.

Today, in America, we have such characters as "Chicago Whitey," "Toledo Teddy," "Moosejaw Marty," and "Pittsburgh Jack"—men who endeavor to conceal their true identities not out of humility, but for reasons not disclosed. Louis beat them to the idea by at least two hundred years. Even in his own village, by his own friends and kinsmen, he was once mistaken for an unsavory hobo, a worthless "moocher," a dangerous tramp. That pleased him. It meant to him—in his own peculiar way of thinking—"local boy makes good."

The saint was born in a big two storey house on the "Street of the men of the Law." The structure is still standing. When he was two or three years old, his father bought a farm at Le Bois Marquer, a league or so from Montfort, in the parish of St. Eloi, and the village of Iffendic. There, when he became old enough, Louis was permitted to serve Mass every morning. The church was about two miles from the stone house at Le Bois Marquer, and the boy had to rise before dawn in order to reach it on time. He might stop a moment to rest, to listen to a bird, to watch the sky catch fire in the east, to pick a flower, or to test the strength of his arm and the accuracy of his aim by throwing a stone at a tree. But he could not afford to dawdle; he had a date with Christ.

There was more beauty and inspiration in the church of St. Eloi than in all the world outside it. A great 16th century stained glass window, high above the main altar, let in the morning sun and scattered its splendor over priest and altar boy and people.

It flamed with many colors. It throbbed with the glory of the Gospels. It contained many pictures, each in its own particular place; and the sun pointed them out one by one, not like a school master with a rod in his hand, but simply by illuminating them. There was Jesus, spiked to His cross, dying between two thieves. A boy could not help seeing Him, even while devoutly serving at the altar. He was too bright, too terrible, too beautiful to miss.

Then the restless sun might light up the picture of the crowing cock —or that of Jesus at the last supper. The sun was never consistent. It varied its light every day. But so many many times it shone on Peter!

The drama of St. Peter was enthralling. One saw him kneeling at the bare feet of Christ, on his boat that was almost sinking with the miraculous load of fish. And he was saying, "Depart from me, O Lord, for I am a sinful man." One could almost see his lips moving. Then the light would shift, and he might be lying blinded by the radiance of the transfiguration of his Master; or he might be swinging a sword, prepared to kill and to be killed for love of the Lord. And, always, there was the rooster crowing! The cock crow of a new life for Peter. The dawn of the first Good Friday.

And, before the sun left the windows, there was Peter with a key. Three times he had denied Christ. Three times Christ gave him the chance to say, "You know I love You." Peter had sinned, but God had given him the key to heaven, not only for himself but for everybody who wanted to go there.

The church contained many people who wanted to go to heaven.

29

They showed that by coming here to the love feast in the Mass—the continuation of the Last Supper. They would go out, presently, like the Apostles. And then what?

One of the Apostles betrayed Christ. Peter disowned Him. And all the others, except John, deserted Him. John! The beloved apostle had a special devotion to Mary. So, naturally, he could not desert her Son. He must stay, even at the peril of his life, at the foot of the cross, with Mary. The people in the church might deny the Lord, under some circumstances. They might even betray him. But those devoted to Mary would be loyal to the end.

Even from his earliest years St. Louis had a special devotion to Our Lady. All his biographers comment on this. He was enraptured by her pictures or statues. He had often been seen praying for an hour or more, on his knees, before her image. She was, it seems more truly his mother than the woman who bore him, or the one who helped to raise him. There was always a new baby in his home, or one was expected. Hence his mother was always too preoccupied to show her affection for Louis. Also there was the house to look after, and the many whims of her cantankerous husband. Mère Andrée was also busy at many things.

But Our Lady was never too busy to talk to a boy, to comfort him, to inspire him. And she was always available! It is no wonder he took her name in Confirmation.

There are no details concerning either his First Holy Communion, or his Confirmation. There are few details about his boyhood that are authentic. We are told he was "an angel of purity." We are told that he once flew at a group of boys laughing at a dirty picture—like a hawk at a flock of sparrows—and tore the picture to shreds. But stories like this have been related of many other boy saints. Sometimes a biographer could find nothing about his subject's boyhood that would indicate his sanctity. So he invented incidents. Without meaning to do so, he molded the boy into a model of himself, making him a smug little monster, a mewling snob, or a pietistic priggish brat.

Take such a character as St. Ipecas, say—if there ever was such a creature—or St. Fantail, or St. Finback. One of them, a reader would discover—to his horror—fasted every Wednesday and Friday from his mother's milk. One, to mortify his little appetite, bless him, would cover his dish of raw oysters with disgusting mounds of sugar. And one would scream in Aramaic, Hebrew, Sumerian, and classic French, when anybody failed to bless himself before or after meals—despite the fact that normally he could utter only a few words of patois.

30

It is possible, though, that St. Louis did attack a group of young hoodlums and tear up their dirty picture.

But the story of how Louis burned one of his father's books—reckless of the consequences—may be labeled "dubious" or "utter fiction."

Jean Grignion was reputed to be one of the most choleric individuals in all Brittany. He was a volcano frequently erupting. And he was constantly goading his eldest son to fury, especially at the table. Often the boy would get up and hurry away—perhaps to the woods, or the lake, or the ruined chapel of St. Lazare, or to the duck-marked altar of the church of St. Nicholas. He confessed to friends that he had a temper as bad as his father's, but admitted he was forever trying to control it. Through his father's outbursts of ridicule and anger, he learned patience, restraint, forbearance, and other virtues. He owed much to his father's anger.

Canon Blain, once one of Louis' closest friends (and one of his first biographers) relates the story of the "dirty book" the boy found in his father's library. Louis, he claims, was so incensed that he tore it up, then burned it, daring his father's wrath and punishment. But Blain cancels this story with a few lines. Louis, he says, "knew so little of what may tarnish purity that when I was speaking to him one day of temptations against that virtue he told me he didn't know what they were." In other words, the boy had never seen an indecent book, nor a pornographic picture.

The elder Grignion was not a rich man and was not apt to spend good money for bad books; and it is doubtful that he was addicted to indecent literature. A man who fathers eighteen children doesn't leave dirty books lying around for them to read. And Louis wasn't the sort of boy who snoops about forbidden shelves to spy on his father's secret vices, if any. Nor was he the type to go around the neighborhood blasting his father's reputation to show what a puritan he himself was.

All the early biographers pay attention to Louis' affection for his sister Louise-Guyonne, whom he often took to church. But they sugarcoat it so heavily few readers can swallow it. Everyone quotes the boy this way: "My dear sister, you will be beautiful and everyone will love you—if you will only do your best to love God."!

Some evidence to prove this is not exactly what he said is contained in a letter he wrote her years later. "God wants you to detach yourself from everybody but Him." She would be happy, he said, if she were "poor in spirit, abandoned, despised, rejected . . ." The boy did want his sister to be good, but certainly not in order that she might become beautiful and win the love of everybody.

He calls her his "dear supplement" in this letter, and advises her to visit the altar more than the table or the bed.

She died in a convent cell thirty some years after Louis died; and nobody in Brittany will be surprised if she too is some day proclaimed a saint.

Perhaps the best way to look at the panorama of St. Louis Marie's boyhood is to climb onto the high wall of one of his books, his "True Devotion to Mary." From there one can get a clear look. In the story of Jacob and Esau, for instance, he can see St. Louis' world.

He is writing about Jacob who had bought his brother's birthright with a mess of pottage, and who has won the blessing of his father, Isaac. Jacob, he says, typifies the chosen soul.

And this, he adds, "is the way chosen souls are accustomed to act. They stay at home. That is, they are spiritually minded. They apply themselves to mental prayer, following the example of Mary, their mother, whose sole glory during her life was within, and who loved mental prayer so much.

"It is true they (these chosen ones) often go out into the world. But they do so out of obedience to the will of God and His mother, and to fulfill the duties of their state in life. However great their outward works may seem, they prize their inner accomplishments much more. They esteem the progress they make within themselves, in the company of Our Lady. They work there at the supreme task of perfection, compared to which all other works are but child's play. They see their brothers and sisters, outside, at work, using great strength, amazing ability, and shrewd skill to win success and the praise and envy of the world. But, through the light of the Holy Ghost, they perceive that there is more good, more glory, and more real joy in remaining hidden in their retreat, with Christ as their model, in complete and perfect submission to Mary. They see clearly that this is better than to work miracles by themselves. The Jacobs truly honor and tenderly love their mother Mary . . ."

Writing of Mary, Louis was, perhaps unconsciously, writing about himself.

4 College Student

ouis was a big boy when he went to the parish school in Mont-fort-La-Cane. He was nine years old. It isn't known exactly why his formal education began so late. Possibly there was no school until that time; possibly his parents needed him at home, to help with the chores, to take care of the babies, to run errands. At any rate his education had not been neglected. His parents, and his uncle, Father Robert, the Rennes priest had tutored him in many subjects, especially in his duties to his God and to his king.

The king was also named Louis. He was known as the Sun King, and the Grand Monarch. He had the most splendid and luxurious court in Europe. He was the richest and most powerful ruler on earth. His armies were the best in the world. They had made France strong and safe—and desperately poor. The king and the nobles were magnificent and rich, the peasants were miserable and in want.

From his earliest days the boy had learned much of France, of Anne of Austria, King Louis' mother, of Condé and Turenne, the great soldiers, of Richelieu and Descartes and Molière, and Mazarin, and St. Vincent de Paul and St. Vincent Ferrer. He had learned about Jacobins and Huguenots, and of Bishop Jansen whose doctrines made a frightful despot of God and a non-entity of God's mother.

One of the first things he learned, naturally, was that God knows all about little boys, and they can never fool Him. He knows when they are good, and when they are bad. He knows when they run away to the woods or the river, or the chapel of St. Lazare, forgetting their little brothers or sisters have need of them. But he learned also that God's mother loves little boys with a great love, and watches over them every minute of the day.

Brittany still remembered St. Vincent Ferrer, the great Dominican preacher who travelled on foot through that region two hundred years and more before, talking of Mary and the Rosary. Crowds of men and women had followed wherever he went, camping in the open at night, sleeping when and where they could; fasting, praying, singing hymns. Some writers assert that it was not unusual for ten thousand people to attend him. They add that never was there a hint of scandal among his followers. His devotion to Mary had taken root in Brittany, and become its greatest treasure.

Louis Marie grew up with a Rosary in his hands. He taught his brothers and sisters how to use it when they were old enough to say the prayers; and at the parish school he induced many of his classmates to pray the Rosary with him.

He was a good student. He was at the head of all his classes. But he was more interested in Jesus and Mary than in any of his studies. The other boys liked him, but thought him odd.

As he grew up, Louis learned much about Gallicanism also, which was almost as great a heresy as Jansenism. It represented an arrogant pride in all things French. Those who practiced it believed in a French church rather than a Roman one. King Louis XIV was, at one time, in bitter opposition to the Pope. He felt the Holy Father wasn't giving him enough consideration, enough respect, enough reverence. Once he called the French bishops into a conclave and tried to make them solemnly declare the Vatican had no direct supervision over France, and that His Holiness must never interfere with the power and the glory and the magnificence of His Majesty, the King of France. He got over this, in time, and died a Roman Catholic.

Jansenism was not French at all; and most certainly it was not a product of any Breton mind. It made familiar things strange, and natural things unnatural. It held that Jesus died not for all men but only for a few, that Communion was only for the elect—or the élite—and that devotion to the Virgin Mother was akin to the idolatry the Pagans gave to Iris and Astarte and other goddesses. It didn't like laughter. It didn't like love.

It didn't like anything most people liked.

Many bishops and priests, some of them powerful and rich, were afflicted with one or both of these odd and gloomy doctrines. A boy must learn his religion thoroughly in order to escape infection.

Louis Marie, clinging to Mary always, emerged into adolescence "with such a horror of vice and such an inclination to virtue," according to his reverend uncle, "that you would have thought him immune from Adam's sin . . . None of those things that amuse the young and charm their elders seemed to touch him. The words 'God alone' were written on his heart."

34

His teachers didn't understand him. (But then nobody else understood him either, because he was "so different" from all other boys.) They couldn't classify him. They couldn't mold him. They couldn't criticize him, for he was never wrong, he was always on time for classes, he was always docile and obedient. He didn't fight, nor provoke fights. He never got into scrapes. There was no horse play in him, no coarse humor. He didn't smile very often, but there was something pleasant about him which everybody could feel but nobody could define, something good and wholesome and warming—something as distinct as the aroma of a flower. He baffled his father especially for he never lost his temper—which can be most exasperating to a man who shoots all the angry words in his quiver, knowing he will never hit the mark.

Louis was so good a student he was considered a genius; hence it is not surprising that he should be sent to college at the age of twelve. The college of St. Thomas a Becket, in Rennes, was chosen for him. Louis was pleased with this, for the school was conducted by the Jesuits, who were fighting both Gallicanism and Jansenism, and who had always shown a tender love for Our Lady. Also, it was known, the Jesuits were excellent teachers, with superb ideas on how to treat their students. They wanted boys to be happy as well as studious; they wanted them to appreciate the beauties of nature, as well as the beauties of Latin and Greek and rhetoric and logic; they wanted them to become saints.

Rennes was only 14 miles away, no distance for a boy used to walking; and there was a room in his uncle's home where he could stay. He could come home over the weekends, so he could teach his younger brothers all he had learned during the week. Thus his parents would get a fine tutor for the younger children, and it wouldn't cost them a sou!

If Louis regretted having to leave his favorite shrines, he solaced himself by finding others in Rennes. The Breton capital was a tremendous city to the country boy; and the people, rich and poor, were extraordinarily busy—even on Sundays—about many things. Rennes was, at first, a bewildering, meaningless, overrun anthill; but he adapted himself to the novelty, after he saw the statue of Our Lady, in the Carmelite church of St. Sauveur, served by his uncle.

There were many legends attached to this statue; and many miracles. Thousands of women, old and young, wives, mothers, and sweethearts had flocked to it during the terrible months of 1356 and 1357

35

when the English siege threatened massacre or starvation. The statue was venerated after the city was saved by the great hero Du Guesclin. And many were the "miracles" related.

Again in 1675 the statue was an inspiration, a hope, a consolation, and a blessing. Rennes had rebelled against the king's tax laws; and the Duc de Chaulnes had hanged and quartered nobles and peasants in the thousands, and had put thousands of others on the wheel.

Louis spent hours on his knees every day before that statue. He visited it at least twice a day, going to college and coming home. He found other statues of Mary in the city, and many pictures of her; but this was his favorite.

Rennes didn't change some of his habits. He still saluted every picture or statue of Our Lady, as he had done in Montfort. The people at home thought nothing of this, but those in Rennes laughed, and mocked him. The boy didn't mind. It was good to become an object of contempt and ridicule for his Lady.

Mary's divine Son had been an object of contempt and ridicule. He had been regarded as a fool. If He was God, and almighty, why did He let a few men kill Him—men He could have blasted into hell with a simple wish? The foolishness of God! What was the wisdom of men compared to it? It was a high privilege to be a fool for Christ, to suffer shame and humiliations, through Him and with Him and in Him. One might not have to suffer eternally without Him.

There were several thousand students in the college; but none were like the friends Louis Marie had known in Montfort. Some, freed for the first time from all family supervision and restraint, were determined to enforce their will on others—especially those younger and smaller than themselves, and those less hardened.

They picked on de Montfort, and, because he never tried to resist their silly or cruel attacks, they thought him a coward and worse. They poured dirty water into the pockets of his new jacket. He only smiled and forgave them. They tripped him, and he did not curse. They slapped and kicked him, and he did not strike back, nor did he show any sort of annoyance or anger. What was the fellow made of? Did he think he was a saint? Was he just a sniveling hypocrite? Or was he just waiting for a good chance to get back at his tormentors? Every man had a breaking point. When would he reach his?

Louis Marie spent more time with the Jesuit teachers than with his fellow students. He loved these devoted priests and scholastics, and learned much from them.

36

Father Gilbert, who taught rhetoric, gave him the wish to be a missionary and—"perhaps, through Your grace, O Lord—a martyr." Father Gilbert was the mildest teacher in the school, and his class the rowdiest. The big boys laughed and talked while he lectured them. They threw books at each other. They tried to turn everything he said into some sort of bawdy joke. The priest never lost his patience, never remonstrated with his hoodlum nitwits.

De Montfort sought him out often, to comfort him, and to ask him questions. The priest was a wonderful example to a boy who wanted to be a saint. His ambition, he told Louis, was to be sent far away, to the Indians or the Chinese, to whom he might bring Jesus and Mary, and make them loved. In time Father Gilbert was given the gift he sought. He went to the West Indies, and died there, teaching the natives the sweetness of the Lord. How many saints does it take to make a saint?

Through Father Camus, his first teacher, Louis became a member of the Sodality of the Blessed Virgin. This, wonder of wonders, entitled him to attend all the services in the Lady's honor, and all the lectures, sermons, and instructions the Jesuits had prepared for these chosen pupils. It also permitted him to recite Our Lady's office every day, and to go frequently to Communion.

Father Descartes, his spiritual guide, wanted him to be more than a good Sodality member. He introduced him to the saintly Father Bellier, the almoner of the City's general hospital, and Louis became one of the priest's small band of helpers, visiting the poor, begging clothing and food for them, praying for the dying, and teaching the little ones. To his anguished surprise, Louis discovered that in this rich city there were people more desperate, more ignorant, more needy than in Montfort—and incredibly more in need of love!

Despite his activity among the sick and the poor, he stayed at the head of his classes. He learned to write Latin verse. He learned to paint and to carve statues. He was so good at this that he sold one of his pictures without the least effort. A rich man saw it, wanted it, paid for it, took it away with him. Hence Louis was able to pay a professional a few francs for lessons. He also learned to mortify himself in many ways.

Those were the days when spiritual directors thought it only their duty to advise using the discipline "unto blood," to wear a hair shirt, or to put chains on arms or legs or around the waist, to mortify the flesh. Fasting and penance helped one to keep his body in control; but he should be moderate in his penances. Yet some authors would have us believe that Louis Marie's shoulders were always red and wet.

37

Some years after Louis entered college his father brought the family to Rennes, believing business would be better there. Louis then became a full-time tutor as well as a full-time student, imparting to his young brothers and sisters not only some of his knowledge but also some of his sanctity. The move was providential, for it brought to Rennes a young woman we know only as Mlle. de Montigny. She came to see Louis' father on a business matter; but someone had sent her especially to talk to Louis Marie.

She had come from Paris, and she was full of the wonder of the grand seminary of St. Sulpice, "the model of all the seminaries in the world"! It was founded by the friend of many saints, Father Jean Jacques Olier—and it was really the house of Mary, the Virgin Mother of God. Father Olier, even in his childhood, never did anything without consulting Mary. He went to Jesus only through Mary. He lived and died for Jesus in Mary. He was a slave of Mary—or rather of Jesus in Mary. He devoutly hailed her pictures and her statues wherever he chanced to go. And he wanted all the priests in his seminary to be equally devoted to her. St. Francis de Sales was one of his teachers. St. John Baptist de La Salle was one of his pupils. St. Vincent de Paul, his friend, was with Father Olier at his death, and believed him to be a saint.

Louis Marie listened with all the wonder and excitement and rapture of a small boy listening to his first fairy story. It was as though God Himself were speaking through this woman. Only a short time before, while praying near the statue in the church of St. Sauveur, he had become convinced that Our Lady wanted him to be a priest. And there was no place he would rather study for the priesthood than in this shrine of Mary. How good God was to let him know such a paradise existed! He would walk to it, every step of the way, to show his gratitude and his joy. Even if it had been a thousand miles away, he would have walked to it.

Mlle. de Montigny seemed to be as enthusiastic as the boy, for she gave him ten crowns, which should be sufficient to pay his expenses to Paris; and she bought him a new suit. Also, she agreed, she would pay his way through the seminary.

Jean Baptiste didn't lose his temper when Louis told him he meant to be a priest. He was sincerely glad. It was not only a great honor to have a priest in the family. It might, someday, be a great blessing too. Many priests take care of their families, once they are settled in a good parish. Jean Baptiste would have someone to help him in his old age!

He permitted Louis to keep the ten crowns—comforting himself with the thought, or the hope, that he was thereby making a wise and holy investment. He suggested that his son ride to Paris, or at least part way. A friend could bring back the horse. But Louis said he would walk.

What were two hundred and some miles to him? He was young and strong. He was a good boy and he could be trusted. He would come to no harm on the way. Jean Baptiste would miss him, and his willingness and strength, but he had other children just as dear to him. He walked a little way with the boy before he said goodbye.

Much has been written about Louis' hike to Paris. It took him ten days. It wasn't a hitch-hike such as the modern boy is accustomed to take when he wants to go somewhere. Louis walked. It rained most of the time, and he couldn't always find a dry place when he needed it. And things kept happening. He saw beggars who needed his money more than he did. He met others who needed his clothes. Before he had gone very far, he had parted with all his money, given away all his clothes, and had put on some wretch's rags. He reached Paris soaked, smeared, rumpled, unshaven—probably with a scraggly black beard—smelling of wood smoke, wet straw, and pungent stables.

He walked alone. Yet, through the years, thousands of people have walked the miles with him, singing with him, praying the Rosary with him, sharing his emotions, sharing his hardships, sharing his love—the love of a bridegroom hiking to his wedding, bringing gifts of humility, patience, charity, endurance, love.

What a sight he must have been to Mlle. de Montigny!

5

Seminarian
in Paris

When she had recovered from the shock of meeting this huge strange man from Rennes, Mlle. de Montigny made new arrangements for him. While he was in college he had seemed to her the very pattern of Father Olier, the perfect candidate for St. Sulpice. Now—now he was a great masculine puzzle and problem. What does one do with a boy like this—a ragged rugged mountain of a man who cannot be made to look like anything but a mountain? Did he belong in the formal garden of St. Sulpice? She didn't think so. He would be as out of place as a giant cactus in a bed of petunias and pansies.

He was something of a hero, in her eyes, and something of a saint. His march on Paris had been a pilgrimage, a journey not only to the priesthood but also to the state of perfection. It had aged him, thinned him, hardened him. It had changed him in many ways. He had given away not only all he had, but also all he was. He had knelt on the dirty cobble stones of some village street along the way, and vowed to live thereafter in holy poverty, depending on Our Lady to take care of him. He had endured slights and insults and curses. Nobody had given him anything, except grudgingly. Even when he begged for it "in the name of God," he had been refused food, dry clothing, shelter from the rain, a decent bed. Yet he was not bitter, he was actually pleased. God had given him many little crosses to carry from Rennes to Paris. Blessed be His name!

This unusual man would like the small community founded by Father de la Barmondière. His room would not be ornate, nor even well-furnished. And the food would not be too good. But, somehow, she knew he would be happy there. She would be happy too, for she wouldn't have to pay so much for his room and board. This was a weighty consideration, for her income, once a golden flood, had become a rusty trickle. France was winning too many victories, creating too many widows and orphans, and too many wretched people. They couldn't buy anything that was for sale. The richer and more powerful

41

France became, the more miserable and the more desperate were her people.

Louis was glad he was not yet to enter St. Sulpice. It was a heavy cross, therefore a holy one. He didn't care about the room. A corner would do. He could sleep on the floor. He didn't need a cot. Food? He never ate much, and he was never particular about what he ate. He was even happier when he met Father de la Barmondière, who greeted him with warm affection, and who insisted that the lady should pay only for his board. The room he could have without cost. But food, alas, had to be paid for. There wasn't too much, and the cost of what one could get at the store was almost sacrilegious!

Mlle. de Montigny's trickle dried up within six months; and she was forced to abandon all thoughts of helping her protégé. Louis must now depend on God alone.

"If the living can't help you," Father de la Barmondière said, "the dead will."

Death was busy in Paris that winter; and there was always a need for someone to "stay up with the corpse" and give the relatives a chance to sleep in comfort. It was cold. People died of exposure. They died of diseases. They died of starvation. They died of wounds inflicted by themselves, or by their friends or foes. They died of murder. They died of neglect. And, in every house where death had knocked, there were a few sous or a few francs, to be earned by the watcher.

Louis spent most of his nights on his knees, in palaces, in hovels, in middle-class homes, keeping vigil over nobles, tradesmen, beggars, thieves; over imperious beauties, notorious flirts, great artists, great sinners. He loved them all, for Christ had dwelt in them. And in their quiet way, they repaid his kindness. They taught him many things. They put ideas into his mind, and made him write them in rhyme and meter. They are difficult to translate; but their meaning is clear:

> *We must die. We must die—*
> *Leave this sad world—you and I.*
> *The tragedy has been ordained.*
> *Nature's law will be maintained.*
> *Vanity, ere your funeral bell,*
> *You will be horror—and a putrid smell.*

In September, 1694, Father de la Barmondière died. Louis was making a retreat preparatory to receiving Minor Orders, and had left

the seminary for a few days. He made no comment when he heard the news. He showed no emotion. Those who knew him called him an unfeeling boor, a base ingrate, a stupid peasant who didn't realize he had lost his best friend and his sole protector. Louis wrote to his family:
"I do not know how things will go with me now, whether I shall remain here or leave. However, I have no anxiety. I have a Father in heaven who will not fail me. . . . I abandon myself to His providence."
Father de la Barmondière, he said, was a saint.

That was all. He might just as well have added, "and who can mourn for a saint—a soul face to face with God, shining in heavenly glory?" He might have added this, but he knew he didn't have to. His folks would understand.

The community disintegrated at the death of its founder, but Louis was not forsaken. Another priest, Father Boucher, who had a small seminary—with a slight connection to St. Sulpice—gave him a welcome. It was a grim welcome. The room was cold and dark and small. Cold indeed in winter; hot indeed in summer. The food was atrocious. Father Boucher couldn't hire a cook, so everybody cooked; and most of the cooks should never have been permitted to enter a kitchen.

A short time after this community welcomed him, Louis was welcomed by the only available hospital, the Hotel Dieu, which was little better than a butcher shop, and almost as clean. Whether it was the food that sent Louis to this awful place, or some infection he had found in his night watches, nobody seems to know. Perhaps his scourgings had weakened him, and thus left him vulnerable to disease or poisonously bad food. All his biographers say about this is that he was near death, that he was happy to be in "the house of God," and that he knew he would not die. All he had to do was lie there on his straw-stuffed cross all day and let the surgeons bleed him—not with the discipline but with dull knives.

Canon Blain says he visited Louis there, and that the patient was happy. The canon undoubtedly tells the truth about Louis, as he remembers it. But one reading his book must come to the conclusion that his memory is not always keen. One must not forget that this dear good friend of de Montfort's, this "constant companion," abandoned him when he was most in need of friends, then went out of his way to avoid meeting him. It is possible that, to make atonement, the good priest poured coals of fire on his own head. Perhaps the smoke and the ashes of those burning coals affected his vision and his recollection. Perhaps, in his remorse, he wanted to prove that Louis was a saint.

But he had the Jansenist idea of a saint—a popular idea at the time, an idea that produced the many rigid plaster or plastic saints you see today in stores that sell religious wares—those in the window, marked down to $1.98.

Writers, painters, and sculptors all jumped in to make the "perfect paragon of virtue." He looks famished, lost, dyspeptic, neurotic, sleepy, dreamy, disturbed. His eyes are cast down. His lips are shut tight, against any semblance of a smile. He has a lily in one hand, a crucifix in the other. And, of course, he has a smear of gilt around his head, for a halo. That's his hallmark, the halo. (If you want to see a real live saint, drop in at the nearest convent, seminary, rectory, or lay apostolic center, and pick out the one with the happiest smile and the most musical laugh—the one with the halo in the eyes.)

We can believe that Louis, in Paris, let a fellow student beat him across the shoulders with a rod, and made no protest. The fellow evidently didn't believe Louis scourged himself, as everybody claimed he did. And also, he wanted to see how Louis would react to a rod not daintily applied. We can imagine his exasperation and frustration when Louis didn't even remonstrate. What satisfaction can you get hitting someone who seems to thank you for your efforts? You wear your arm out, and don't get even a nasty look!

But when we are told that Louis Marie half killed himself every time he used the discipline we begin to wonder. We wonder also if it is possible Louis was the churl, the lout, the snob, the pious pharisee Canon Blain unconsciously portrays for us. Listen to this:

"His first sacrifice as he entered Paris was the curbing of his curiosity. He struck a bargain with his eyes, not to see anything of the affluence, the magnificence, or the multitude of rarities and art masterpieces which made Paris the most beautiful city in the world . . . he kept his decision as if it were a vow. He closed his eyes to all that might lead him from perfection. I stress this. He closed them. Ten years later he left the French capital as he had entered it, without having seen anything that could have gratified his senses. He might as well have been blind. He cast his eyes downward so much that he was able to see nothing other than his feet . . . yet he knew where all the images of the Virgin were . . . not looking anyone in the face."

Yes he might as well have been blind. He might as well have been an ostrich looking for some sandy place in which he could bury his silly head.

My! My! Whatever became of the little boy who looked at everything he saw, and found God in it; who listened to every sound and heard God's voice? Maybe he had three eras in his life, the pre-Blain, the Blain, and the post-Blain!

Louis' main ambition was to be a missionary. To be a missionary he had to know people. He had to look at your own clumsy shoes. You have to meet them face to face. You have to work with them, pray with them, eat with them, love them, bring them to God. And you don't rush to God by rushing away from them—even the least of them.

One wonders, too, how Canon Blain can be so certain Louis kept that odd bargain with his eyes. He saw very little of his old friend in Paris. Louis often walked alone, without Canon Blain to guide him.

And listen to this:

"Outside of his recreation time, M. Grignion made no more use of his tongue than of his eyes. His silence was so exact that one could not get even one word from him unless it were absolutely necessary; and then he spoke so low and so succinctly that one wasn't tempted to distract him from his contemplation of God . . ."

Whatever became of the little boy who was always preaching to his friends about Jesus and Mary? Whatever became of the lad who was forever urging people to say the Rosary with him? Whatever became of the child who stole away from people (to contemplate God) only when he didn't have something else to do? Did he forget that God knows when big boys are good, and when they are bad, and when they run away when they shouldn't?

And listen again:

"His forgetfulness of mortal creatures went so far as not wanting to speak to, or see, his fellow countrymen or his student companions; and if he met them in the streets he turned aside, or appeared not to know them."

He did this, the canon explains, to avoid unnecessary visits and conversations—which might take him away from contemplating God. And, he adds, Louis "exhorted me to imitate him."

Surely the canon is confused in this recollection. He was the one who didn't want to see de Montfort. He was the one who took short cuts or ducked into alleys when he saw Louis approaching.

He is also confused about his old friend's skill with brush or chisel. Louis sacrificed his love of art, he assures us, "either through a spirit of mortification or the fear of being distracted from God!" The death of M. de la Barmondière "left him free to bury his various natural talents in eternal oblivion!"

Louis Marie must have forgotten that he made this most noble sacrifice, for he went on painting pictures of Mary, and carving statues of her for many years after leaving Paris—and his biographer friend.

It may be that Canon Blain wanted to remember Louis as walking like a man deaf, dumb, and blind. Many priests and bishops—including those who had been students at St. Sulpice—did try to walk that way. Theologians of the period wrote much about "custody of the eyes," especially for religious. A devout young man should always walk with his head down. The sky was not for him. The birds in the trees were not for him. The balconies opening on the streets were not for him. And certainly the women coming down the street, directly toward him, were not for him. Women, to some of the clergy, and particularly to the Jansenists, were temptations to be most scrupulously avoided. One peek and a boy might lose his vocation and his soul!

Blain relates anecdotes of de Montfort's early Paris days that also make us wonder. There was the time he saw two men about to duel in the street—and, quick as thought, he thrust his crucifix between their gleaming blades. This was once a stock situation for every saint one had to write about. Our hero, walking modestly down the main street never encountered fair damsels; but he was forever running into bravos armed with daggers or poignards or javelins or pikes or swords or iron maces. And he was always stepping in between them with sweet words and the cross—to shame them, and to turn one at least (and sometimes both) into a holy penitent monk or friar. Of course it may have happened. I know a young man, then a lay apostle in Harlem, who boldly thrust himself between two husky Negroes who were threatening to carve each other with switch blades.

That young man eventually became a Trappist priest. What happened to the fighting cocks I do not know.

And then there is the story of St. Louis' meeting the man who was selling filthy songs, or pamphlets, or pictures. He happened, somehow or other, to have quite a little money with him. So he bought up all the smut the fellow had to sell, and destroyed it. You believe that? If St. Louis Marie de Montfort had money enough to do that, he would have given it to the poor who needed it so sorely. He would never have been fool enough to think he could keep the dirt peddler from buying a new stock with his unexpected profits.

Louis knew God had not abandoned him when he was taken to the hospital. On the contrary. The Lord had awarded him a tremendous cross; one he didn't deserve. How could God be so generous to him?

There was pain, and suffering, and plenty of blood-letting. But there were blessings too. The nuns and nurses were fond of him. They waited on him night and day. (Evidently he wasn't looking at his feet in that wretched hospital.) They talked to him, they told him stories, they said the Rosary with him, and they brought him books. Through these women he encountered the "Letters of Father Surin, S.J.," a book full of glorious thoughts about the folly of the Cross, and about the Incarnate Eternal Wisdom. The slaughterhouse had become a treasury!

Lying in bed, reading Father Surin, Louis had his first dreams of spreading devotion to Wisdom, to the Cross, to Jesus in Mary, and to Mary herself, the Mother and the Queen of all mankind.

Through the nuns and nurses Louis also met two women who insisted on helping him enter the Little Seminary of St. Sulpice. It wasn't the Grand Seminary, of course. It was the same, but different. The fees in the big seminary were higher—and the beds were softer, and the meals more appetizing, perhaps. But—Louis was happy. He had never been so happy.

One can be gloriously happy, carrying a cross. But one really doesn't need even a little cross, to be happy. One who lives for God alone can never be wholly unhappy, with or without a cross. And Louis, following the holy Jesuit's letters, was learning to live for God alone.

6   **Saint or Fool?**

Father Brenier, superior of the Little Seminary of St. Sulpice, and Father Bouin, his associate, had heard stories of Louis Marie's sanctity. The nuns and nurses had told Paris that the young man was a saint. They were as convincing as church bells saying the day is Sunday. The priests, confident that they were about to take charge of a saint, ordered the *Te Deum* sung on the day of his arrival.

This wryly delighted biographer George Rigault. "Montfort," he wrote, "was not the kind of present Providence usually sent to the Sulpicians . . . they might well have sung the *Te Deum*, but with a stress upon the 'Have mercy on us, O Lord, have mercy on us!' They thought the world of him, yet were not sure of him. They ended by cold-shouldering him."

Louis probably sang the hymn more fervently than anybody else in this delightful garden of Mary, this oasis in the desert of the world, this earthly abode of Incarnate Wisdom. He could have had no idea of the wicked thorns growing in that garden, nor of the poisonous shrubs. Undoubtedly he added his loud voice to the chant of the angels.

There was so much for which he should praise God. He was, at last, in the holy of holies created by his hero, Father Olier, the devoted slave of Mary. He was, at last, on the direct road to the altar of Mary's Son. He was surrounded by young men who, he was sure, also wanted to be great saints. And he had caught a glimpse of Wisdom in the books he found in the library and in the quiet of his room. Like St. Paul, he had merely "looked through a glass, darkly." He had looked only with his intelligence and his emotions. Had he used his eyes, he would have died of sheer delight and love, or he would have been blinded. Yet he had seen Wisdom, Incarnate Wisdom! He had seen Reality! Is there anything more real than the Creator of all real things? He must share that Reality with his fellow students.

Wisdom is not just a word. It is THE WORD! It is THE WORD that was made flesh. Wisdom is God Himself, and the Son of God, Jesus Christ.

49

"The Eternal Wisdom," Louis wrote, "is the substantial and everlasting concept of the beauty of God as shown to St. John . . . when he exclaimed, 'In the beginning was the Word and the Word was with God, and the Word was God. The same was in the beginning with Him, and without Him was made nothing that was made. In Him was life, and the life was the light of men. And the light shineth in the darkness, and the darkness did not comprehend it.' "

St. John! The beloved apostle! The young man who had rested his head on Christ's bosom and listened to the beating of His divine heart, who had stood beneath the cross on Calvary, the only one of the twelve to dare the consequences, who had taken Mary for his own!

Since he was the only Apostle there, he represented Christ's Church. Eternal Wisdom gave Mary to the Church, through John. She was the mother of the Church, as well as the mother of the Apostle.

The Word that was made flesh contained the wisdom of the Godhead. The Wisdom of God was exemplified by the Word of God. This divine Wisdom chose to come to us through Mary. This Wisdom Incarnate chose to redeem man by dying on the cross. Man, therefore, guided by Wisdom, should go to heaven through Mary. Man, knowing himself a sinner, should not try to avoid the cross so loved by sinless Wisdom.

De Montfort loved St. John. He loved Solomon too. The wise kings words were meadowlarks singing in the clean blue sky, bees humming in a field of clover, God's clean winds rustling the palm grove's fans.

"The Lord begot me, the firstborn of his ways, the forerunner of his prodigies of long ago; from of old I was poured forth, at the first, before the earth. When there were no depths I was brought forth; when there were no fountains or springs of water; before the mountains were settled into place, before the hills. I was brought forth: while as yet the fields were not made nor the first clouds of the world. There I was beside him as his craftsman, and I was his delight day by day, playing before him all the while, playing on the surface of the earth (and I found delight in the sons of men) . . . he who finds me finds life and wins favor from the Lord . . . Come and eat of the food and drink of the wine I have mixed . . ."

The Sulpicians might well have asked for mercy; for the next five years were going to be hard on them. That is, Louis Marie was going to be more than a burden. He seemed to live on top a mountain they could not climb, to breathe an air too rarified for them to inhale. He was so far from them, in everything, they were not sure whether he was a saint or a fool pretending to be a saint. Whatever he was, he was certainly not one of them. He didn't belong to them. He was the ugly duckling, who, one day, would be revered as a swan.

But Louis, even if he had known how difficult the coming years would be, still would have praised God with all his heart and soul. For he had fallen in love with the cross; and God sent the most crosses—and the heaviest ones—to those He loved.

It was a heavy cross to realize he couldn't share the Wisdom that had been given him. He had tried many times. But he had failed, through some fault of his own. It was a strange thing, but a fact. These young men who wanted to be priests, and therefore saints, laughed at him when he talked of Jesus as Incarnate Wisdom, or of Mary as the woman who brought that Wisdom to mankind. Or they walked away as though they were insulted, or bored, or tempted to anger far beyond annoyance. Or they insisted on telling him stories, ordinary stories.

They liked, it seemed, to talk about the king and his court, the extravagance of Versailles, the queen mother, Mazarin and his love for power and possessions. They even liked to discuss King Louis and his mistresses and his queen! They mentioned Louise de La Vallière with some vague sort of reverence, because she was spending her life then in a Carmelite convent; and they had a certain respect for Mme. de Montespan, though most of them did think her something of a witch. They liked to refer to these women and the queen as "the three queens." The Sun King, who would never travel alone, always took his queen and his mistresses with him.

Louis was wise with the Wisdom of God. The words of Solomon were more familiar to him than the speech of his friends. And he felt as Solomon felt about Wisdom . . . "I pleaded and the spirit of Wisdom came to me. I preferred her to scepter and throne, and deemed riches nothing in comparison with her . . . all gold in view of her is a little sand. Beyond health and comeliness I love her, and I chose to have her rather than the light, because the splendor of her never yields to sleep. Yet all good things together come to me in her company, and countless riches at her hands; and I rejoiced in them all because Wisdom is their leader, though I had not known she is the mother of these."

Solomon referred to Wisdom as a mother and as the craftsman, the maker of all things—a mother who loved what she had made. He did not know, of course, that Wisdom was the Word of God, the Word who would be made Flesh, and who would die for men. Yet he must have

51

felt that Wisdom was divine, for he says: "Such things as are secret I learned, and such as are plain, for Wisdom, the artificer of all, taught me . . . she is an aura of the might of God and a pure effusion of the glory of the Almighty; therefore naught that is sullied enters into her. For she is the refulgence of Eternal Light, the spotless mirror of the power of God, the image of his goodness, and she, who is one, can do all things . . . passing into holy souls from age to age she produces friends of God and prophets . . . she is fairer than the sun and surpasses every constellation of the stars. Compared to light she takes precedence . . . she reaches from end to end and governs all things well."

Louis Marie could hardly speak of Wisdom to himself. He confesses it in his book. "We must exclaim with St. Paul: 'O the depth and immensity, O the incomprehensibility of the Wisdom of God' . . . Who is the angel enlightened enough, who is the man daring enough, to venture to explain His origin? Let all human eyes be closed, lest they be blinded by the glowing brightness of His radiance; let every tongue be silent for fear of tarnishing His perfect beauty by trying to reveal it; let every intelligence bow down and adore, lest, trying to fathom Him, it be oppressed by the immense glory of the Divine Wisdom."

Louis lived with Divine Wisdom, but he could not explain it to his friends. But the day would come when he would share it with all the people in the world.

Father Bouin, who acted as Louis' spiritual director for two years, decided the young man was too severe with himself. He bade him moderate his penances, and try to enjoy his hours of recreation. "Mix with your friends," he advised. "You need them as they need you. Their talk may be empty, silly, vain, extravagant. Learn to endure it. And learn to tell funny stories."

Louis learned a number of stories—probably some of those current today. There are no new stories. Some we think are new go back to the days of Noah—or beyond him. Like the story of the French peasant going home with his last bottle of good wine. He was near his home when he slipped and fell. In panic he reached for the pocket where he had put the bottle. He found something wet and sticky there. And he called out in agony, "Dear God, let it be only blood!" That story, naturally, was used again in prohibition days in the U.S.A., and credited—of course—to an Irishman with a flask.

Louis learned his stories word for word, apparently; but, when he told them, his audience laughed at him. They laughed until they wept. They rolled on the floor, or on the grass. They acclaimed St. Louis as

52

the greatest clown that ever came out of the sticks into polite society. A buffoon of a man! A fool! A clumsy country bumpkin!

The fact that he had been told to stay away from the Sorbonne added to his reputation as a lout and a dunce. Most of the seminarians were sent to this great school, the pride of France, to learn theology. Louis had studied there before he came to St. Sulpice. Nobody knew why he was now banned; yet everybody thought he knew.

So everybody gossiped about him. They were not essentially mean. They were simply young. Youth, like death, loves a shining mark. And where in all sophisticated France was there a mark more tempting than the man from Montfort La Cane, "the duchy of the duck?" To these intellectuals, these ardent French aristocrats, Louis was the stupidest goose uncooked. Except, of course, in the classroom. And that was an unexplainable thing. For in spite of everything, Louis was a tremendous scholar! They couldn't understand it, but they had to admit it. One day when he was defending the doctrine of grace, they thought it would be fun to listen to him for awhile, and then to attack him with questions. The subject the backward boy was about to expound had made nervous nellies of many a would-be theologian.

Scarce had Louis begun to speak than they swarmed around him like so many woodpeckers looking for juicy grubs in the bark of a tree. But the goose from the town of the duck answered their questions so easily, so quickly, and with such profound wisdom and authority, that they scattered in dismay and wonder—and perhaps in some admiration of the goose and some disgust at their own foolishness and ignorance.

Later they tried again. He would be entirely different they thought, teaching catechism—especially to those wretched and uncouth little hoodlums Father Brenier had chosen for him. It should be fun to see how those gamins would react to his peculiar ways. But it was so touching that some of the visitors wept. Louis had put a spell on those little devils, and they acted like budding saints.

After directing Louis Marie's soul toward perfection for two years, Father Bouin died, and left him friendless indeed. Father Bouin had sometimes let him see he loved and admired him. Father Leschassier, his successor, "a holy but severe man and an enemy to everything he regarded as new," had never liked Louis—had never even tried to like him.

When a boy enters a religious congregation and evinces a desire to be a priest, the superiors are pleased, and sometimes proud. They have "a new vocation," a sinner who wants to be a saint. He has, they are glad to realize—and acknowledge—come to the right place, to the right saint-factory. They take pains with him. They cannot do too much for him. They spend all their energies making him the perfect representative of the institution.

But when the applicant is already a saint—and a great saint—the superiors are perplexed, unhappy, and horribly suspicious.

Is it possible this soul has already achieved a high degree of perfection without their permission or their blessing, without any sort of help from them? Without even their knowledge? How can they be sure? It isn't a new trick for a wolf to dress up in a lamb's white wool. It isn't a novelty for Satan to make himself look "angelic." He is an angel.

Woe to the young man who looks, and acts, "too holy!"

In every Sulpician there was a suspicion that young Louis Marie de Montfort was too good to be true. Father Leschassier, the new superior general of St. Sulpice, let his suspicion fester. Louis made him his spiritual director, but Father Leschassier was not appeased, nor reassured. He had begun to doubt Louis when the boy knelt in the classroom, before lessons, blessed himself, and said some secret prayers. Did he think he had to say grace before and after classes? Was he "showing off?" He studied Louis, but from a distance. He wanted as few contacts with him as possible. Hence, he appointed Father Brenier to look after him—and he put the priest under obedience to be severe. Father Brenier had liked and admired Louis. Now it was different. The man had been handed to him—like a sweet and spicy dish to a dyspeptic, or a glass of heady wine to a man with gastric ulcers. His task was not to train Louis but to test him for any symptoms of disobedience or pride; to make sure, by discipline, that his apparent sanctity was not a sham.

Louis would go often to Father Leschassier, to ask a question he thought important, to seek advice, or to discuss a matter that troubled him. But the grave priest always repelled him. He listened grudgingly, impatiently, with evident dislike. He made it clear that Louis was unnecessarily bothering him, that he tolerated him only because he was filled with paternal charity. (But charity could go too far in some cases!) He frequently dismissed him abruptly, as a master snaps at his dog, and sent him to Father Brenier. For chastisement?

It distressed Father Brenier that he had to be his superior's rasp, his whip, and his spur. He was a gentle soul, yet he devoted himself to the task assigned him. Through the grace of God, he managed to become a stern, implacable, bitter, disdainful, overbearing, and even hateful slave driver. He gave Louis as many distasteful jobs as he could invent. He worked him day and night, at many things. He scolded him for obeying, and for seeming not to obey more quickly. He chided him in public whenever possible, and with as much sarcasm as he could summon. He changed his orders frequently, countermanded them, and scolded Louis for being too dumb to understand them. He took away privileges, added penances—and commanded him to forget the penances he was used to inflicting upon himself.

Louis obeyed promptly, sweetly, never showing any signs of anger or resentment, never asking any questions, never seeking any escape. He listened to scalding reprimands as though he deserved them. He was always ready to confess himself the most wretched of sinners. He always humbly thanked his persecutor for his "kindness." Some biographers say that Father Brenier became an "expert at murdering nature," and destroying all vestiges of self-love in a man.

But the saint's docility and patience and love were more merciless than all Father Brenier's inflictions. The rasp lost its teeth and became no more abrading than the tongue of a month-old calf. The whip became a mess of string. The spur, through constant use, became rusty and dull; and it hurt the rider more than the gentle horse he rode. At the end of six months Father Brenier begged for mercy. Let somebody else try to show that de Montfort was merely a hypocrite! Father Leschassier relieved him and took the task himself.

Had Louis not consecrated himself to Mary, as he has taught so many millions to do, he might have bucked and reared and thrown his rider not once but many times, for he still had a villainous temper. But since he had become a slave he had grown strong; and he was free. He could bear everything. Why didn't everybody see that if he wanted to be stronger than the devil he must come close to God? Why didn't everybody realize that the closer he drew to Mary the nearer he came to Father, Son, and Holy Spirit?

Didn't St. John, who wrote about Eternal Wisdom, also write about the Mother of Wisdom, the woman clothed with the sun and crowned with a dozen stars? Eternal Wisdom had come to men as fruit comes from the tree. Whoever wanted that Fruit must go to the tree. Whoever ate of that fruit would be strengthened against all trials.

"Like a vine I produced a pleasant aroma, and my blossoms turned into fruits . . . in me is found every gift of the way and of the truth, and all hope of life and virtue. Come to me, all you who desire me, and fill yourselves with the fruit I bear . . ."

55

Mary was the mother of the Way and the Truth and the Life. She gave her graces lavishly to those who gave themselves generously to her, or to Jesus in her. If they will permit her to do so, she will mould them into perfect images of her Son. Let a man melt the self-love in him and throw it onto the desert sands; then let him pour the molten gold of his love into the heavenly mould of the Mother of God. The gold will be shaped into perfection.

How does a man empty himself of self-love? By enduring with patience, even with joy, everything that attacks and harms that self-love. By accepting all the crosses heaped upon him, and carrying them willingly to his own Calvary. Father Leschassier, and Father Brenier, and all those others who ridiculed and harassed him would make him a saint, if he let them.

God bless them—and give them many little crosses!

7 Wisdom Through Mary

Some of Louis Marie's companions felt sympathy for him, admired his docility and the obedience he showed his superiors, and praised his devotion to Mary. But most insisted he was either a fool or a pharisee, or maybe both. If he was sincere, those holy priests wouldn't treat him so abominably. Many followed the example of the priests. (St. John Bosco once said that a priest takes many with him, to heaven or to hell.)

The majority agreed it was good and proper to love and reverence the mother-maiden. But did a man have to mention her name aloud so often—like a homesick school boy mooing for his mother or his rustic village belle? Did he have to flaunt her Rosary everywhere, and try to make everybody say it with him? The beads meant more to him than the flag of France! Did he have to sing songs to her, or recite impromptu verses in her honor? Did he have to kneel, unmoving, for hours, before her altar in the chapel? What was he trying to do, make a goddess out of Mary? The man could not be sincere. He was merely posing as a mystic. He deserved all the priests rubbed into him.

De Montfort's love for Mary was unique and extraordinary. No man of his era was so openly, so completely, so ardently hers. No one had such a childlike trust in her. Few men of any age have given themselves so fully into her guidance. But not even those closest to him knew, or suspected, that he loved God far more than he loved the Virgin. They had no idea that the principal reason he loved Mary was that she brought him closer and ever closer to Eternal Wisdom.

De Montfort, in his cold, dark, cramped, bare room, wrote many verses to Wisdom—and even in a poor translation they are beautiful.

> *Forgive my ardor,*
> *Wisdom Divine,*
> *But You are the master*
> *Of my whole heart.*

57

I cry to You.
Come to my help;
Lend Your ear
To my poor words.

Son of God, Beauty Supreme,
Come! Come!
To be without You
Is to be damned!

Come! With You I shall be king—
Yet a king submitted to Your rule.
O Word equal to the Father,
Come!

Light of Light,
Come dwell in me.
With You I shall most clearly see;
With You I'll fight all hell.

All virtues follow You.
Come! Dwell in me.
With You is charity, humility, and poverty.
Come! Dwell in me.

I want to own You, Wisdom.
Come! Dwell in me.
I want to gamble with You—
To lose all things—
And win You—You alone.

They were all like that. But some stand out, because of the passion that gave them birth. This is another example:

Divine Wisdom, I love You unto folly.
I am Your lover.
You alone in this world I seek,
You alone I desire.
I am a man gone mad with love,
Forever chasing You.

Tell me who You are.
For I'm half blind.
I can discern only
That You are a secret I must fathom.
Show Yourself fully to my soul
Which dies for love of You.

Where do You live,
Wisdom Divine?
Must I cross continents or seas
To find You,
Or fly across the skies?
I'm ready to go wherever You are,
Not counting the costs, to possess You.

De Montfort was most sincere in his determination to acquire Wisdom at any cost; and to share that Wisdom with all the world. But, he felt, one must first know Wisdom, then desire Him, then pray to own Him, continually mortifying oneself. And, of course, one must have a real devotion to Our Lady. Without Mary, a man might easily lose his way.

Louis was a product of the 17th Century French school that stressed Christ's Incarnation rather than His passion, death, or resurrection. The teachers of this school believed God's glory was most apparent when it was most hidden, when it reigned in Mary's virgin womb. Their favorite ejaculation was: "Jesus, living in Mary."

Mary was the first cathedral in Christ's kingdom. Unnumbered choirs of angels sang therein all day and all night. Her pregnancy gave more joy to God than all the splendors of the millions of billions of galaxies of worlds His shining hands have made—those love lights He has been flashing since long before our world began.

In this chaste and most exquisitely designed edifice, Infinite Wisdom prepared Himself to enter our foolish earth. Divinity therein eagerly put on our pitiful humanity. Unlimited Majesty and Power took on flesh to become "the most abject and despised of men." Eternal Life, because He loved us and because He bewailed our sins and our possible damnation, most willingly accepted the seeds of death. Power Unlimited became a helpless and most dependent slave.

The students of St. Sulpice knew all this. But evidently the dust of the Jansenist heresy had stung their eyes and coated their mouths.

59

They could not see the doctrine clearly; and they had quit discussing it seriously. Talk of the Virgin Mother had become "old-fashioned"—"bad form"—"infantile goo." They had no idea that devotion to Mary was a prelude to devotion to God. To Louis it was simple.

A boy hurrying through the Breton fields stops to lift a flower. He cannot help himself, for the flower is so attractive, so compelling. He holds it in his hands, feeling its stem, its leaves, its petals. He looks at its design, its colors, its divine construction. He inhales its aroma. And he remembers the words of Jesus: "Consider the lilies of the field; they toil not, neither do they spin; yet Solomon in all his glory was not arrayed as one of these."

The glory of God is revealed in this flower, which begins to wither as soon as it is plucked. And there are millions of them scampering gaily through the world! They are God's gifts to men. They cry out His name. And, if a boy listens, he will hear the grass and the grain and the clods of earth, and the distant clump of trees, and the silver of blue river, and the rock piles, and the rising sun, and the fast fading crescent of the tired moon all join the flowers in a hymn of praise; "Holy, holy, holy, Lord God of Hosts!"

What is the glory of Solomon compared to the glory of God? What is the glory of a flower compared to the glory of Mary? The flower has lifted a boy toward his Creator? Mary will lift him higher—as high as he desires to go. The flower is more than a flower. It is a proof of God's presence, of His might, of His love. Mary is more than a woman; and she is still alive!

Wasn't she assumed bodily into heaven? God lifted her up as easily as the boy the flower. And God gave her to us not only as a proof of His love, but also as an all-powerful mother. She transmits His love. She radiates it. We transmit our love of God through her.

The flower is perfect? Mary is the one perfect creation of the Most High, and dearer to Him than all the rest of His miracles of perfection. Who does not love her does not love God.

Mary was, to St. Louis, not only the gate to the Way to Paradise; she was an earthly paradise herself: "the true paradise of the new Adam . . . filled with untold riches, with beauty, with delights, with all sorts of good things the new Adam left there."

"In this Eden," he wrote, "this weedless garden . . . one may find trees which were planted by God and maintained by His grace. There is the tree of life which bore Jesus as its fruit. And there is the tree of the knowledge of good and evil, whose fruit was Incarnate Wisdom,

60

the light of the world. There are, in this most beautiful place, flowers of virtue whose fragrance thrills the angels. There are fields of flowers, meadows of hope, towers of strength, and mansions of simplicity and trust . . .

"The air is pure. Day reigns here. Day without night. A beautiful day, the day of the Sacred Humanity. The sun does not cast a shadow. It is the sun of the Divinity.

"The Holy Spirit speaks of Mary as the sanctuary of the Divinity, the resting place of the Trinity, the throne of God, the city of God, the altar of God, the temple of God, and the world of God."

De Montfort could not write anything about Mary without also writing of Father, Son, and Holy Ghost.

He reveled in the mystery of the Incarnation; but he was always aware of the mystery of our redemption. The cross was a great part of his life. It flamed in his mind as it did when he was a boy serving Mass in the church in Iffendic and the sun lit up the stained glass window high above the altar. Who could forget Mary, standing beneath Him, nailed to her own most dreadful cross?

Did he, as a boy or as a man, ever suspect that Mary, in her own sweet feminine way, had helped Jesus to carry His cross?

She came upon Him just after He had fallen because of the weight of the cross. An ordinary mother would have rushed forward, cursing the centurion and all his men, demanding help for her boy. Or she would have pleaded, or coaxed, or tried to shame the guards into commanding the broad shoulders of some man standing there looking on. Mary, apparently, did nothing. Yet, suddenly, the centurion was touched with concern—or was it pity? And he commandeered the aid of the young African, Simon of Cyrenaica. Simon became a Christian because he helped to carry that cross. The Centurion became a Christian too. Isn't it like the Mother of God to help her children when they stagger under the cross? Isn't it like her to lead all men to Christ?

Nobody knows whether he suspected this or not. But most certainly he knew the Lady was helping him carry the cross Father Brenier had pressed upon him. And most probably he felt it was she who arranged to have it lifted from his shoulders. For Father Brenier not only ceased to harry him, he also gave him something of a reward for his patience. He appointed him librarian of the seminary, put him in charge of Mary's own little chapel in the church of St. Sulpice, and made him Master of Ceremonies at all the celebrations to be held there. Now Louis had not only a respite, but also a shrine where he could be alone when he had no pressing duties. Now he had all the books he had ever wanted to read. Books about Wisdom. Books about the Cross. Books about the Rosary. Books about the "slavery to Mary."

Father Boudon's "Holy Slavery of the Admirable Mother of God" was among these books. And there were the writings of Father Olier, Cardinal de Bérulle, Father de Condren, the Venerable Mother Agnes of Jesus, a Dominican nun, and others, including St. John Eudes, and St. Bernard.

Father Olier, who had founded the seminary of St. Sulpice and intended it to be "a little kingdom of Our Lady," had put a silver chain around his neck in token of his bondage. The Mother of God is said to have appeared to him, while he was in the church of Notre Dame, and to have given him the plans for the seminary. When the building was nearing completion, Father Olier carried its keys all the way to the shrine of Our Lady of Chartres. There he begged the Lady to take possession of his house and bless it forevermore. Regarding his consecration to Mary, as her slave, he wrote:

"I owe the happiness and glory of my bond-service to Jesus Christ to that which I vowed to the Virgin Mary, for that incomparable Mistress draws all souls first to her own love and service, in order to lead them afterwards to Jesus Christ, our Lord; the great aim of the mother being the honor of her Son. This is what she meant by her words at the marriage feast of Cana . . . 'Whatsoever He shall say unto you do ye.' "

Father Olier, like his friend, St. John Eudes, never separated Mary from Jesus. They were always together in his mind, his biographers assure us. St. John Eudes gives them one heart. "Most loving heart of Jesus and Mary, we revere thee, we praise thee, we glorify thee, we love thee . . ."

When Louis had absorbed all that was written about slavery, he consecrated himself, solemnly, to Jesus, in Mary, and through Mary; and gave up to Him, and to her, everything he owned, everything he had, even the value of his prayers and his good works.

He gave himself first entirely to Mary, believing that the more truly a soul is consecrated to her, the more truly is it consecrated to her Son . . . This is what he means by "True Devotion to Mary."

"True Devotion to Mary," he wrote, "is an easy, short, perfect, and safe road to perfection, which means union with Christ. To a Christian, perfection is nothing else than such a union. It is an easy road. It was opened by Jesus when he came to us. The road of Mary is gentle, peaceful. One finds there, it is true, great difficulties and fierce battles.

62

But our mother is ever near, to light the darkness, to clear away doubts, to give strength, to banish fear, to help in every way. The Virgin road to Jesus, in comparison with all others, is a stretch of roses and bee-trees packed with wild honey. There have been a few, not many, saints who have walked that way—Ephrem, John Damascene, Bernard, Bernardine, Bonaventure, Francis de Sales. The Holy Ghost, Mary's spouse, had revealed it to them . . . The road is a perfect one by which to reach Christ and be united to Him. Mary is the most perfect creature, the purest and holiest.

"The Most High, the One Beyond All Understanding, the Untouchable God, He Who Is, came down, perfectly and divinely, to us mean little worms, through the humble Mary. He came without losing anything of His divinity. Therefore it is through Mary that we little ones must, perfectly and divinely, and without fear, ascend to Him."

To give his consecration added significance, St. Louis renewed the baptismal vows that made him a child of God. A man professing himself the slave of Mary—or of Jesus in Mary—must, he thought, repeat his renunciation of Satan and all his works. In this act, one commentator says, Louis, like the beloved St. John, "took Mary to his own," never going to Jesus without her.

Almost immediately he began to urge his fellow students to bind themselves to Mary—so that they too might be set free—and he asked permission of his superiors to establish a group, or an association, or a congregation of such slaves. Father Louis Tronson, retired superior general of St. Sulpice, who had to be consulted by de Montfort's immediate superiors, gave him permission, with his blessing, but suggested that those enrolling themselves in the movement should be called not Slaves of Mary, but "Slaves of Jesus in Mary."

Years—many years—later, when the book "True Devotion to Mary" was published, those who loved Our Lady best found this form of consecration, and recited it, on their knees, with joy and awe:

"O Eternal, Incarnate Wisdom; lovable, adorable Jesus, only begotten Son of the Father and of Mary ever Virgin, I adore You profoundly in the bosom and the splendor of Your Father, in eternity, and in the virgin womb of Mary during the time of Your Incarnation. I give You thanks for annihilating Yourself and taking the form of a slave to set me free from the cruel slavery of the devil. I give you thanks, and I glorify You, because You consented to submit to Mary in all things, in order to make me Your faithful slave through her.

"I, a faithless sinner, renew and ratify today, in your hands, O im-

63

maculate mother, the vows of my baptism. I renounce forever Satan, his pomps and works; and I give myself entirely to Jesus Christ, the Incarnate Wisdom, to carry my cross after Him all the days of my life, and to be more faithful to Him than I have ever been before.

"In the presence of all the court of heaven I choose you this day for my mother and mistress. I deliver and consecrate to you, as your slave, my body and soul, my goods, both interior and exterior, and even the value of all my good actions, past, present, and future; leaving to you the entire and full right of disposing of me and all that belongs to me, without exception, according to your good pleasure, for the greater glory of God in time and in eternity. . . . Faithful Virgin, make me in all things so perfect a disciple, slave, and imitator of Jesus, Your Son, Incarnate Wisdom, that I may, through you and after your example, come to the fullness of His age on earth and of His glory in heaven. Amen."

Incarnate Wisdom! All men should be united to Him. Slavery to Mary —or to Jesus in Mary—would unite them perfectly!

8 Madame de Montespan

If St. Louis was ever tempted to self-pity, he had only to remember that crosses come from God. To carry them was a privilege. To complain of the weight was to be ungrateful. And whining would weaken a man.

All God's children were stumbling along together on the road to Calvary. They should help and love each other. One had to be strong enough to carry his cross well, and to help all those who needed his aid. The added strength would come from Christ. Incarnate Wisdom had given power to Simon of Cyrene. The man couldn't lift the heavy wood at first. Then, suddenly, the burden had no weight at all. Christ still lived, still gave His strength to those who wanted it, especially to those who would be other Christs. He gave His peace. And His patience.

How shameful it would be to resent the insults and indignities and absurdities heaped upon him! The men tormenting Jesus thought themselves superior to Him, because they could kick Him and punch Him, because they could spit on Him, because they could revile and taunt Him, because they could nail Him to a cross and mock Him as they watched Him die. And all the time Jesus was using their hatred, making it serve His love for them. He was using their weaknesses and their wickedness against them—so He might die for them and bring them to His Father. A man who wanted to follow Jesus must, like Him, live and die for all men, especially those who despised and hated him.

And one had only to look at the wretchedness of other people to see how miraculously light his own cross was.

It was in this period of his life that Louis met a woman who carried the heaviest cross in France, perhaps in all the world.

Historians are confused, and somewhat contentious, about the exact year these two met. Father E. C. Bolger, a member of the Montfort Fathers, says it was 1697, three years before Louis was ordained. Another biographer, whom we know only as "A Secular Priest," insists it was in 1701, a year after the ordination.

A letter Louis received from his sister Louise led to this meeting. The girl was in danger of being ousted from her convent. Mlle. de Montigny's death had forced this crisis.

It was not only St. Sulpice Seminary that relied on the prudence of men rather than the providence of God. Many convents operated on the same principle. These religious were desperately poor themselves; and they felt that they had to say, in effect, "your money or your (religious) life." Unless one could pay for room and board he could not take vows of poverty, obedience, and chastity. Louis had been forced to visit the homes of the dead when Mlle. Montigny could no longer support him. A man could do this; he could find work most anywhere. But a girl—

The "secular priest author" prints a letter Louis wrote his sister and dated it "February, 1701." It seems to deal with this situation—yet does not refer specifically to it. It could have been written before or after the event.

"God wishes you to be separated from everything that is not Himself," he wrote, "perhaps to be forsaken by all creatures." (He could have been reflecting that God wanted him also to be separated from everything except 'God Alone.') "Rejoice, spouse and servant of God, if you thus resemble your Jesus, who was despised and rejected, like the dirt swept out by a housewife's broom . . . If you serve God and His mother faithfully, you will want for nothing in this world or the next . . ."

He wasn't worried. Saints never worry. When they are helpless they look to heaven for help. Undoubtedly Louis talked to the all-powerful Queen of Heaven, and let her "worry" for him. Then he talked to the women who had paid his way into St. Sulpice. They sent him to a bishop, who sent him to a priest, the tutor of the young children of King Louis XIV and his cast-off mistress, Madame de Montespan.

Athenais de Montespan, the daughter of a duke, met the king when she was chosen maid of honor to his queen, Maria Theresa. Two years later she was married to the Marquis de Montespan. She was the mother of two children when the king decided she should belong to him alone. Her husband was helpless against his master's majesty. He protested by draping his coach with black and decorating it with antlers, then driving it to the palace of Versailles so that everybody could see he did not believe in the divine right of kings. The royal Louis didn't like this form of criticism. He had the marquis jailed. Later he exiled him to his estates in the Caribbean.

Exile, to the nobles of Louis' court, was looked upon as the worst possible disgrace. Few of them survived it very long. They sulked, pouted, spleened, pitied, ate, or drank themselves to death. They were out of favor with the court. They could impress nobody, not even their own peasantry; and there was nothing—nothing, nothing, nothing—to do on their estates.

Athenais shared the king, willy-nilly, with his wife and a younger mistress, La Vallière. The Grand Monarch took his women—and his horses and household goods and servants—wherever he traveled. And everywhere he went, crowds of people came running to see "the French queens." She liked that. She liked to be thought a queen. After she had rid herself of La Vallière, and had turned the Queen into a tame tabby cat, she lived in the full glory of the royal sun. She gave the king seven healthy children. She was accouched in public, like a queen, and the babies were made legitimate by Louis' own decree.

She had power unimaginable, riches unlimited, friends innumerable. The court centered about her, reacted to her whims and follies and moods. She had beauty and wit and charm—and a fang-like tongue. It bit deep when it bit. And it was always biting. Eventually the sun king began to hide himself—behind bright young clouds—and to cast long and longer shadows on the mother of his brood.

Athenais attempted to win him back by desperate and devious methods—which led to the belief that she was a sorceress, a witch, a user of love charms that might poison the king, or make him her slave for life.

One day the woman had few enemies, if any. The next day the palace swarmed with them. And that day the royal sun did not shine on her. Eventually she was thrust out into the night—a long night. The king made no effort to protect her. He made no effort to punish her. He did not stop her royal pension or banish her from her children. He simply moved her out of his light.

In her gayest and most lavish days, the queen who wasn't really a queen, was called "the humiliation of France." Now she was the disgrace of France.

She hid herself. She could not sleep at night. She was afraid. There were people she had ruined by a word, a look, a bit of sarcasm or satire. She had had men jailed, exiled, beaten, degraded. Any one of them might find his way into her bedroom and kill her while she slept. She hired a woman to stay on guard in her room, with all the candles lit. She had to play cards all night, one solitaire game after another, so that if her employer awoke she would be reassured that all was well, and might go back to sleep.

She sent letters to her husband, humbly begging his forgiveness and imploring him to take her back, even as the least of his servants. The Marquis would not even answer her.

Athenais, abandoned by everybody, scorned by everybody, made her peace with God, Whom she had abandoned. Eventually she learned to carry her terrible cross with patience—even with a sort of joy, the joy that comes with the strength Christ gives to those who follow Him.

She was living in a convent when Louis de Montfort went to see her about his sister's plight; and she was trying, in every possible way, to atone for all her sins.

No biographer has bothered to tell us anything about this dramatic encounter between France's "greatest sinner" and France's "greatest saint"—the greatest of their time, that is. But we suspect that Athenais must have found Louis the most exciting man she had ever met—more exciting even than that other Louis. For this one wanted nothing for himself, only a pittance for his sister. He didn't pity her. He didn't scorn her. He didn't flatter her. And there must have been something in his eyes to show her how much he admired her in her role as a penitent. Her hair had turned white. Her face had softened. Her tongue had lost its bite. She was more beautiful than ever. It is impossible to believe Louis did not see her beauty, or that he did not enjoy it. It is impossible to believe he stood before her, looking only at her shoes—or his own—as Canon Blain pictures him. He must have seen, instantly, that she was a friend, and undoubtedly the one ordained to help him bear his cross.

She agreed to care not only for Louise, but also for two other sisters. She made provision for Louise in the convent of St. Joseph, in Paris. Sylvie she placed in the Royal Abbey of Fontevrault, then "the queen of all the abbeys in France."

It had been founded in the Eleventh Century, in honor of the Blessed Virgin; and it had prospered gloriously in these six hundred years. It contained several monasteries, one for monks, one for nuns, one for repentant women; and there was an infirmary. The "queen-abbess" was in complete charge of everything and everybody, including the monks. She was always of noble blood. Sometimes she was a royal princess. In spiritual matters, she took orders only from the pope; in material matters, she listened only to the king.

68

The abbey was revered not only for its royal flavor, but also for its long history of pious men and women, for the crowds of distinguished pilgrims who visited it, and for the beauty of its buildings, its art treasures, and the country it graced. It was one of the great shrines of the country; and it seemed—between wars—to attract almost as many Englishmen as French, for the early Plantagenet kings were buried there, including Henry II and Richard the Lion Hearted, his son. Henry's aunt Matilda had been one of the abbesses. Another, incidentally, was a sister of Mary, Queen of Scots, and a third was an illegitimate sister of Louis XIII, and of Henrietta Maria, queen of England.

The fame of the abbey was spread through the veins and arteries of Europe by the minnesingers, the troubadours, the wandering minstrels, all singing the story of Henry and his son.

Henry II, once the most powerful monarch in the world, was brought, dead and naked, into the abbey church for burial. During his reign he had never travelled anywhere without a coterie of bishops and archbishops. When he died, in 1189, there were no clerics near him, not even a simple priest. His men took everything he had, even his clothes. As the body, covered by a page boy's old coat, lay before the altar, Richard, the new king of England, knelt beside it. And, so the story had it, blood ran from the nostrils of King Henry.

Henry was a mad man when he was enraged. Often he threw himself to the floor in his fury and chewed the rushes. In one of these rages he had asked to be rid of his friend Thomas A Becket, whom he had made archbishop of Canterbury. In one of those rages, after the battle of Le Mans, he had shown his hatred of the Almighty.

"O God, since you have today, to heap up confusion on me and increase my shame, taken so vilely away from me the city I love most on earth, where I was born and reared, where my father is buried, I shall pay you back . . . by taking from You the part You love best, my soul."

In one of those rages he died, crying: "Shame, shame on me, a vanquished king."

Ten years later, Richard's body was borne to the same altar. He was buried at the foot of the father he had helped to destroy, and near the body of his mother. King John, Richard's brother, came to Fontevrault for the funeral.

It is not odd, perhaps, that, in time the historic abbey should become a prison, a home for those awaiting the guillotine.

But at this time, whether it was 1697 or 1701, the abbess was Madame de Montespan's sister, Gabrielle de Rochechouart-Mortemart.

69

God often sends special joys to his saints, to supplement the joy of carrying his cross. Louis must have relished this joy of knowing his sister was safe. He must have relished the joy of meeting a sinner who was trying with all her might to be a saint.

There were other joys sprinkled in his path at this time. He was ordained sub-deacon, then deacon. He knelt before his Lady's image in the Cathedral of Notre Dame, solemnly renewed his consecration to Mary, and took a vow of perpetual chastity. And, about this time, he was chosen as one of two seminarians to visit the Cathedral of Our Lady of Chartres.

Two men were selected every year to walk the long road from Paris to Chartres, as Father Olier had first walked it. It was, to each new crop of students, a legacy of love.

Louis, to quote Canon Blain, "received the commission with all the joy of his soul . . . he went to Chartres as if he were going to some earthly paradise . . . His companion, Father Bardou, later vicar general of the diocese of Narbonne, was a model of holiness. With him Louis had no need to restrain his devotion."

The Canon does not say, this time, that Louis walked like a man in a trance, his eyes lowered against the beauties of nature, his ears shut tight against any friendly—and distracting—word from his friend. The Canon was not present. He learned the story from Father Bardou. So he had to admit that Louis did leave the highway now and then to talk to people working in the fields. However, he manages to convey the idea that the saint spoke to these people only of God.

It apparently did not occur to him that Louis might also have discussed crops with these fellow-peasants, and their domestic problems, and the glory of the day, and the wonder of the sky. Nor did he consider that Louis might have spent happy minutes looking at houses and barns and animals and orchards and fields and vineyards and trees and piles of manure, the "farmers' gold"—and maybe a line of ducks coming up from the water.

He tells us that the travellers arrived at their destination sometime during the night, and that Louis "hurried to throw himself with every sign of tender and sensible devotion at the feet of the image of the Blessed Virgin, which is honored in the crypt chapel." He adds that the long journey appeared to have "caused him no fatigue." He doesn't say where the pilgrims slept that night, or if they slept. He hurries on to assure us that Louis spent most of next day, unmoving, kneeling before the statue.

70

Most every one of Louis' biographers wonders, publicly, what froze him there at the feet of Mary. Father Bolger asks: "Did he recall the martyrdom to which he had been subjected? If he remembered at all, we can be sure it was with regret that it had not been greater. His intense love of Jesus and Mary must that day have blazed with almost unbearable intensity; his desire to make them more loved must have tortured him as no ill-treatment could possibly have done . . ." Others believe he was thinking ahead to the day of his ordination, or backward to his friendship with Claude Poullart des Places, his friend in the Jesuit College in Rennes. He and Poullart had formed a sodality in honor of Mary, and Poullart had decided that someday he would found a seminary that would give the world many holy priests—especially priests in love with Mary.

It is quite conceivable that Louis' thoughts were full of the priesthood that awaited him. It might not be a bad guess to say he expected to be a missionary, probably among the Indians in the heavy snows of Canada. He had yearned to be a missionary ever since his days at Rennes.

Louis wanted, of course, to be a priest. That was all he wanted in this life. Yet he wouldn't let himself be rushed into the priesthood. He kept putting it off, apparently because he thought he was too unworthy for such glory. A saint, in the bright light that shines on him from above, can see, more clearly than most of us, his weaknesses and his faults and his imperfections—his utter unworthiness of God's love.

On March 9, 1699 he wrote his uncle in Rennes, describing how he felt: "Would to God I might be left in peace, as the dead in their graves or as a snail in its shell. Hidden in his shell, the snail seems to be something beautiful; but when it comes out of that shell it is only dirt and nastiness. This is what I am. Or perhaps I am even worse . . ."

His superiors finally commanded him to present himself to the bishop. He hesitated no longer. This was the will of God, the call to obedience. He became a priest on the 5th of June, 1700, Ember Saturday after Pentecost. The bishop was a man Louis loved and admired, the Most Reverend Bazan de Flamanville, Bishop of Perpignan.

He spent most of this day also on his knees before the Blessed Sacrament. And he took several days to prepare himself for the celebration of his first Mass. No other altar than that in the chapel of Our Lady, in the church of St. Sulpice, would do for this momentous occasion.

Canon Blain was one of the few who attended this Mass.

71

"I stood by his side," he assures us, "and in him I saw an angel . . . Nor was I the only one struck by his angelic appearance . . ."

This, really, is pure gabble-babble. Few men have ever seen an angel. How could the canon know what one looked like? Why compare an angel to a priest, or a priest to an angel? Can an angel, with a few words, bring Christ down from the right hand of the Father, and hold Him in his fingers? Can an angel feed men with the Body and the Blood of Christ, the Son of God, the Son of Mary? Can an angel forgive sins? Can he properly prepare a man for death? Can he ever become another Christ?

Father Louis Grignion de Montfort, saying his first Mass, looked like a priest of God!

9　First Assignment

Seminarians today know what awaits them after ordination. They are being fitted for certain tasks, and these will be given them. Some will preach. Some will teach. Some will be missionaries. Some will be assigned to country or city parishes; and, in twenty years or more, they will become pastors.

But St. Louis de Montfort, in the seminary of St. Sulpice, in Paris, in 1700, had no inkling of his future. He knew what he wanted to do. He wanted to go to Canada, where it was unbelievably cold during the winter and incredibly hot during the summer, and live with the Indians, and their dogs, and their fleas, and their frightful foods, and tell them about Christ and Mary. But he must have known his superiors would never permit him to do that. He must have known he had only to express a wish, or a preference, to be instantly and firmly denied.

His superiors had no plans for him. They didn't know what to do with him. He did not fit any priestly pattern they approved. He would never be a real Sulpician, one they could respect and honor. All they could think of was to ordain him, and let what was going to happen happen. They made him a priest, but didn't bother to secure for him the faculties most desired by a priest—the right to hear confessions and to preach the Word.

This was a cross Louis had not expected. It was an especially cruel one. But a cross, accepted as a gift of God, shrinks in weight. A cross that is welcomed has no weight at all. Louis hugged the cross and thanked the Lord Who sent it.

For fifteen years, ever since he had come under the influence of Father Gilbert, his gentle Jesuit teacher, he had been preparing himself for the missions, praying, studying, reading about the great missionaries of the ages, writing sermons, scribbling poems, making up songs he would sing in the forests of Canada, or perhaps in the jungles of Africa or South America, or in the islands in the Caribbean. He would

73

go alone, and, in time—perhaps—others would join him, a band of saints. In one of his prayers, spread over twelve pages, he writes of this.

"What do I ask? Nothing for myself. Everything for Your glory . . . priests free with Your own freedom, detached from all things . . . priests without fathers, mothers, brothers, sisters, kin of any kind, without worldly goods, without cares, without even a will of their own . . . slaves of Your love . . . who will overthrow Your enemies with the staff of the Cross and the sling of the Rosary . . . men who will suffer everything with You and for You . . . true servants of the Holy Virgin . . . who will set the world ablaze with your love."

He asked Father Leschassier, as he was supposed to do, to send him to the Indians in Canada. The good priest laughed at him, made a joke of his dreams. "You in Canada? No. No. Looking for the Indians, you'd get lost among the trees." He had no suggestions to offer. It didn't seem to matter what de Montfort did.

Louis, thus forced to remain in the seminary, continued to prepare for his life as a priest. Fifteen years of dreaming of the missionary life are not erased by a witless joke. One who wishes to be another Dominic, or Francis, or Vincent Ferrer or Francis Xavier, submits to authority, but does not surrender. Louis was no longer a hero-worshipping boy. He was twenty-seven. Yet none of his heroes had lost his lustre.

St. Dominic was especially close to him, for he was essentially a missionary preacher, a tireless walker, a happy troubadour of Mary; and he brought the Rosary wherever his feet directed him.

Dominic! The man went singing everywhere, breathing the beauty of God's world into his lungs and heart, breathing it out like perfume. The glory of the earth became heaven when the saint inhaled it. Love transformed it, made it almost like the breath of God. Dominic exhaled heaven! He went through the world like a giant, adoring God with his body as well as his soul, bringing the truth into all the sorry untruthful world.

St. Francis of Assisi, wed to holy poverty, in love with all God's creatures and creations! There was another man to dream about, to study, to follow.

St. Vincent, who had set all Brittany afire with his love of God!

St. Francis Xavier who had claimed a continent for Christ!

St. Ignatius Loyola, the soldier-saint who had sent St. Francis—and how many others?—into action!

These were men who could not be driven away by a superior's sneer.

They still called to Louis. He could not go to them. But he must have known that in God's time he would join them—and bring an army of saintly missionaries with him.

He waited patiently for the Sulpicians to think of something for him to do. He kept up his daily chores, taking care of Our Lady's chapel, teaching young hoodlums the Way and the Truth and the Life, studying, writing, doing penance, growing in wisdom and in grace.

It was three months before any sort of comfort came to him, any indication that some of his holy dreams would soon come true. Father René Lévêque had organized a group of priests and seminarians in Nantes, which was known as the Community of St. Clement. He stayed there most of the time, but every so often he felt compelled to return to St. Sulpice "to renew his spirit." He liked Louis. And Louis liked him. He was happy when the old man asked him to join St. Clement's and become a missionary. Louis went immediately to Father Leschassier to ask permission. The superior granted it without hesitation—an ominous surprise.

St. Sulpice was, at last, rid of the saint it could not shape, remake, or reassemble. Possibly the good fathers sang another Te Deum as de Montfort left, bound for Nantes with Father Lévêque.

How did Louis feel as he trudged along the roads to his new life? He had to travel slowly now, to keep step with his venerable companion, and he must have had to stop here and there to give the old man time to rest. There were probably long golden hours of silence as they walked. They were two of a kind. They had not much need of conversation. They talked continually to God. Louis has written:

> *God speaks rarely from without,*
> *But forever deep within.*
> *O lovely lesson of God!*
> *O Model so supreme!*
> *Christ lived for thirty years*
> *In holy silence!*
> *Does not that radiant fact*
> *Light up the gold of silence?*

We can imagine these two men singing, sometimes, as they walked. It was September. The world was turning red and gold and purple. The days were shortening; but the sun was warm and bright while it shone. There was much to sing about. We cannot imagine them gossiping of common things, or talking about themselves. Louis had also written:

> *A great talker is usually*
> *A trunk without a lock,*
> *A big balloon of wind,*
> *A pretty bag that smells.*
> *When he is all poured out—*
> *With no latch upon himself—*
> *The devil soon may use him*
> *For his own evil ends.*

We can imagine that Louis felt something like a young knight setting out on his first crusade to find the Holy Grail. And we can imagine him thanking God that his prayers had been answered. "O great God, who can raise up children to Abraham out of these lifeless stones . . . send good laborers into the harvest, good missionaries into the Church. Your divine law is transgressed, Your Gospel misunderstood, Your religion abandoned. Torrents of iniquity deluge the earth. Impiety sits on the throne . . . May the divine fire that Jesus brought to earth be kindled anew, before the fire of Your wrath reduces everything to ashes. Arise, Lord. Why do You seem to sleep? Arise in Your omnipotence, in Your justice, and also in Your mercy. Form a company of bodyguards to protect Your house, to defend Your glory, and to save the souls that cost You so much blood!" He was, at last, a missionary, a laborer going into the harvest, one of a company of soldiers dedicated to Our Lady and Our Lord.

After many days of travel they reached Orléans. And after Father Lévêque had been rested and refreshed, they took a river boat to Nantes. Father Lévêque, it seems, was too weak to walk.

It could have been a beautiful outing on the Loire. Days of rest and relaxation. Days of silent prayer and meditation. Days of songs and psalms, and the writing of new sermons. But there were three men aboard who made the trip anything but pleasant. They were drunk. They were loud. They were vulgar and obscene. And they uttered blasphemies that Louis could not endure. He spoke to them, gently. They mocked him, big as he was. They ridiculed him. They taunted him. They cursed him. And, just to shock him, they uttered more terrible blasphemies than before. Was Louis angered? We do not know. There are few details of the trip; and there is much confusion, and many contradictions, in the books of his various biographers. But one thing is certain, Louis predicted that God would punish them, and very soon.

Within a day or two one of the three died of alcoholism; and the others, quarreling over the dead man, drew their swords and cut each other severely.

Some biographers declare that Louis traveled with Father Lévêque all the way to Nantes. Others say he left the old man at Saumur, and went from there to the Abbey of Fontevrault to visit his sister Sylvie, who would soon take the habit.

"We learn," writes one, "from a letter of Father Leschassier, that Louis must have visited Fontevrault before the month of November. Whether he came from Nantes or Saumur, he must have gone to the abbey before settling down in the Community of St. Clement, and it was on this occasion that he placed his new life under the protection of Our Lady of Ardilliers, whose church at Saumur became, to him, a favorite place of pilgrimage."

The shrine at Saumur was as well known then as Lourdes or Fatima is today. Pilgrims from all over Europe journeyed there, to show their love, to ask favors, to beg for cures. And many miracles have been recorded in the ancient books.

In 1454 a man digging in the earth near the town found a small statue of Our Lady of Sorrows holding her Son's body on her knees. So many wonderful things happened to people who came to see the statue, that they enthroned it in a small chapel. The wonder grew with the years. Eventually not only the hierarchy of the church but also the king and all his court became interested.

In 1554, one hundred years after the statue was found, a church was built to house it. Cardinal Richelieu enlarged it, so did King Louis XIV. The church was given a great dome; and much money was spent on decorating its interior and exterior. Kings and queens and lords and nobles of all kinds, rich men and poor, artists, writers, scientists, scholars, peasants, came in the hundreds of thousands to visit the shrine, each for his own reasons. Among these, Louis knew, was his hero of heroes, Father Olier himself.

How long Louis stayed in Saumur, silent and still before the statue, nobody knows. He was there alone. He may have spent a day, as he did in Chartres. He may have spent a week. And, when he wasn't in the church, he may have rambled around the town. It must have reminded him of Montfort-la-Cane. It had a fortress high on a hill. A man could see a good portion of God's beautiful world from its eminence—and remember the church of St. Nicholas, and the ruins of St. Lazare, and other places dear to the boy St. Louis had been.

At any rate, Louis walked the dozen miles or so from Saumur to the abbey of Fontevrault. Undoubtedly he was tired and hungry when he reached the gate. Undoubtedly he needed a bath and a shave, and perhaps a haircut too.

He bowed to the sister-portress, who greeted him with a stare—almost a frightened stare. He asked for "charity, for the love of God."

Maybe he wanted to prove, if only to himself, that charity did exist in this land "deluged with the torrents of iniquity." He was a man in rags. He was a creature covered with dust. But he was "one of the least of these." He was another Christ. Surely the good sisters of Fontevrault would receive him gladly.

The sister at the gate asked him who he was. He repeated his words, begging charity for the love of God. She asked where he had been. He asked again for charity—"for the love of God."

The sister kept questioning him. Finally she was exasperated enough to call the Lady Abbess, the noble Louise de Rochechouart, the sister of Mme. de Montespan. That great lady also tossed aside Louis' plea for charity, demanding to know who he was, what he was, where he had come from, where he was destined. Eventually she turned him away without a bite of food, a drink of water, or a kind word.

Louis, as he walked out of the gate, may have remembered the story of St. Francis of Assisi. The Saint and Brother Leo were walking toward a monastery somewhere near Perugia on a blustery winter day. The wind was whipping through their thin habits. There were icicles on their eyebrows. They were tortured by hunger and thirst. They were weary, for they had walked a long way. And now a rain began to fall—a chill, chill rain! Brother Leo thought it would be perfect joy to get to the monastery, the fire, the dinner table, and the bed. But Francis had other ideas.

"Write down, Brother Leo," he said, "that perfect joy is not to be found in giving good examples of holiness." He did not intend that the miserable, shivering, chattering, starving brother should then and there put those words on paper; merely that he should remember them, and record them later. He went on: "If a man could heal the sick, give sight to the blind, hearing to the deaf, and sound limbs to the lame—even if he could bring the dead back to life—he would not know perfect joy. If he could speak all languages, could read the Word of God in all its fullness, could prophesy, and could work great miracles—he would not know perfect joy. If he knew all that science knows, of the world and the moon and the sun and the stars, and all

78

the creatures God had made—he would not know perfect joy. If he could convert whole nations by his preaching—he would not know perfect joy."

Brother Leo, warmed a trifle by his curiosity, asked: "Then how can a man find perfect joy?"

And Francis answered, in words to this effect: "If, when we get to our shelter, faint with fatigue and hunger, soaked with rain and coated with ice, the brother porter takes us not for Friars Minor, but for thieving knaves, and beats us furiously, and drives us away, back into the rain and the snow and the ice and the endless leagues of darkness and emptiness—Brother Leo, if we accept this with patience, believing it is a cross the good Lord wishes us to bear, then we shall know perfect joy! The greatest gift God can give us is the grace to subject our self-love to bearing the cross of humiliation, or affliction, or danger, or torture, for the love of God."

St. Francis had merely thought of this perfection of joy. St. Louis had found it.

He wrote about it to Father Leschassier. His letter was lost or destroyed, but the answer from his superior remains in the archives. It is dated November 2, 1700, and can be translated thus:

"I was glad to hear of the consolation you had at Fontevrault. It is my sincere wish that you be no less favored at Nantes. There is, indeed, every reason to hope so . . . for all things will contribute to give you that joy which the spirit of the Lord allows us to taste in the midst of tribulations."

Evidently he expects his young priest to be snubbed, humbled, mistreated, and even abused in the Community of St. Clement.

After Louis left the abbey, the nuns could not help talking about him, how big he was, how wretched and lean, how ragged, how covered with dust, how bold and stubborn. And they talked of how he kept saying: "Charity for the love of God." When the portress described him as very tall and strong, with a great nose, and an obstinate chin, and eyes that disturbed her terribly—for no reason at all—Sylvie Grignion cried out that the man must have been her newly ordained brother!

This caused a tremendous stir, even consternation and panic. Sylvie was a protégé of Mme. de Montespan. And her brother Louis was the pet saint of this penitent mother of the royal children! They had actually ousted a priest who had begged shelter for the love of God—and not only a priest, but a most influential one! Why, Mme. de Montespan

79

could make him a bishop if she chose to. How dreadful! He must be found at once. He must be welcomed with a most special welcome. They must strew ashes on their heads, kneel humbly at his feet and beg his forgiveness. He must have the best food in the larder, the best wine the cellar boasted. He must have the softest bed, the most comfortable pillow. Look for him through the village. Search every house.

"Go to the poorest house first," Sylvie advised. "If the man is my brother, you will find him there."

Servants went to the poorest house and found him, but he would not return to the abbey.

"Tell the Lady Abbess," he said, "that I cannot accept, for myself, the charity she denied for the love of God."

10   The Call of the Poor

Louis Marie used to beat himself with extra severity every now and then. He discovered this not only gave him control of his strong and obstinate body, it helped him in many other ways. It also helped all sinners.

> 'The discipline,' he wrote,
> 'is a medicine.
> If everybody beats his back
> Until he bares his bones
> He will find that all
> Tepidity has gone.
> This is a remedy
> Hell despises.
> It is one that wakes a sinner
> In a second.
> All sins are put to flight
> By the old, old, remedy—
> The discipline, the scourge.'

It is probable that before he left Fontevrault he mercilessly bloodied his back, and offered his suffering as atonement for the sins of uncharity; and that he went, fasting rigorously, to Nantes, praying for the nuns who had denied him "charity for the love of God."

Perhaps, as he neared Nantes, a feeling of exultation overtook him, quickened his step, brightened his eyes, and lifted his face to the sky. For, naturally, he expected that when he reached the Community of St. Clement, he would begin the life of a missionary.

Thus he was building himself up for a descent into horror, shock, frustration, and temptation to anger, rebellion, and despair.

For the Community was nothing at all like the cluster of saints he hoped to find. It was more like a country club for privileged priests and seminarians. They dressed and spoke and acted like men who had never heard of Christ or His virgin mother. They wore silks and satins and much lace. They wore gaudy velvet jackets. They delighted in gold buttons, jeweled snuff boxes, lacquered boots. Some even carried swords. Few wore the prescribed clerical garments. Few said Mass. Few went to Communion. Their talk was mostly blasphemy, politics, or scandal. Nobody preached. Nobody went on missions. Not even Father Lévêque. He was too old.

If he had tasted heaven in St. Sulpice, Louis tasted purgatory in St. Clement. He wrote Father Leschassier, asking to be released, yet assuring him he would wait for orders. The chalice was bitter. He would let it pass, if he could. Yet not his will be done! He was torn between two desires, he said. He wanted to "commune in solitude," and he wanted to work for sinners, to preach devotion to Mary.

"And," he said, "I cannot help praying for a little company of good priests who may do this under the patronage of the Holy Virgin. I try to calm these desires, assured that I am in the arms of Providence, to forget all the difficulties shutting me in, and to live in perfect submission to your counsels, which will always be commands."

He remarked that he would like to associate himself with Father Leuduger, a missionary, and go with him to Rennes. He knew "a good priest" in that city who might place him in the general hospital, as a chaplain. There he could devote himself to the sick and crippled patients.

But he left his fate to his superior. Father Leschassier must tell him whether he was to stay, or to go.

This letter was written on November 6, 1700; but Father Leschassier waited until the last day in the year to answer it. He said he didn't know Father Leuduger. He said he was surprised Louis wanted to leave 'so soon." He said nothing at all about the reasons that made Louis eager to leave. He said: "Give yourself to our Lord and ask Him to let you know His will." Perhaps he forgot that the will of God is made known to a subordinate through his superior.

It was evident to Louis that God didn't want him merely to taste the bitter chalice. He wanted him to drink it to the lees, in further preparations for the day when he would go, fully equipped, into the vineyards waiting for him. God would not keep him in this purgatory forever.

In March, Father Leschassier received a letter from Canon Blain, Louis Marie's "good friend." Apparently Louis had written Blain about conditions in St. Clement's. The canon wrote Father Leschassier. Only the latter's letter to Louis has been saved:—

82

"I add to the letter Father Blain has written you that, having well considered the matter, I do not think you ought to quit the Community of St. Clement this year at least, unless Father Lévêque should leave. In that case, when he has set out on some journey, you can also withdraw, should you think it advisable. I recommend myself to your sacrifices, and am, with all my heart, yours. . . ."

Louis could grow rich on the crosses so carefully arranged for him by his good friends, and by those chosen to guide and protect him. A whole year? So be it. God always had a divine reason. He never sends anything but good, even when the good seems evil.

Perhaps Louis was tempted to pray for the early departure of Father Lévêque—wherever the blessed man might go.

The Lord rescued him a few weeks later, through Madame de Montespan. She invited him to the Abbey of Fontevrault to witness the clothing ceremonies attending his sister Sylvie's simple vows. She was to receive the habit on the second day after the fourth Sunday of April.

Louis wrote Father Leschassier, asking permission to accept the great lady's invitation. Father Leschassier answered immediately. (Nobody kept the king's ex-mistress waiting; nobody interfered with her desires.) He gave Louis a grumpy assent. It was as if Providence had upset all his plans and left him powerless and puzzled.

As soon as Father Leschassier's letter arrived, Louis set out. He walked swiftly, for the way was far and the time was short. The air was the pure air of God, unpolluted by any remarks against the mother of God, or against frequent communion, or against devotion to the Blessed Sacrament, or against His Holiness, the pope. It was spring. There were wild flowers everywhere along the roads. Trees were in bud. Birds were singing. The sun was warm and bright. And Louis, a man suddenly released from prison, must have chanted praises to God as he walked.

> *Let us adore the Lord forever.*
> *Let us adore Him in His mercy.*
> *Let us bless His gentleness and*
> *His divine compassion.*
> *Let us exult in His almighty power.*
> *Let us adore Him forever.*
> *He is good by nature—*
> *He is sweet and never bitter.*
> *He is beautiful, without blemish.*

83

He is immense beyond all measuring.
Let us adore Him forever.

He arrived the day after the ceremonies, but was welcomed not only by Madame de Montespan, but also by her sister, the Queen Abbess, and by all the nuns. He was asked to stay several days, and he wrote he "had the honor of several private conversations with Mme. de Montespan."

"She questioned me about myself," he said. "She asked what I wished to be. I told her I had an attraction toward working for the salvation of the poor. She approved of this. She knew how neglected they are. She said I could have a canonry, if I wished. It was hers to give. This I declined, explaining that I would never exchange the Providence of God for any canonry, benefice, or certain income. At this, she asked me to talk to the bishop of Poitiers. I agreed to this, although I didn't want to, because it meant I must walk seventy miles or so. But I saw God's holy will in this, which was the only thing I looked at; and I obeyed her."

It is recorded that St. Louis performed a miracle in the Abbey but whether it was on this or a subsequent visit is not clear.

He had just finished Mass on the marble altar donated by Mme. de Montespan, and was about to leave the chapel when he saw a blind man. He was inspired to ask him if he wanted to see. The man, puzzled as well as startled, said that of course he wanted to see. Louis put his wet fingers on the sightless eyes, and immediately the man saw.

The facts were sworn to by Mme. Hilaire Nicolas, in November, 1725, in the presence of two royal notaries. Mme. Nicolas, by the way, expected her testimony would be used not for the cause of the priest who had performed the miracle, but for the woman who had donated the altar on which he had said Mass. It was Mme. de Montespan's chapel—hence, the lady reasoned, it was her miracle. Some biographers see something of a parallel in this incident. The spittle of King Louis—his repudiation of her—had opened her eyes "to the beauty of holiness, which is above all other beauty."

Writing from Poitiers on May 4, 1701, Louis tells Father Leschassier that he had to wait four days to see the bishop, hence he had made a "short retreat," shut up in a little room in a big city, where he "didn't know anybody."

"I went to the hospital to serve the poor patients," he added. "I went into their little church to pray. There, while waiting for supper, I spent four hours. It seemed a short time to me; but others thought it a very long time. The fact that I stayed on my knees all this time, and that I was dressed like the poorest of the poor, touched them, made something of a stir. They bade the porter not to let me out of the chapel until they had taken up a collection for me. When I went out, to ask about supper and to beg permission to serve those at table, the people surrounded me and forced their alms upon me. Then I learned that they did not take their meals in common."

The hospital was a combination poor house, old folk's home, clinic, and surgery. It sheltered the most miserable in the city; the sick, the maimed, the blind, the senile, the desperate, the degraded poor. Louis "thanked the Lord a thousand times," for letting him pass as a poor man, and for permitting him to wear "the glorious livery of poverty." These people wanted him to be their chaplain. They hadn't had a resident priest in that wretched place for years.

Louis busied himself with these new friends until he was summoned to the bishop's palace. His Excellency had been out of town. He didn't know exactly how to greet this scarecrow priest who had caused such holy commotion. He had met Louis before. He was Father Girard then, tutor to the children of King Louis and his mistress. It was he who had sent Louis to Mme. de Montespan, on behalf of Louis' sister, Louise Guyonne. Evidently he had forgotten all this. How could he have forgotten so ragged a man?

"On the bishop's return," Louis wrote, "I told him in a few words what Mme. de Montespan had bade me say. He thanked me dryly, which was what I wanted. But the authorities of the hospital, in the name of all the people there, had presented a petition to the bishop's brother, Father de Bournat, asking me to be their priest. Therefore, the bishop spoke more pleasantly to me the second time I saw him, and commanded me to write you all these details. He wanted you to judge what I should do.

"I will tell you, my very dear Father, that I do have a great inclination to work in the hospital, but not so great as to settle down there and attach myself permanently. I place myself, however, in a state of indifference, desiring only to do God's will. And I will gladly sacrifice my time, my health, even my life, for the salvation of the poor in this neglected place if you think I should. I shall never take leave, I hope, of your guidance and friendship in Jesus Christ and His holy mother, in Whom I am wholly subject to you.

"I have been urgently requested, on several occasions, to ask your

85

permission to get myself approved for hearing confessions; but I have hesitated, because, for so difficult and dangerous an office, a particular mission is required."

Louis had intended to return immediately to Nantes, to acquaint Father Lévêque with what had happened, and to ask his permission, as well as that of Father Leschassier, to put himself under the direction of the bishop of Poitiers. But the bishop kept him in town for a month or so. He wanted to appoint the tattered and battered young priest as permanent chaplain of the battered and tattered old hospital; but first he wanted to know a little more about him.

He wrote to several of Louis Marie's former superiors; and was puzzled by their answers. They all said he was a saintly young man. They all hinted he was strange. They all said they didn't know whether he could take charge of the hospital or not. The bishop would have to judge.

Meantime the people in the hospital were clamoring for him. To add to his problems, the bishop was forced to leave Poitiers for a few weeks. He asked Louis to stay until he could give him a definite place in the diocese. He obtained a room in a seminary for him, and bade his vicar general use the young priest in any way he wished. Louis stayed.

He taught catechism to children, and to many grownups—whom he gathered together in the market sheds. He visited the hospital at least twice a day, giving alms to the poorest.

He found time also to talk to the city school students, and to form a religious society among them. This was but one of many lay organizations founded by St. Louis. He recognized the power of the laity two hundred and fifty years ago!

He was busy night and day. He loved it. The exhausting work refreshed him. He asked for more. So he visited the prison and ministered to the convicts and those awaiting trial.

He made such an impression on Poitiers that he was "news." The news spread to Nantes, and even to Paris. The people in St. Clement's, and the people in St. Sulpice's, began to wonder about him, and about the bishop of Poitiers. Perhaps, also, they began to wonder about themselves and their neglect of this extraordinary priest. Letters came to Louis from his old superiors and friends, chiding him, not praising him.

Father Leschassier criticized his "treatment" of Father Lévêque. The venerable old priest, the superior said, had been put to expense on Louis' behalf, and Louis was sadly neglecting him.

86

In this letter, however, he answered a question he had ignored many times before . . . "About getting yourself examined by some capable and experienced person, in order to see if you are fit to hear confessions, I answer Yes. You should not put it off any longer."

There was no one so capable and experienced as Father Leschassier himself in judging Louis Marie's fitness, no man living who knew so much about his soul. Yet he wanted someone else to judge him.

Louis felt he owed more than money to Father Lévêque. He owed him gratitude for his paternal friendship, for his many kindnesses, and for his affectionate good will. He had never tried to obtain the proper faculties for Louis; he had never suggested any missions for him; but he had asked him to try to make his fellow priests in the Community as zealous as himself. It is hard to be a missionary to Jansenistic priests, to fanatically Gallic priests, to indifferent priests, to worldly priests. Louis had tried and had failed; lamentably, he thought.

Maybe he should go back to them, if only for a time. The bishop would not return for weeks. The vicar general had no special work for him. The matter of his chaplaincy would not be determined for months. Therefore it seemed advisable to Louis that he put on a pair of stout shoes and hike to Nantes, settle matters with Father Lévêque, and await God's holy will.

A tremendous surprise awaited him in Nantes. A day or so after he arrived, he was given all the rights and privileges he had sought, and was sent to preach a mission in the little town of Grand Champ. God had spoken! Louis Marie Grignion de Montfort was at last a missionary priest!

With a word
He has brought forth all things from nothing.
Let us exalt the Lord.
All things exist through Him and by Him,
All things obey His laws—even His enemies,
Who ultimately know and feel His power.
This wondrous God creates the cities,
Fills the air with birds
And the earth with animals—
Even unto little green frogs, and reptiles.
His hand holds the lightning,
Rattles and rumbles the thunder,
And stirs the tempests of the sea,
Let us exalt the Lord.

Grand Champ, Louis wrote his superior, was "a rather neglected country parish." He remained there ten days, teaching catechism to the children, preaching three times a day to their elders, begging alms and giving them to the poor and distressed; baptizing, confessing, consoling the sick and the dying; working such a spiritual transformation that Nantes and Paris were chagrined and amazed.

From Grand Champ he went to other small communities. He was at Le Pellerin when Bishop Girard asked him to return to the hospital in Poitiers as soon as possible. The people there were continually demanding him. The bishop was sure this was the will of God for him. Louis wrote for permission:

"The urgent and continued prayers of the poor and the sick in the Poitiers hospital, joined to the desire of the bishop, and also of Mme. de Montespan," he said, "oblige me again to importune you, dear Father."

He added: "For three months I have been laboring without intermission in several parishes."

He had no inclination to shut himself up in a hospital for any long stay. Father Lévêque felt he might leave the Community, since God did not, apparently, mean him to stay there constantly. He had promised to keep a small room for Louis, where he could retire from time to time when he wanted solitude. Louis remarked about this promise: "I doubt he really means it."

He didn't want to return to St. Clement, he said, any more than he wanted to be confined to work in the hospital. True, Poitiers was a big city. It had more need for missionaries than these country hamlets, but he was not summoned for the general need, merely for a particular niche.

"Only the hope of eventually extending my labors," he said, "could give me any inclination to go to the hospital. My calling is to catechize the poor of the city and the country. But the great thing is to give implicit obedience to your wishes. I venture to declare myself, my very dear father in Jesus Christ, wholly subject to your orders."

In his reply, Father Leschassier avoided, as usual, making any decision for his spiritual son. He contented himself with saying, in a rather brusk way, "Follow the ordinary rules."

Late in October Louis returned to Poitiers. Father Lévêque had given him his blessing and a sum of money—both of which Louis gave to the beggars he met on the way.

He went by way of Saumur. He made a novena to Our Lady of Ardil-

88

liers, and stopped for a few hours at the Abbey of Fontevrault, to talk to his sister Sylvie, and to his friend Mme. de Montespan. That ex-sinner, he realized, had done more for him and his priestly career than all the priests who could have and should have helped him, and who had only hindered him.

Early in November he was back in the little room the diocese of Poitiers had provided for him. And he was back in the school, and in the streets, and in the market place, and in the cells of the prison, and in the hospital. Everywhere people greeted him as a long lost friend. He had never experienced so much affection.

One of the first things he did was to write to Father Leschassier for advice.

The "young lady directors" in the hospital wanted him to take his meals with them. He had refused, wanting to eat with the patients. Did he do right?

He did not want to separate himself from Divine Providence. So he would take no money for his work, and he would eat the food of the poor. Was he doing right?

He slept on straw. He took no breakfast, and ate but little in the evening. Was he doing right in this? He was in good health. Might he take the discipline every week—"beside the three ordinary ones"—and might he wear a girdle of horse hair once or twice a week!

Father Leschassier couldn't take any more. He was not going to be responsible for penances that might or might not make Louis a saint; nor was he going to be responsible for forbidding him these penances. He told Louis to get another spiritual director.

"I shall always be," he finished his letter, "with the same esteem, and the same affection, devotedly yours . . ."

But the next time he saw Louis Marie, he was neither affectionate nor devoted.

11 Storm Clouds Gather

St. Louis knew that in accepting the management of the general hospital he was accepting a heavy cross. But he had no idea how heavy it was. He soon began to call it Babylon. Babylon the wicked! Babylon the cursed! It was a pitiless place and it had a pitiless system. The strong fed on the weak. The weak debauched themselves to lessen their miseries. They suffered from their ills, their wounds, their wretched surroundings, and from the treatment of those paid to care for and protect them. They wandered into town, when they could, and begged or stole money for drunken orgies. And some lived in scandalous conditions.

The staff ate regular meals in the refectory. The patients ate alone; and often only on bread two or three days old, issued in the morning. If the management had chickens for dinner, the patients might be offered the bones in warm water, with perhaps a small chicken feather in each bowl—to make it a festive affair. Sometimes a man known to have gone into the city the day before was denied his daily ration—because he had come too early or too late—until he surrendered the coppers hidden in his poisonously dirty pockets.

All France—except the royal court—was suffering great poverty. Budgets were stingy everywhere. But the saint must have known that the management cheated the poor, even on this most stingy budget. And undoubtedly he knew it was best that the poor should eat in common, and at regular times.

To fatten the lean revenues, he borrowed a donkey and a couple of stout wicker panniers, and went about the city, begging from the merchants and the principal citizens. A few people helped him collect the food, clothing, blankets, and linens the generosity of the people provided. He became, like several other beggar saints, an object of intense interest and curiosity. Crowds followed him now and then; and spread stories about small boys trying to steal from the donkey, and the cleverness of the beast in foiling their attempts. The same stories have been told about other saints.

Many people, civic authorities among them, came to see the amazing reforms in the wicked Babylon. They noted that St. Louis served at the table, while someone read from the Gospel of the day or from some other holy book. They learned that he ate with the poor, and that he ate only what was left of the food he had begged for them. They also learned, and were mildly shocked, that he slept in the room intended only for contagious patients, that he took no pay from the city for all his work, and that, besides managing the place, he swept the floors, washed dishes, even scoured bed pans.

In addition to his work for the hospital, the saint taught a class in the city college, preached little homilies to the sick and the poor, said Mass, spent many hours of the day hearing confessions and giving religious instructions to the poor outside Babylon.

All went well, or comparatively well—for he had to fight continually against the grafters and the vicious—for the first three months.

"The superiors and subordinates of the hospital, and indeed, the whole city, were delighted at my arrival," he wrote. "They looked upon me as one sent by God to reform the place. The bishop and all the officials authorized me to make the poor take their meals in the refectory, and to collect something for them to eat with their dry bread. This I did in spite of many rebuffs, which constantly increased until, due to a certain person and the lady-superior, I was forced to give up charge of the refectory tables. The gentleman, who was embittered against me without any reason I know of, ceaselessly and harshly opposed, contradicted, and insulted me inside the house, and decried my management throughout the town. This stirred up a strong feeling among the inmates, who were all attached to me—except for a few men and women of bad life, who leagued themselves with him against me."

St. Louis calmly put the matter in the hands of Jesus and Mary, and went to his beloved Jesuits to make an eight day retreat. "At the end of the retreat," he wrote, "I learned that the gentleman I have spoken of was ill. He died a few days afterward. The superioress, who was young and vigorous, followed him to the grave within the week. More than eighty of the patients fell sick, and many died. Although I assisted all the dying I was not taken ill.

"Yet among all these troubles, God has been pleased to make use of me, working great conversions inside the house, and outside . . . Vocal prayer, the Rosary in common, the singing of hymns, and even mental prayer, are still observed, in spite of all the opposition . . . God has given me many spiritual lights . . . ease in expressing myself, perfect health, and a great opening of heart to all around me.

"There is in this house a young woman, the most cunning, artful, and at the same time the proudest I have ever known. It is she who has caused all the troubles. I fear that the new bishop will be deceived by her, as was his predecessor. If you judge it well, you may put him on his guard as to this."

Louis never underestimated the power of a woman, for evil or for good. He was afraid of this woman. He feared her more than he feared the devil. He knew how to handle the devil.

Many witnesses testified at his beatification that they had heard him in loud and angry combat with the prince of hell. They had not seen the adversary, but they had heard Louis talking to him, taunting him, and vanquishing him, eventually, with the names of Jesus and Mary. They also testified to hearing not only the sounds of a struggle, but the pummeling of fists and swish of whips.

The devil came every so often to Louis, in his nights at the hospital. And sometimes, undoubtedly, Louis suffered physically. But he was big and strong, and he could take it. The devil was just another cross.

The young woman worked by day and by night. She leagued some of the inmates against him, made them mutiny, made the insane attack him. The drunkards insisted on drinking what they could and when they could. Some of the feeble minded insisted on eating alone. Give them their rations every morning. If they wanted to eat it all at once, and go hungry the rest of the day, who should prevent them? Was a man free, or was he a slave?

The young woman also aroused most of the parish priests in the city against the priest of Babylon, to such an extent that they complained to the bishop. Father de Montfort had said this and that against them; Father de Montfort had called them dirty names. Also, she kept the doctors and nurses, and most of the attendants, in a constant state of hostility.

Louis devoted only one paragraph to the devil's deputy in this letter, which is dated July 4, 1702. He could not put all his fears on paper. He sent the missive to Father Leschassier as a plea for help. It was not a ruse to ingratiate himself with the new bishop. He was mostly concerned for the welfare of the souls of 21 women who possessed the power of good—and who, in time, might do much to bless the stricken and the poor all over the world.

93

He had taken time, and care, despite all his work, to select twenty women from among the paupers and the patients. They were to be the nucleus of an order of Religious, to be known as the Daughters of Wisdom. He gathered them together, whenever he could, in a room he called Wisdom.

People openly laughed at the idea that these poor wisps of womanhood should attract this crazy priest, and that he hoped to "turn them into nuns." Some of them were aged and ugly. Some were crippled. And—this is the real funny part of it—the superior picked for this odd group was a blind woman!

Louis talked to them frequently about Mary, about the joys of the cross, and about the love and the mercy of God. He put a large cross in the room, and made it a sort of shrine. He gave his élite congregation a rule of life. They were to be a leaven. Their holiness should beatify the whole house—and, perhaps the entire city. They were not nuns; but their lives were dedicated to "God alone."

Sometime in 1701 St. Louis had found the rare soul he was seeking. She came to his confessional in the city of Poitiers. He knew her immediately, though he could not see her.

"Who sent you?" he asked.

The girl was surprised.

"Why," she said, "I guess it was my sister Elizabeth. She heard you preaching. She said I must go to you. I want a priest who will help me. I am sure I have a vocation. I want to be a nun."

"You will be a nun," the saint promised. "But it was not your sister who sent you. It was Our Lady."

The girl was 17 years old, the daughter of a crown lawyer, the darling of a rich and important Poitiers family. Her name was Marie Louise Trichet. She was beautiful, holy, and full of fire. The saint asked her to join his group of lay apostles. She did so, despite objections from her family.

She came into Babylon not as a pauper—how could she be a pauper, everybody asked, when her people were so comfortably rich?—but as an assistant to the head nurse. She worked from four o'clock in the morning until ten or eleven at night, lived on the poor food, lived with the sick and the degraded and the insane and the helpless and the despairing and the dying poor. And she gave strict obedience to her blind superior. De Montfort tested her virtues in many ways. He was sure this bud would blossom into a lily that would perfume the world.

Father Leschassier did not deign to answer de Montfort's letter until nearly a month had passed. And he didn't really answer it. He said Louis didn't need his advice. He was a big boy now and could make his own decisions. He penned a few pious platitudes, and mentioned, most casually, that the bishop, M. de la Poype, had gone to Lyons—"so I couldn't tell him what you want him to know." He ended with the words: "I am, in the love of Jesus and His holy Mother, devotedly yours!"

Louis decided to go immediately to Paris and see Father Leschassier face to face. He evidently didn't understand how desperate the situation was. At the same time Louis might be able to do something for his sister Louise. She was about to be ejected from her convent in Paris, where Mme. de Montespan had placed her. If any of the biographers knew the facts about this incident they have muddied, or concealed, them. Some modern writers feel that the king's ex-mistress still had a few influential enemies here and there, even in the convents.

Louis also might have felt that he needed to get away from this battleground, even if only for a few weeks. Walking in God's fresh air, through His lovely country, singing with His birds as he walked along, begging his way, preaching sometimes, sometimes talking to groups of peasants or crowds of children, sleeping under the stars or under some well-weathered roof, might strengthen him for the crosses he would have to carry when he returned.

He left Babylon early one morning in early August, after a short talk to his ewe lambs. Paris was nearly three hundred miles away, but what was that to a man? He stopped in Saumur, to talk to Our Lady of Ardilliers—who, for all we know to the contrary, might have directed this journey. He went on then to Angers, where he learned that Father Brenier was in charge of the Sulpician seminary. The news refreshed and brightened him.

The old man had been stern. He had done everything he could to insult and humiliate Louis. But Louis had always believed Father Brenier liked him, and that he abused him only for the good of his soul. He went, singing joyful hymns, to see and embrace this dear old man. He was led into the recreation room where Father Brenier was talking to his priests and novices.

To the saint's consternation, lovable old Father Brenier turned on him as though he were the foulest creature on earth. He shook his head wrathfully, indicating he didn't want to hear a word, and pushed him out of the door.

"Nor," says a biographer, "did he even offer him a morsel of bread!"

St. Louis, as he walked through the building was heard to say: "How is it possible that a priest should be so treated in a seminary?"

Back on the dusty roads to Paris, Louis thanked God for this foul blow which he could not understand, and comforted himself with the thought that he would soon see Father Leschassier, and have a friendly long talk with him. There had been misunderstandings between them, yes, but this had been in their correspondence. Seeing him face to face—that would be different. "I am, in the love of Jesus and His holy Mother, devotedly yours!"

When he reached Paris he learned that Father Leschassier was at the house in Issy. It was vacation time, and many priests were with him. Louis had walked nearly three hundred miles. He almost ran the rest of the way to Issy.

"M. Leschassier," says a historian, "received the humble servant of God (still bearing traces of his rude foot journey) with a countenance cold as ice; and haughtily and disdainfully dismissed him with a wave of the hand, not favoring him with a single word of welcome or hearing a word of what he had come so far to say."

St. Louis went back to Paris slowly, thanking God for this unexpected additional cross. And, humanly, he sought solace from the only other holy priest he knew in Paris, Father Chétardie, the Curé of St. Sulpice.

This venerable old man had been more than kind to Louis when he was a student. He had held the young seminarian in such high reverence that, several times, he had made profound bows to him. It was as though he realized de Montfort was a saint, and was glad to do him honor.

Louis hastened to St. Sulpice. He sent in his name to Father Chétardie. And he was told that the wonderful saintly old priest wanted neither to see him nor to listen to him!

Perhaps he and his sister Louise found consolation in praying together when they finally met. Both were homeless and without money or friends. Our Lady came to their rescue.

Someone told them of a place in the Rue Cassette, the convent of the Daughters of the Holy Sacrament. The Blessed Virgin had been chosen, by these nuns, as their first superior. Every day they showed their love for her by sacrificing a part of their dinner. This was to be given, through her grace, to some poor hungry son or daughter.

Louis went to visit the convent, and was offered "Our Lady's portion." The sisters knew he was the poorest of the poor. They seemed to recognize his sanctity. They loved him for his poverty, his humility, and his love of Mary; they invited him to come every day. And they did what they could for his sister Louise.

She became a guest in their convent. Louis asked if he could give her to them as a lay sister. This gift they declined. She was too delicate, they said, and too refined. They would take her gladly into their order, if they could. But there was that rule about a dowry!

Mother Superior had an inspiration—a gentle nudge from the Mother Superior of heaven?

"We have two postulants ready to go to our house in Rambervilliers. Why couldn't Louise go with them, and offer herself as a postulant?"

Louis would have to pay part of the fare. He would also have to pay the dowry. He had no money. He had no friends. Who could help him? He knelt and talked to Our Lady.

Before the three young women set out for their new life in Rambervilliers, a lady whom de Montfort had never seen before, had never heard of, came to him out of the shadows and begged him to accept enough money for the trip to the convent, and for his sister's dowry!

God sometimes permits a man's old friends, idols, heroes, to turn and rend him. And how often he sends strangers to take their places!

Louis remained in Paris for at least two months after he had said goodbye to his sister. The nuns who had been so kind to him, fed him every day, and he managed to find a hole-in-the-wall sort of room, under the stairs in an old house in the Rue du Pot-de-Fer—a place where he could be alone with God, where he could meditate, write poems, paint, or carve.

"He was an outcast," says Father Bolger. "He lived like a beggar . . . Stupid rumors were rife. He had been placed under an interdict by the bishop of Paris, he had been thrown into prison, etc. He just could not please his critics. One day he preached in the crypt of St. Sulpice; the sermon was a paraphrase of the Magnificat, and all who heard it were thrilled by the beauty of the words and sentiments. Yet as soon as it was over, some made of it a pretext for criticizing him . . . It was enough to break even his lion heart; yet strange to say, it served only to increase his desire for crosses and humiliations. His letters to his sister, and to Marie Louise Trichet, all have the same theme; crosses, slights, insults; and begging their prayers that he might receive the gift of Divine Wisdom."

He was constantly thinking of the great order of holy women he must give to Jesus and Mary and of the order of priests he intended to organize.

Sometime before he returned to Poitiers, he encountered an old friend who still loved and admired him. This was Claude François Poullart des Places, who had studied with him in the Jesuit college in Rennes. Louis revealed his intention of founding "a small company of priests" who loved Mary and would spread devotion to her. He asked his old friend to be one of them. Des Places said he would like to, but he could not. He was about to open a seminary for men who wanted to be priests but were too poor to enter a seminary.

"I can't give you myself," he said, "but I will form generous-hearted priests for you. You shall have the holiest and the best."

Louis walked back to Poitiers, singing the praises of God all the way.

One of the first things he did, when he returned to the horrors and the delights of Babylon, was to give Marie Louise a religious habit. Ever since she had first met him, the young lady had been pestering him about her vocation. Many a time she had asked: "How much longer must I wait? When will you let me be a nun?" He had never said anything to her but, "Have patience. You will be a nun."

Somebody, on the road from Paris, had given him ten crowns. He gave this to Marie Louise and told her to buy her habit. He directed it should be of rough cloth, and should be ash gray in color. He even designed it himself.

She was clothed with a solemn ceremony, kneeling before the statue of Mary, the Seat of Wisdom, which the saint had placed in the chapel of the hospital. The twenty old women, bent, wrinkled, crippled, blind, sick, knelt around the altar and wept with joy. St. Louis presented the habit to her, and the white cap, and told her that henceforth she was to be called Marie Louise of Jesus.

The date was February 2, 1703. It was Candlemas day, the Feast of the Presentation in the Temple, and of the Purification of the sinless Virgin. St. Louis presented his religious daughter to Jesus and Mary, as Mary and Joseph had presented Jesus. On this same day, Louis learned later, his sister Louise took the habit of the Daughters of the Blessed Sacrament in Rambervilliers. He wondered how much happiness a human heart could hold.

After the service in the Babylon chapel was finished, and two score of eyes had been wiped dry, Louis directed Marie Louise of Jesus to show herself to the city.

"Walk up and down in the most frequented places," he said.

"In those days," a historian relates, ". . . uncloistered nuns were not so numerous, nor was the religious habit so familiar in the public streets. Naturally then, the sudden appearance of the gray habit startled the whole town; not the less so because she who wore it belonged to so well-known a family. Everyone spoke of it. Few there were to approve it; the greater number denounced it as either extravagant folly or excess of zeal, on the part of the confessor and his penitent."

De Montfort watched Marie Louise calmly accept all the snubs, the outcries, the insults, the lewd derision. The habit was receiving the baptism of the cross. It would endure. And Marie Louise would endure. The twenty holy old women would die soon. They would die barren. But Marie Louise of Jesus would be given thousands and thousands of holy daughters.

Mme. Trichet had permitted her daughter to receive the habit, but the excitement it caused among her neighbors and her friends and her relatives made her hurry to the hospital and demand that her daughter "get rid of that thing."

Marie Louise refused. The habit had been given her by God, she said. She would wear it so long as she lived. Mme. Trichet rushed with her to the bishop, sure that he would "put an end to this nonsense." But the bishop resisted her.

"Do you wish to destroy your daughter's vocation?" he demanded. She could not answer him. "She belongs to God now," he reminded her, "not to you." Then turning to the girl he smiled. And he blessed her.

"My daughter," he said, "my dear daughter! Keep your habit always."

Mme. Trichet was not to be put off by all this. Not she! She made a daily and nightly nuisance of herself, storming into the hospital and demanding that her daughter come home with her.

She always went away weeping. She began to inflame the city—already smoldering—by telling how de Montfort made her poor Marie Louise carry heavy piles of linens from one end of the hospital to the other, how he made her slave from dawn until nearly midnight, and how he publicly snubbed and humiliated and bullied her. She did not understand that de Montfort was training his beloved daughter in humility, obedience, and charity—and in carrying heavy burdens and heavy crosses for the love of God.

Complaints against Louis piled up on the bishop's desk. They came from the clergy and the laity—among whom were many of the city's most influential citizens.

So—as Rigault puts it—"one morning Louis Marie Grignion found himself turned out of the General Hospital, the town, and the diocese."

The devil and his cunning disciple seemed to have won. But never underestimate the power of a saint!

12   Wisdom Through the Cross

One of de Montfort's biographers likens him, poetically, to a rain cloud going somewhere to shower God's blessings on some arid patch of earth. This is true, in a way. But does a rain cloud sing as it travels? Does it stop, and praise the Lord, every so often, for some new ache, or pain, or insult, or cruel rebuff? Does it shine with the light of Mary— who reflects the light of God? Does it look up at the stars at night, or in the early morning, and see the eyes of God? Does it make love to the Morning Star that brings the Dawn to men?

Louis, walking back to Paris, was like a cloud, in that he didn't know where he was going and didn't care. He trusted God. He knew Divine Wisdom was guiding him. So he could sing joyfully:

> *O Wisdom come!*
> *The poor beseech You*
> *By the blood of my sweet Jesus*
> *And by the womb of Mary.*
> *We will not be confounded.*
>
> *In spirit I throw myself*
> *At the foot of Your throne.*
> *If you care not for me, Lord,*
> *Give me at least an alms*
> *For the poor who are filled with faith.*

It was late in September or early in October when he began to walk. The dying world was at the peak of its beauty. The air was soft. The people were generous. There had been an ample harvest. And it was good for the most despised of men to walk with God—wherever God wanted to go.

Years later Louis wrote: "Why is it that the most faithful slaves of Jesus in Mary are the most despised of men? It is because these slaves, being her favorites, receive from her heaven's best favors, best graces, which are crosses. And I maintain it is the slaves of Mary who carry these crosses with more ease, more merit, and more glory."

When he arrived in the lonely city of Paris, he went immediately to the Salpêtrière hospital, which once was used by those working in saltpeter. There were many priests in the tremendous building. They made no objection to de Montfort's working with them, but they were never enthusiastic about him.

"I am at the general hospital," he wrote Marie Louise of Jesus, "with five thousand poor, in order to die to myself and make them live to God. My Master has led me here in spite of myself. He has designs in this which I adore without knowing them. I know no friend here but God alone. The friends I had have forsaken me."

Marie Louise had been sent away from the hospital in Poitiers, but she received his letter. It began, as most all his letters did, with the words: "May the pure love of God reign in our hearts together with Divine Wisdom."

He assured her he knew she was praying constantly for him—"pitiful sinner that I am." He relied on her prayers. He asked her to redouble them—"that is, if you are asking utter poverty for me, humiliations, abasement, a heavier cross."

There was no bitterness in him. Rather he seemed to live in bliss!

"Oh what riches," his pen shouted. "Oh what glory! Oh what pleasure if all this obtains for me Divine Wisdom, for which I sigh day and night!"

He believed that it was not impossible to obtain this infinite treasure, "even though all the angels and all mankind and all the devils should argue against it." He believed he would eventually find it because of the persecutions he had undergone—"and still undergo, daily, day and night."

He begged her to gather some "good souls, good friends," around her, and ask them to pray for him, and to pray with them, "every Monday between one and two o'clock."

Marie Louise found sixty young women to join in her prayers. One of these was Catherine Brunet—who, in time, became the second Daughter of Wisdom.

In a second letter he wrote:

"I am under boundless obligations to you. I feel the effect of your prayers. Never have I been so impoverished, so crucified, so humbled. Men and devils in this great city are making pleasant and sweet war against me. Let them calumniate me, jeer at me, tear my good name to pieces, put me in prison. How precious are such gifts! How delicate are such meats! These are the equipment, and the consequences, which Divine Wisdom brings into the house in whom it wishes to dwell! Oh when shall I possess this unknown and greatly to be loved Wisdom? When will it come to dwell with me? When shall I be sufficiently adorned to serve as its resting place—in this city where it is despised and has no home?

"Oh who will give me to eat of the bread of understanding, by which Wisdom nourishes great souls? Who will give me to drink of the chalice, which quenches the thirst of the servants of Wisdom? Ah, when shall I be crucified and lost to the world?"

One of de Montfort's biographers comments: "What a contrast to the harsh and ironical letters sent to him by his own spiritual director, when he was craving for the bread of counsel and advice and there was none to break it with him!"

Louis also wrote, from the Salpêtrière, to his sister Louise: "I thank our God daily for the mercies with which he visits you. Try to correspond with them by an entire fidelity to what He asks. If God alone does not open the door of the convent to you, do not enter it even if you have a key of gold—for it would become the gate to hell. A high vocation is required for the Daughters of the Blessed Sacrament . . . every true nun is a victim in body and soul. She is nourished by sacrifices; continual, and of every kind. She dies daily by living, and she lives by dying."

Louis worked late and early in the hospital, zealously attending all who needed him; thus winning the suspicion, distrust, and contempt of his fellow priests. He was not surprised when, four or five months after his arrival, he found a note in his dinner napkin which informed him he was no longer wanted.

He went back, joyfully, to his hermitage in the Rue du Pot-de-Fer (The Street of the Iron Pot) to the nook beneath the stairway, and to the table of the Daughters of the Blessed Sacrament. His "den" was near the novitiate of the Jesuits; and in this place he discovered two old friends, one of whom became his spiritual director. He was quite happy in this new life. Nothing disturbed him; not even the news that Louise was ill, and afraid she would not live to take her vows of poverty, obedience, and chastity.

"I rejoice," he wrote her, "to hear of the sickness which God in His kindness has sent to purify you like gold in the fire. You ought to be a victim sacrificed on the altar of the King of kings, to His eternal glory. How high a destiny! How sublime a calling!

"I almost envy your happiness . . . Have no fear of the evil spirit who will try to make you believe you will never be professed . . . Let your body suffer, but let your heart rejoice, for nothing is better for you at the present time than sickness."

Divine Wisdom permitted Louis Marie to rest awhile—to meditate and write and paint and carve and fast, and mortify himself, and pray; then sent Him to Mount Valérien, also known as Mount Calvary, a suburb of Paris, to bring peace to a brotherhood of hermits who could no longer stand one another nor the life they lived. Perhaps the Jesuits arranged this with the Abbot, and with the cardinal archbishop of Paris.

It was winter, and it was biting cold and Louis wore only light underwear and a thin cassock. He did not even think of begging warmer clothing. God would provide.

"It was not by making a show of his authority"—(from cardinal and abbot)—"nor by parading his extraordinary power before the hermits," says one commentator, "that Louis began his work, or hoped to accomplish it. His first aim was to gain their confidence; and this he very soon did by his virtues . . . which simply astonished them. He asked them to do nothing beyond their rule, which he himself kept to the letter. He never missed an exercise . . . he was sure to be found kneeling in the chapel, trembling with cold but rapt in prayer . . .

"Moved to pity by his mortifications . . . their hearts were soon gained, obedience was again observed, and peace was reestablished. Those who had done wrong asked pardon and made reparation; those who had anything to forgive forgave from their hearts.

"So pained had the hermits been at the sight of his scanty clothing, that they insisted he clothe himself with one of their warm habits; and it was their pleasure to see him walking among them in their own white garb, as though he were one of them."

His work done, Louis hurried back to the Street of the Iron Pot. Here he had something new to think about. The monks at Mount Valerien had built a reproduction of Calvary on the hillside; and a great cross brooded there, looking down on Paris. Maybe he should build Calvaries in other parts of France, when the Lord permitted him to leave his nook beneath the stairs.

In the Spring of 1704 God sent him back to Poitiers—this time in tumultuous triumph.

The bishop of that city had tried again and again to find him and bring him back. The governors of wicked Babylon had also tried to reach him. And the poor . . . ? Four hundred of them finally succeeded in getting a man of some education to write a letter on their behalf. They begged him to return.

After the letter was written they wondered where to send it. Their good friend was somewhere in Paris, or in that vicinity, but his address was not known. They decided finally that, since he had written to only one man in Paris, that man must know how to find him. So they sent the letter to Father Leschassier.

Poor Father Leschassier! He had to read phrases like these:

"By the death and passion of Jesus, for the glory and the love of God, please send back our beloved chaplain, our angel, Father de Montfort, the shepherd who so dearly loved his sheep!"

They were not worried about temporal matters, they explained, for God had sent them a rich and saintly woman who provided all that was necessary. They wanted Father de Montfort for their souls. The devil had destroyed most of his work; many had been seduced in his absence. Some had seen the devil laughing at them, mocking them because of his victory over them.

They asked his pardon for putting him to any trouble, "knowing that his heart is too full of love for God's glory to refuse," and begged him to help them, "for the love of Jesus and Mary."

Father Leschassier, whatever his emotions on reading these praises of the one he so despised, did try to find de Montfort, and finally succeeded. The letter was given to Louis, by one of the Jesuits, or by Canon Blain, about the same time he received a letter from Louise. At last, on February 2, 1704, she had become a solemnly professed Daughter of the Blessed Sacrament! Louis wrote to her before he started back to Poitiers.

"I cannot thank God enough for giving you the grace to make yourself a perfect victim . . . a reparation for so many bad Catholics and unfaithful priests. What an honor for your body to be supernaturally immolated during an hour of adoration of the Most High! Be of good heart and rejoice while you consume each day like a burning light. The more you give of your own, the more you will receive of what is God's. I triumph in you and in all your holy sisters . . . I set out immediately for the hospital at Poitiers. I beg you to love Jesus alone, Jesus in Mary, and through Mary."

News of his coming reached Poitiers long before he arrived; and, days before he was due, scouts went out to meet and greet him, and bring him into the city as though he were its most important and beloved son. As he neared the city, great piles of timbers were set alight; there was dancing in the streets; and the entire city, especially the hospital, held wild festival.

Louis looked at the bonfires blazing in the night, and realized that his sudden popularity would last as long as they did, no longer; and that it would end as the fires ended, in ashes and charred wood.

He accepted the post of director, now offered by the bishop and the civic authorities. What else could he do? He resumed his labors in and out of the hospital, and waited for the disaster that must inevitably come crashing down on him.

The petty annoyances began at once. They doubled. Then, so the story goes, he ran into real trouble. As he was hurrying through one of the principal streets in Poitiers he heard a military officer swearing at his men. He was so outraged at the colonel's profanity, and his wickedly irreverent use of the name of God that he forced him to kneel in the street and beg God's pardon—this while his men looked on and laughed and cheered.

Whether the force Louis used to accomplish this was mystical or muscular, nobody seems to know. The incident, however, appears to be authenticated. The colonel became the priest's enemy for life—and the cause of some of his suffering.

The bonfires of welcome burned out swiftly; and the cold rains fell on them. Nothing is so dead as a drowned bonfire.

Louis decided it were better for the hospital if he should not wait to be ousted. The matron was really a saintly woman. She would do her best to maintain order; and she would keep the respect of the bishop and the town.

He debated the matter of resigning with Father de la Tour, a local Jesuit who had become his spiritual guide, and with Marie Louise of Jesus. They agreed it was better for him to resign, and to trust in the Lord to send him where He would.

Louis had never wanted to be the chaplain of a poor house or a hospital. He had always wanted to be free to go wherever God directed. Now was the time to make that old dream of going to the Indians in Canada come true! Indians? There were thousands of souls right here in the diocese who had more need of a missionary than any Canadian Indian.

"I will resign," he told Marie Louise. "I must. But you must stay. Do

106

not leave this hospital for ten years. If it should take that long to establish the Daughters of Wisdom, God will be satisfied; and His designs for you will be accomplished."

"I will stay," she promised.

Bishop de la Poype readily accepted Louis' resignation, then asked what he wished to do.

"Let me be a missionary in this diocese," Louis said, "going from parish to parish, wherever you may need me, preaching missions, giving retreats, teaching catechism, hearing confessions, looking after the poor in every way I can."

"How will you live?" the bishop asked, wondering what this was going to cost.

"God who feeds the swallows," Louis said, "will provide for me. I do not want any money. I do not want any certain place to live. I shall go where I am most needed, do what God wants me to do, and, perhaps, build up some of the old and ruined churches I have seen here and there."

"You sound like St. Francis of Assisi," the bishop remarked, "isn't that rather out of date?"

"St. Francis will never be out of date," Louis said simply. "There will always be men to follow where he led."

"All right," the bishop assented, finally, "do as God directs you. But you must have a headquarters. For this I give you the chapel in the house of the Pénitentes. And for your first mission I give you Montbernage."

Louis knelt for the prelate's blessing, and arose eager for new crosses.

13   The Gentle Priest

There were no painted Iroquois lurking in ambush in the Montbernage district; but the territory was more hostile to missionaries than any part of Ontario or Quebec. Some of its people had never heard of a priest. Others had been taught that a priest was to be treated as an enemy, and given no mercy. Attack him. Stone him. Drive him away.

There was a church in the parish, but few people ever went to it. The streets were filthy. The house of the average citizen was filthy, and dark, and cramped, and frightful to smell. The people of Montbernage blamed their wretchedness on the Church. The Church was rich, they said, and getting richer and richer out of the blood and bones of the poor.

De Montfort's arrival among them, says Rigault, "created a sensation. The shabbiness of his cassock, his worn-out boots, showed that he was as poor as any of them. But he was a priest . . . Groups would form to discuss him as he strode through the muddy alleyways, insults would be hurled at him by men and women to whom life meant only keeping body and soul together. He accepted such signs of hostility as invitations, joining groups, speaking gently, kindly. They could insult him if they liked, he never grew angry, for he knew it was not really the priesthood they insulted. Gradually he beat down the wall of suspicion, grew friendly with the folk, joined in their discussions . . . His first direct step was to gather the children and make them ambassadors to their families. He had a winning way with children. Then, as more and more people came to listen to him, he looked around for a meeting place."

He found a suitable building, a dance hall that looked like a barn and was called La Bergerie—the Sheep Fold. Why it had been given that name nobody seems to know. Maybe it had once been a sheep fold. That was good. It was a place for his sheep. He would buy it.

109

The place had a bad reputation, even in Montbernage, which gallons and gallons of holy water could not wash away; but someday he would preach the Word of God to these poor wicked people in that poor wicked barn!

He begged for the money he needed. He begged from the people he knew best, the people in the slums of Poitiers, and in the poorhouse and hospital. If you must have money, ask the poor for it.

He had a place of worship. He needed a congregation. He got it. He said Mass in the morning, with many of the savages, big and little, in attendance. He said the Rosary in the evening. Great numbers of men and women bowed their heads, and some said the Rosary with him. He organized processions through the streets, young boys leading them, proudly holding lighted candles high, proudly bearing statues of Our Lady and Our Lord, proudly keeping the crucifix steady, so that all could see it.

But what won Montbernage for him was his method of hearing confessions. Men were afraid to go to him, at first. Such a great ruffian of a priest would most certainly punish sinners like themselves.

"Well, let's find out. He can't put us in jail. Let's see how tough he is!"

They were stunned by his gentleness. They were softened. They were changed. All their sins had been forgiven? Every one of them? They were supposed not even to remember them? Not even the worst of them? And there had been no scolding? The priest was even gracious to them? Such things had never been heard of in Montbernage. The miracle of it shook the district to its roots; and sent the devil howling in protest back to hell.

"If I am too lenient with sinners," Louis once said, "I will gladly suffer for it in Purgatory. I would rather suffer thus than be harsh with them, or sparing of God's infinite mercy."

The Sheep Fold soon became the shrine of Mary Queen Of All Hearts. It still exists, and it has two treasures it will not part with. One is the statue of Our Lady that St. Louis carved. The other is a rock he often used for a pillow. Pilgrims visit the place every year.

Louis, spending hours and hours every day in the confessional, gave all the credit for the success of his first mission to the recital of the Rosary.

"There is nothing more powerful in bringing Divine Wisdom down into us," he explained, "than the welding of mental and vocal prayers in the Rosary, uttering the prayers and meditating on the mysteries.

110

Saying the Rosary is the best way of praising Jesus in Mary—and through Mary."

When he left Montbernage everybody said the Rosary every day—except the babies. Before he left, however, the devil tried to get his revenge.

Louis saw a trio of naked little barbarians on the river bank, and might have passed on, had he not observed that they were making lewd gestures at a group of women washing clothes at the river's edge. He reached into his pocket for the cords with which he disciplined himself; and managed to belt one of the imps before they vanished, screaming insults and threats.

Nothing might have happened had not some one taken the mother of the "victim" to the bishop. It was a long way from Montbernage to the prelate's residence, but someone helped her get there. She wailed about the outrage to her innocent little angel, and demanded justice against the brutal, ruthless, monster of a priest.

What sort of priest was it that could be shocked by the sight of a naked boy about to enjoy the cool water of the river? What sort of priest was it that could half murder a child one-sixth his size?

There were now witnesses to sustain the woman's story. The bishop did not ask for any. He did not ask Louis for an explanation. He immediately barred him from saying Mass in his diocese.

"If I can't say Mass every day," Louis said, "I must go somewhere else."

Paris? What a dreadful thought! He hurried to his friend, Father de la Tour, who persuaded him to be calm. The Jesuit went to see the bishop. He explained the situation. The bishop lifted the ban. But he was annoyed, just the same. Why was this zealous priest always getting himself into trouble? Why couldn't he act like all the other priests in the diocese? Why couldn't he use a little tact now and then? Why did he always get on people's nerves?

When he had thoroughly prepared the congregation, and the barn-like edifice, Louis began the mission in earnest, preaching several times a day, hearing many confessions, marshalling many parades and processions. He had painted banners for each of the fifteen mysteries of the Rosary, and the boys who carried these felt highly honored.

There were days devoted to general Communions, one when all the men went to the altar rail together, another devoted entirely to giving the Host to the women, and a day set apart for the children. There was a day devoted to prayer for the dead and the dying, a day for the re-

111

newal of Baptismal vows, and a day for the planting of a big cross—a token of Calvary, which should remain as long as possible to remind the people that they had given themselves to Jesus—Who had given Himself to them.

When the mission began, everybody in Montbernage had a Rosary, and wore it openly. After the mission, everybody was eager to kiss the statue of Our Lady which de Montfort held out to them; and most of them repeated, after him: "I give myself wholly to Jesus Christ, by the hands of Mary, to carry my cross after Him all the days of my life."

"Lastly," says a commentator, "he himself made—and this he never failed to do in every other mission—a public reparation to the Blessed Sacrament, with a rope around his neck and a torch in his hand. On this occasion he preached with more than usual tenderness and emotions. During the whole mission at Montbernage, Our Lady seems to have obtained most abundant graces for the people, the missionary reaped a rich harvest."

In Montbernage he left a lasting devotion to the Rosary. In other communities, it was perpetual adoration of the Blessed Sacrament, or a mystic association with the Daughters of the Blessed Sacrament, by which they shared in the prayers, good works, and indulgences of the holy nuns.

"What he did to build up the legacy of the Rosary for his children in Montbernage," wrote Father Picot de Clorivière, "is incredible. What he did to spread it, and to plant it deep into their hearts is impossible to say. It would be impossible to count the pious confraternities and congregations he established."

The "secular priest biographer" has this to say:

"When, at the end of the century, the woes foretold by de Montfort fell on France, the Vendeans marched to battle in defence of the altar and the throne, with Rosaries around their necks or arms, or fastened to their belts; and, in groups, or in common, they recited the Rosary which Blessed Louis had taught their fathers to value and to love."

Long after de Montfort's death, the Sheep Fold became a church; the Daughters of Wisdom came to Montbernage to teach, and, quite probably, the naked little imps of Louis' time grew into Christian men.

Sometime during this mission, or shortly after it, Louis began recruiting for that "company of priests" that had been in his mind for years. In the chapel of the Pénitentes, he saw a young man saying the Rosary with great fervor. He interrupted his prayers.

"Who are you?" he asked.

112

"Mathurin," the boy said. "Mathurin Rangeard. From Anjou. I am looking for the Capuchins. I want to be a lay brother."

"Follow me," Louis said—the words Christ used to catch fishermen on the shore of the sea of Galilee. The boy arose and followed him—and became his constant companion.

The Jansenists were enraged at the saint's tremendous success in Montbernage, and doubled and tripled their efforts to thwart him. But he went, at the bishop's request, from one town to another—everywhere making thousands and thousands of fervent Catholic men and women. Everywhere he went he introduced the Rosary, held processions and parades, preached to tremendous crowds, founded lay apostolates of various kinds—and here and there repaired a ruined church or chapel. The Jansenists ground their teeth in helplessness. Here was an oafish priest exalting Mary with old-fashioned methods! Exalting the one they hated most! And driving the people to frequent Communion—which was strictly against their rules! He was making them look foolish—and all because a silly old bishop believed in him!

An extraordinary miracle decided them to take action.

Father de la Tour begged Louis to say Mass for Mme. d'Armagnac, the wife of the governor of Poitiers. She was dying. The physicians were in despair. They didn't even know the nature of her disease. The Governor was going mad with anxiety and desperation. Louis said the Mass in the Jesuit chapel, and told Father de la Tour the lady would not die.

"Go tell that to the governor," the Jesuit said. "Go immediately."

Louis went to the governor's palace, let himself in, and went to the lady's bedroom. He was smiling as though he had good news. The weeping old man sitting by the bedside almost threw him out. How dare he come into this sacred place, smiling like that?

"Madame," Louis said to the patient, "God does not want you to die. He has many years for you yet. He knows of your charities to the poor."

The lady opened her eyes—for the first time in many hours—and smiled as the saint smiled. She sat up. She rose and knelt and prayed. She looked up to thank this strange and gentle priest. But he had gone.

He had gone. And, in the minds of the Jansenists, he had gone to war. This was an act of war.

Led by the General of the diocese, in the temporary absence of the bishop, they attacked him in the Calvary church of the Benedictines, where he was preaching the wisdom of the folly of the cross.

113

"At that time," says a historian, "a very pestilence of unclean books and pictures seems to have spread over France. There were not only writers, but gifted writers as well, and painters . . . who spread the contagion among all classes of people, at least in the large towns. The servant of God had spoken strongly against this great evil, and many of his hearers felt moved to bring him books and pictures they had."

There were at least five hundred dirty books, and perhaps as many dirty pictures given to St. Louis to be destroyed. He intended to burn them in a solemn ceremony, outside the church, when he had finished preaching; and then to erect a huge cross.

Rigault, writing of this incident, remembers St. Paul at Ephesus, where "many who had followed curious magical arts brought together their books and burnt them before all, and they counted the price of them and found the money to be fifty thousand pieces of silver . . ."

The monetary value of the books, engravings, and paintings piled up outside the Benedictine church, was never ascertained—but men pay more filthy lucre for filthy literature and pictures—even in our own day —than for any other kind.

While St. Louis was preaching, his enemies made a somewhat lascivious effigy of the devil—or was it just an evil woman?—and fastened sausages on its ears for earrings. Then they spread the word that Father de Montfort was going to burn the devil with the books and pictures—and the sausages too.

One of the proud and wealthy matrons of the parish, and a priest who didn't like all this "fol de rol and nonsense," hurried to the home of the bishop to complain that Holy Mother Church was being ridiculed. Perhaps they knew the bishop was not at home. Perhaps they didn't. However the Vicar General, the Reverend M. de Villeroy, was there; and he was delighted to help save Holy Mother Church from such a Marian fanatic as Louis Marie de Montfort.

When his panting horses brought him to the church he found that Louis was still in the pulpit, and the congregation still in the church. He was in time!

"At once, without asking for any explanation," says a chronicler, "he reprimanded the Servant of God, heaping upon him the bitterest and most undeserved reproaches. The holy man knelt, then came down from the pulpit without a word . . . Not the slightest sign of pain or confusion or anger passed across his face."

When the great and dignified and righteous man had strutted out in triumph, Louis spoke a few words. "We had meant to plant a cross at

114

the door of this church. Evidently it was not God's will. Our superiors are opposed to it. Let us then plant the cross in our hearts. There is no better soil."

Meantime, scores of boys, learning there was to be no bonfire, stole all the dirty pictures and all the dirty books, and put them back into circulation—among the innocents of the parish.

The devil had had his day.

"Why have they not taken away my life," Louis cried, "rather than poison so many of these my little ones? If I could buy back those evil books and pictures by shedding my blood, I would shed every drop of it."

When the bishop learned of the incident he sided with Louis, and against his Vicar General. He needed Louis. Yet when the Vicar General's friends—and most of them were powerful in the hierarchy, in the army, and in the civic government—kept complaining about Louis and his "unusual ways," the bishop surrendered. He commanded Louis to leave his diocese.

Before he shook off the dust of Poitiers, Louis wrote a circular letter to his various flocks, parked Brother Mathurin with the Jesuits, said a cheery and courageous farewell to Marie Louise of Jesus and Catherine Brunet; and made arrangements for the care of his patients in the parish of St. Saturnin.

This parish was as vicious, in its way, as Montbernage had been. But it was much more immoral. It was famous for its "Garden of the Four Figures." The place was so called because there was a great rock-hewn statue on each side of it. Evidently they were not the statues of saints. Historians hint they could have been Greek or Roman gods—or goddesses. Saints would never draw the amorous crowds these four figures drew. The visitors came in couples. Sometimes robbers awaited them, sometimes jealous lovers with stilettos. In our day we use the terms "lovers' lane," and "mugging."

De Montfort, when he opened his mission there, spent nights face down in the garden, in imitation of Christ in Gethsemane, scourging himself, praying, pleading for his sheep. On the last day of the mission he led his flock to the garden in a parade of Rosary banners, lighted candles, and singing and praying boys and girls and men and women. And he prophesied to them.

"This garden will, in due time, become a house of prayer, served by holy nuns."

A hospital rose there, years later, to care for incurable patients.

115

Eventually it was served by the Daughters of Wisdom. It was begun by Louis himself. He saw a man, obviously sick, lying near one of the great statues. In that day, and in that place, nobody touched such a man. Nobody knew anything about germs; but everybody knew about plagues. When a man was down with the plague everybody deserted him, even his relatives and friends. That was wisdom—practical wisdom.

Louis knelt and lifted the man into his arms. This was divine Wisdom. What should he do with him? No hospital would take him. No house would permit him to enter. But Louis was not going to let the man die there, alone, exposed to the sun and the rain and the chill of night. He looked around, and found a nook in one of the figures—perhaps a womb-like niche in the statue of Venus or Aphrodite. He placed the man carefully there, obtained a sort of mattress for him, and a few blankets. Then he arranged for a number of women to care for him, night and day. Before long there were six men lying in various stone nooks in this al fresco hospital.

Louis had left St. Saturnin and was starting a retreat for a group of nuns when he received the bishop's order to get out of his diocese. The vicar general, the angry colonel, the cunning young women, and other Jansenistic souls had won a battle.

He was neither dismayed, nor bitter. With the Rosary and the image of Our Lady he had "clobbered" the enemy everywhere he met them. Now, if they lurked in ambush, awaiting his approach, it was only that they might get his blessing!

He was going to Rome. He was going to see the Pope if he could. He was going to learn what he must do with the rest of his frustrated life.

14
Journey
to Rome

When Louis walked away from his friends and his foes, in Poitiers, at the beginning of Lent in 1706, he also, unfortunately, walked away from his biographers—and they didn't pick up his trail until many years after he was dead. The trail was cold, but it did supply a few details.

Nobody knows which route he took to Rome, but it is certain he went many miles out of his way to visit the Holy House of Loreto—said to be the house in which Mary lived, in Nazareth, where the Angel Gabriel came to visit her—the holiest place on earth. It was believed to have been flown, by angels, from its original site, to save it from destruction. Certainly there was nothing in its construction or its materials to suggest it was Italian—and everything to indicate it was Galilean.

"From the fact that he visited Loreto," says one biographer, "it seems probable that he crossed the Alps into Italy, and passed through Lombardy into the Marches of Ancona. With what burning love he must have knelt within the hallowed walls, and said the Angelus as it is said there—'Here the Angel of the Lord announced to Mary!' "

Some biographers say he travelled, for a time, with a mysterious "Spanish student"—but not until the young man had given all his money to the poor. They had a hard time. They were snubbed. They were badly treated. They were, several times, taken for spies, because there was a war in Northern Italy. They went hungry many a day. They slept in the open many a night.

At the first sight of the dome of St. Peter's, St. Louis fell to the earth, we are told, and "shed hot tears of joy." Then, taking off his shoes, he walked barefoot the last few miles of his long pilgrimage. He rested a few days. He was exhausted. He had to rest. Then he went "sight-seeing"—to all the holy places. Somewhere he met the Theatine priest—Blessed Giuseppe Maria Tomasi, who was later made a cardinal —and Father Tomasi secured him an audience with Pope Clement XI.

117

There is undoubtedly a good story in the meeting of these two saint-ly men, but history has muffed it. Maybe the Theatine priest saw the ragged French pilgrim kneeling in rapture before a statue or a picture of Our Lady. He was devoted to Mary also. Perhaps he too was a slave of Jesus in Mary. It is well known that the Queen of Heaven loves to bring her favorite slaves together. St. Louis in his book, "True Devotion to Mary," says the Theatine Fathers had established the devotion in Sicily and Savoy.

Father Tomasi was the pope's confessor; so it was simple for him to arrange the reception at the papal throne. Louis says he felt he was looking at the majesty of Jesus Himself, as he knelt and kissed the little cross on the Holy Father's slipper. He began to talk in Latin, but the pope asked him to speak in French.

Louis told his story, his boyish desire to be a missionary to the Indians in Canada, his experiences as a priest, his mission in and around Poitiers, and his conclusion that only from the lips of the successor of St. Peter, could he learn exactly what God wished him to do.

Did he, at any time during his trip, or while he was kneeling before the pope, remember the stained glass window in the little church in Iffendic, and the morning sun that showed so many pictures of St. Peter?

"Go back to France," said the voice of Clement—or of Peter—"and work. It is a field big enough for your zeal. Work against Jansenism. Teach the children their catechism. Teach all Christians to renew the promises they made, by themselves or through their godparents, in Baptism. And always be obedient to the bishop of the diocese."

He conferred the title of "Missionary Apostolic" on Louis; granted him privileges he had never expected, and blessed the crucifix he carried. He gave it the power to confer a plenary indulgence on all those who might kiss it on their death beds, providing they were truly sorry for their sins, and providing also that they pronounced the names of Mary and Jesus, or tried to, before they died.

Louis, as soon as he had left the Holy Father, planted the indulgenced crucifix into the top of his staff, and set out immediately for France. It was June, and hot. His feet became so chafed he could not walk. He took off his shoes and kept going, barefoot.

The biographers learned a few facts, too, about his return journey. It was as dreary and painful and difficult—and happy—as the trip to Rome. Once he went to the home of a village priest, because he was weak with hunger. The priest was entertaining a group of clergymen. The table was

118

covered with savory dishes, and with cool looking bottles of wine. But Louis was sent to eat alone in the kitchen. There a dour servant gave him a piece of hard black bread and a sip of sour wine.

When Louis, rejoicing, came out of the kitchen into the room where the priests were still eating and drinking, one of them tried to poke fun at him for walking "all that way."

"Why don't you get a horse and ride?" he jeered.

"The apostles walked," Louis said—and resumed his hike to France.

Late in August he arrived at the Jesuit priory where he had left Brother Mathurin. That young man didn't know him at first, he was so sun-tanned, so thin, so weak, so ragged—and he had such bloody feet. But when Louis smiled, Brother Mathurin leaped toward him, thanking God for his return.

"Now," said Brother Mathurin, "you must have a long rest." "Exactly," said all the Jesuits. "You must rest! Nobody ever needed it more."

Louis was willing enough, and thankful to his friends for their suggestion. But he was not permitted a rest. Some righteous and respectable citizen of Poitiers had seen him walking into the priory and had hurried to the home of the bishop. And presently the bishop sent word to the priory that Father de Montfort was not to say Mass in his diocese, and was not to remain in his diocese.

"But this is cruel," one of the Jesuits cried. "If the bishop knew your condition, he would not do this to you."

Louis remembered that Pope Clement had told him always to obey the bishop. He began, at once, to walk out of M. de la Poype's diocese. Brother Mathurin went with him. They walked eighteen miles that day, then found refuge in the home of a kindly priest. There Louis stayed eight days, making a retreat, regaining his strength.

Perhaps he grieved that he had not been able to see his two Daughters of Wisdom. Perhaps he thanked God that he had this cross to bear, with all the other little crosses.

During his retreat, he prepared for the war on Jansenism. He would walk to Saumur and talk to Our Lady of Ardilliers. After that, he would walk to Mount St. Michel, to obtain the help of the Lady's greatest general, the Archangel Michael. Long miles of walking. Days of begging. Nights without rest. Snubs. Insults. Slights. More blisters. More bruises. Happy, happy days!

At Saumur, after hours of kneeling in silence before his Lady's statue, Louis was inspired to ask shelter for himself and Brother Mathurin at the convent of the Sisters of Providence.

119

The foundress of these nuns, Mother Jeanne Delanoue seemed to recognize at once that Louis was a saint. She welcomed him sincerely. She needed his help, his wisdom. For many years she had been using severe methods of punishment against herself, and her daughters were worried about her. Some openly criticized her.

She was doubtful. Was her mortification an inverted sense of pride? She had made a vow—and was keeping it. But should she have made that vow? It allowed her one meal a day—and the poorest kind of food. It denied her the right to go to bed. She slept in a chair. And she practiced secret penances, day and night.

She took the visiting saint into her confidence and asked him to decide whether she should continue to live as she did, or to find some milder forms of mortification. Louis asked for time. He spent some days at the shrine of Our Lady of Ardilliers, and visited the convent frequently. One morning, to test the Mother Superior, he declared, before all the nuns, that her austerities were born of self-love and pride, and that, hereafter, she should live as all the others lived.

"Jeanne Delanoue," says Father Bolger, "was convinced that she had honestly been doing her best to serve God; and here, in the presence of all her nuns, she was stigmatized as a proud fool! Montfort watched her, waiting for her eyes to betray outraged pride, but he waited in vain. She submitted humbly to what she took to be the voice of God, and resigned herself to His wishes.

"Montfort's next words were puzzling in view of the very categorical statement he had made: 'I am now going to offer Mass for your intention; go to Communion at this Mass, and be sure that God will then let me know what I ought to tell you.' Humbly she followed him into the church. When she entered the sacristy after Mass, she found Montfort radiant. 'Continue as you have begun,' he said. 'It is the spirit of God that animates you and drives you to this life of penance.' "

He stopped in Angers, and visited the hospitals. Then he trudged on to Mount St. Michel. He picked up a beggar along the way, an old man carrying a heavy burden. He took the load on his own shoulders, and pushed merrily on. That evening a charitable innkeeper offered shelter free to him and Brother Mathurin; but he had no charity whatsoever for the beggar. Louis paid for the man's food and lodging.

"He arrived at the holy mount," says a chronicler, "on the 28th of September, the eve of the feast of the Archangel . . . Hearing some men uttering horrible oaths and blasphemies, he immediately rose and ran among them; and *so earnest were his reproaches* that they at once withdrew."

120

Louis could, we see by this, be something of a fiery archangel himself, playing hell with the devil and his pals.

The early biographers describe Mount St. Michel as "a glorious shrine," as a "marvel animated by the spirit of the Benedictines," as a "power house of prayer," and as "an inspiration to all of Christendom."

"The monastery itself," says Father Bolger, "is of unbelievable beauty, rushing upward from the sea. One marvels that man's puny hands threw it on the rock on which it stands. Montfort's artistic soul must have dilated under the spell of its sheer beauty."

Today it is little more than a tourist trap—a granite peak rising out of a waste of sand at low-tide, out of a shallow sea at high tide—almost completely commercialized. A long rambling stairway leads the tourist up, up, through sunshine and shade, up, up, up, to the top. On either side of the stairs are shops of all kinds, and restaurants, and museums, and a theatre or two. And everywhere are exhibited curios of various kinds. Pictures and statues and cartoons of the devil can be found in almost every shop, at any price one cares to pay. But nowhere, except in a vacant church half-way up the tortuous climb, can anybody find a picture or a statue of St. Michael.

Perhaps this is symbolic. The world has certainly forgotten St. Michael; and it has surely gone to the devil. One doesn't have to visit Mount St. Michel to find the images of the Prince of hell. They flood the earth.

All the world, it is said, loves a winner. St. Michael, in a great battle, hurled Satan and all his cohorts into flaming hell—but the world has picked the loser as its champion!

Louis had met the devil many times, in and near Poitiers. Is it possible he had met St. Michael too, before he ventured to his shrine? Nobody knows. Did he go there to thank the Prince, as well as to ask his help? What does it matter? He came away strengthened, and determined to fight the devil more fiercely than before.

15

Among His Own

From Mt. St. Michel, Louis went directly to Rennes, to his old friend Father Bellier, who was still the almoner at the general hospital. It is possible that Father de La Tour, at the Jesuit priory near Poitiers, had advised him to do so. Father Bellier had influence in Rennes. He might introduce Louis to a bishop who would be a father to him.

The town had fond memories for him. It was there Our Lady had made known to him her wish that he should be a priest. It was there he first drank the intoxicating wine of missions and martyrdom. It was there he had been given his first opportunity to go unto the altar of the Lord.

He was there some few days when his uncle, Father Robert, rector of the church of St. Sauveur discovered him. He was living in a dismal house kept by one of the poorest women in the city, and he was working with the patients in the hospital and with the poor in the slums. Father Robert chided him gently for avoiding his father and mother and all his other relatives in Rennes, and induced him, finally, to visit his home and have dinner with the family. Louis was glad to oblige; but he would not stay at home. He had given his family up to God. He must live on whatever Providence should send him. Before he left he gathered up all the choicest food from the table that he might serve it to the poor. All the story tellers are in agreement that it was a pleasant meal. His father didn't turn purple; his mother didn't weep. And his little brothers and sisters didn't ask too many silly questions.

He spent two weeks in Rennes, and was asked to preach in many convents, seminaries, and churches. He had, to his dismay, become famous. The fact nettled him, especially in the Calvary church, which was packed with those waiting to hear him. He had never seen this edifice filled before.

"Evidently," he said to them, "you have been told that I am a great preacher, or an extraordinary missionary. That is nonsense. I am not

123

going to preach to you. I shall simply make a meditation, as if I were alone in my own room."

He knelt in the nave, and talked about suffering.

"Many who listened to him," says Father Bolger, "were in tears. He ended with the Rosary"—and with a collection for the restoration of the church of St. Sauveur.

Then he was on the road again, headed for Dinan. Father Bellier had told him about an old friend—and his ideal of a missionary—Father Leuduger of St. Brieuc. Once before, while he was a student, Louis had wanted to join this priest and his little band of missionaries.

The road to Dinan led through Montfort-la-Cane, but he went on without stopping. He pushed ahead with Brother Mathurin, to the area of La Bachelleraie—where his father still owned property, and where his old nurse, his second mother, Mère Andrée still lived. He wondered how she was, what she had been doing all these years, whether she might need anything he could obtain for her. And he thought it might be good to spend the night under her roof, if everything were well. He sent Brother Mathurin to see her. He was to beg her, "for the love of Christ," to give a night's lodging to a poor wretched priest and his companion.

Mère Andrée, Mathurin reported, had not appeared. But her son-in-law was home. He said the old lady was "out." He also said that he wasn't taking in any beggars, priests or laymen.

So she had a son-in-law! That runty little girl who had always tagged after him and Louise had grown up and married! And the son-in-law was emphatic? No, no. He was merely carrying out Mère Andrée's directions. Mère Andrée would never let her son-in-law make such a decision. She didn't believe in free will for men.

Louis begged at other houses, and was turned away. He sought out the poorest hut in the village, and was welcomed by the old man who opened the door. He had only a little bread and water to give his guests, this man said, and a little poor straw for their bed, but he was more than glad to share it all.

As he knelt for the priest's blessing, and saw him plainly in the light, the old man recognized him. He hadn't seen him in twenty-one years, but he knew him. And, before dawn, everybody for miles around knew that the eldest son of M. Grignion de la Bachelleraie had come home— the priest, you know, the one everybody calls a saint, the giant in rags.

While Louis was still asleep, a crowd gathered outside the house, wailing because they had turned him away. They came to beg his forgiveness, and to implore his blessing. Prominent among them was Mère Andrée, weeping like a new-made widow. He consoled her by accepting an invitation to breakfast in her home; but he felt he had to scold her, mildly, before he went on his way. He might never see her again.

"You have committed a great fault," he said, "not against me but against Jesus. You are making it up to me now, but not to Him. You are showing me your affections, not because He is in me, but because I am in me. Jesus abides in the poor, even the least of them. The next time a poor man asks anything of you, give what you can—for you give it to Jesus as well as to him."

After he had been accepted by the Dinan missionaries, Louis went to the Dominican church to say Mass. In one of the priests in the sacristy he recognized his brother Joseph Pierre—his favorite brother and his best pupil. But Joseph didn't recognize him.

"I wish to say Mass on the altar of your Blessed Alan de la Roche," Louis said. "Will you, dear brother, please let me have what I need?"

Joseph was a priest, and he didn't like to be called a brother. He didn't say so, but he made it plain by his actions. He produced the oldest vestments he could find, the smallest candles, the crudest cruets, and the least ornamental of all the chalices.

"Thank you, dear brother," Louis said, smiled at him, and went into the chapel. Brother Mathurin started to follow, but the angry Joseph stopped him. "Who is that impudent, ignorant oaf?" he demanded. "Can't he tell a Dominican priest from a lay brother? What is he? A country boor? A lout that never uses his eyes? Was he having fun with me? Why did he 'dear brother' me?"

Brother Mathurin looked dumb. The priest kept after him. Finally Mathurin said his friend must have been distracted. He asked the priest's pardon for him. But he would not reveal his master's name. The priest had to know. He kept badgering the young man. Mathurin could stand it no longer.

"He called you 'dear brother,' " he said, "because that's what you are. He is your dear brother Louis!"

"My dear brother Louis? And I gave him the shabbiest vestments I had!"

The next time Louis said Mass at Blessed Alan's altar he wore the richest and most beautiful vestments in the monastery. He couldn't help feeling good about this; for the vestments really honored the saint, "the darling of the Blessed Virgin," one of his own great heroes.

The Dinan missionaries gladly granted Louis' wish to teach cate-

125

chism to the children. This was a task below them. Anybody, they held, could teach Catechism. But you had to be a man to preach.

Louis taught the children about Mary, and about Eternal Wisdom, and about the great Archangel Michael, who would always help a little boy or girl fight all the devils that tempted them. He heard confessions too. He tended the sick. And, because none of the other priests wanted to take the job, he was permitted to preach to the soldiers in the garrison, "men devoted to drink, dames, dice, and destruction."

"Montfort," says Father Bolger, "accomplished what a more worldly wise priest could never have done. He completely converted that rough soldiery, made them forget human respect to such an extent that they walked meekly through the streets bearing lighted candles in their hands. He left, in the barracks, a beautiful painting of Our Lady, before which they promised to keep a light continually burning. And they promised to say the Rosary daily."

As usual, Louis visited all the poor districts during the mission, and begged food and clothing for those who were in need. He began to organize the first "soup kitchens" in the world. He also, in a way, helped to found a hospital.

One night, in a house in the slums, he found a man wasted with disease and covered with vermin. He threw him over his shoulder, and ran to the home where the missionaries lived. He pounded on the door, and, in his most powerful voice, shouted: "Open up, open to Jesus Christ."

When he was let in, he took the man to his own room, put him in his bed, did what he could to warm him and to cleanse him, then knelt beside him and prayed. The next day he took his patient to the castle of La Garaye, where he was accepted.

The count and countess of La Garaye had lived the empty gay lives of French nobles until the sudden death of relatives and friends made them realize they had wasted their years, and that it was time to redeem themselves and to do something for humanity and for God.

They changed their "stately chateau and roomy stables" into a medical school and hospital. The count studied medicine and surgery, and chemistry. (King Louis XV honored him publicly for some of his discoveries, and gave him an award of 50,000 livres.)

Count and countess welcomed Louis when he came, and insisted that he stay with them several days. They assured him they were glad he had brought the sick man. The hospital was just starting. Louis' patient was one of the first.

126

Years later, the noble couple asked the Daughters of Wisdom to assist them, and gave them half the royal award. They extended the hospital and the medical school, added a general school and an orphanage.

In February, 1707, the famous Father Leuduger invited Louis to join his mission band in the diocese of Saint-Brieuc. Louis rejoiced. An old old dream had blossomed into reality. He was to work for souls with a "master missionary!"

"But," says Rigault, "Montfort clashed with the dark background of average humanity. It was in vain that he practiced heroic obedience, aspired to contempt and to nothingness where he himself was concerned. He was too different from the rest. He did not fit in; like Father de Foucauld in our own day, for whom the Trappist rule was not strict enough. Such men are trying to their superiors. Father Leuduger had learning and influence, but he was neither enthusiastic, nor deep, nor really eloquent . . ."

A clash was inevitable. It came in the little town of La Chèze. There Louis had found the ancient chapel of Our Lady of Pity, which was a wilderness of rubble. He was told by many of the natives that, a long long time ago, the great Saint Vincent Ferrer had looked on these ruins in sorrow, and had made a prophetic statement. "The chapel will be restored by a man whom the Almighty will bring into the world in due time. He will come as a stranger. He will be insulted and abused. But he will rebuild the chapel."

"I am that man," Louis said. "Let's set to work." He begged money. He recruited workmen. He made a plan for the new building and directed the work of restoration. In a few months he had accomplished the work. The new chapel of Our Lady of Pity had an altar "in the Roman style, surrounded by a fine balustrade on which there were eight life size statues. On the altar were three great crosses, having at the foot of the middle one a beautiful statue of Our Lady holding the dead Christ in her arms."

For nine successive nights, during the last phase of the building, Louis had fires lighted on all the surrounding hills. On the last day he arranged a tremendous procession. People came from everywhere around the village to march, holding lighted candles, singing hymns, saying the Rosary aloud, and carrying the new statue of Our Lady of Pity.

One commentator notes that La Chèze was "particularly dear" to St. Louis, and was "the scene of many miracles."

127

When food ran short, Louis multiplied it. He cured an epileptic girl. He cured many cases of fever by sprinkling them with water. A sort of "holy water." Plain water with strips of linen bearing the Holy Name dipped in it. Father Jagu, parish priest of the village church, bore witness to all this in a letter to the bishop—38 years after the saint had died. Louis' bed there, he added, had been made of "three bundles of branches and a stone for a pillow."

It was here too that Louis first became known as "the saint who could put a curse on you." He was shocked, on the Feast of the Ascension, to find that the people of La Chèze were dishonoring the day by holding their annual fair, buying and selling horses and cows and pigs, and products they had made. In a loud and indignant voice he told them what he thought, and asked them to postpone the fair until the next day so they could really honor their Father in heaven. Most of them listened, abandoned the fair, and went home. Some even went to the parish church, or to the new chapel, to say the Rosary. Only two peasants chose to ignore him. One bought a cow from the other. The beast died the next day or so. The man lost the use of his legs. The man who sold the cow lost all his money.

All this bothered and annoyed Father Leuduger. There were other things that angered him.

A high-born lady well known to Father Leuduger decided it was scandalous that Louis dressed the way he did. So, with great charity, she sent her favorite tailor to him, to measure him for a new cassock. Louis didn't like this.

"My body can do without a new cassock," he said, "but the members of the Body of Christ cannot do without food. Tell your lady to spend her money on food for the poor."

Father Leuduger asked him to preach a retreat for the Daughters of the Cross. He obeyed. But he sent Brother Mathurin to them first, to test their charity. Brother Mathurin asked for a piece of bread "for the love of God." It was refused. One of the sisters told him the convent was very poor and had no bread to give anyone. Then Montfort knocked on the door and asked bread "for the love of God." The sister was about to send him away when, through the accidental appearance of another priest, she learned that the beggar was the one who had been chosen to give the retreat. She had prepared a lavish breakfast for him.

De Montfort shook his head in astonishment and sorrow when he looked at that repast.

128

"You had not even a crumb to give a beggar for the love of God," he mourned. "Yet, at the same time, you have all this for me, a common sinner! You are wanting in charity and in faith."

The mission had begun. The nuns talked about it for years. It accomplished wonders, they said. But it troubled Father Leuduger.

In Moncontour, Louis found a group of young men and women dancing to loud and lascivious music in the public square—and this on a Sunday morning when they should have been in church.

He rushed at them and into them. He snatched the instruments violently from the musicians and tossed them into a heap. Then he threw himself on his knees and begged his auditors to kneel also, and repent for the "outrage done to God's divine majesty." Most everyone of those present did as he asked. Then, giving back the musicians' property, he went to see the mayor and to implore him never to let such a thing happen again. Sunday was the Lord's day. It could be enjoyed; yes; but it should be kept holy.

A few days later, when he had finished Mass in the hospital, he invited the congregation to kiss his indulgenced crucifix. But he refused to put the cross anywhere near the lips of a certain few—several women with low-cut gowns, and a number of nuns. The Sisters were modestly dressed, of course, but to de Montfort they were lax in the way they brought up their young girl students.

It was Louis' eagerness to help the souls in Purgatory that settled the matter with his stern superior. Father Leuduger spoke to an immense congregation about the value, and the necessity, of praying for the dead, and of having Masses said for the release of their souls. Father de Montfort was so affected that immediately he took up a collection, to be given for Masses for the holy souls.

That was it! Father Leuduger had made a rule, a long time ago, that no missionary working with him should ever ask for money from the people. Louis had fractured that rule; and it didn't help him at all that the collection was big. Father Leuduger summoned him into his presence, and, with thirty or more of his missionaries around him, cast him into an earthly Purgatory.

It was not enough for him to say, in effect, "go and sin no more." He recited all Louis' "sins" aloud, before he expelled him from his holy band!

Years later, too many years later, he realized what he had done; and he sent word everywhere, asking Louis to come back to him, and to take his place as the superior to all the missionaries in Brittany.

Louis walked away with Brother Mathurin, and another young man he had picked up—Brother John—rejoicing in a brand new heavy cross, and in the knowledge that now he had many new "enemies" to love.

16   The Miracle Worker

Every so often, ever since his boyhood, Louis had to flee to some hermitage, or place of solitude, some desert where he could be alone with God, where he could renew his courage, and find new strength and new determination to carry his crosses all the way to Calvary. How often, when he was a child, had he fled to the serenity and the comfort and the security of St. Lazare! He could sit near that pile of ruins and rest his eyes on green hills, a lush green valley, a laughing stream, great rocks, and towering trees. And, through these wondrous works of God, he could forget the petty ambitions and devious methods of the world.

He remembered now, outcast that he was, how close he had come to Jesus and Mary in those visits to St. Lazare; and he remembered that, once, long ago, he had promised himself that, when he was a man, he would come back and rebuild the chapel.

Once there had been an abbey here, and a hospital for lepers. They were built, according to legend, by Crusaders, sometime in the 14th century. The monks of the abbey, named in honor of St. James, would say Mass in the chapel two or three times a week. All that was years and years ago—years of wars and ashes. The abbey was still standing, in part; but it was unoccupied.

"We will go to St. Lazare," Louis told his two lay brothers. "We will ask permission to sleep in the abbey. We will live as hermits for awhile, until God shows us what He wants us to do. And perhaps we shall place ourselves in the hands of the Bishop of the St. Malo diocese. Meantime, while we are resting, we shall give Our Lady a new chapel."

St. Lazare was the most peaceful spot on earth—for a day or two. When the peasants discovered who was there, they came like sheep at eventide. Hundreds of them, thousands of them. Whole villages emptied themselves to rush to St. Lazare. They brought food. They brought money. They brought materials needed for the chapel. They

131

brought the labor of their hands and the love of their hearts. They brought their sorrows and their hopes and their frustrations. They brought their crippled, their wounded, their maimed, their sick.

De Montfort preached to them, listened to their stories, fed them, provided clothing for them, healed them, sent them home rejoicing. The chapel was built; but it wasn't big enough to hold the crowds—and the crowds grew in numbers. Louis talked to them under a big oak tree near the chapel—and his voice could be heard distinctly by all, even by those furthest from the oak tree pulpit.

Eventually two priests in Montfort asked him to preach in their churches. He went first to the church of St. Jean, where he had been baptized. He went next to the church of St. Nicholas—and saw that the duck's leg carving was still there.

His father and mother came from Rennes to hear him deliver his sermon in St. Jean's. They opened their big house in Montfort for the occasion, asking Louis to dine with them, and to bring all his friends.

Jean Baptiste Grignion thought he had enough cash to provide a good dinner for Louis and his friends. He bought all the things he needed. He was as generous as his purse permitted.

But he was aghast, chagrined, scandalized, frightened, and overwhelmed with horror and dread, when he saw the friends Louis let loose on his banquet table. His son had more friends than the king; and each one of them could eat more than any dozen duchesses or dukes. They were the poorest of the poor, the lame, the halt, the blind, and the hungry. This bounteous repast wouldn't last a quarter of an hour with that munching mob. He would have to hurry out to the stores. He would lose his house. He would lose everything he had. His wife and children would starve. He must do something. But what? He could not drive this army of vultures out of his dining room. His honor was at stake. How the town would jeer! How all Montfort and Rennes would laugh!

But maybe he was going crazy. Or maybe something was the matter with his eyes. Look at that skinny old man with the leg of a chicken partly in his grimy hands and partly in his yellow fangs!

He had seen a dozen men like that. A score. Two score. More. They were everywhere, gnawing the leg of a chicken. How many legs, for heaven's sake, do three cooked chickens have?

And how could those chickens, lying so quietly in their gravy, still have their legs? The table was still fresh-looking. The dishes were still full. The floor was piled with crumbs, and chickenbones, and orange

132

peel, and the skeletons of fish. What was all this? An echo of the story of the loaves and fishes?

He went out of the room shaking his head. And perhaps he remembered dinners at home, when Louis was a boy and he, Jean Baptiste, had so deviled him that he had rushed out of the room to keep from losing his temper.

He was even more affected the next morning when Louis said Mass in the old family church. He waited eagerly, with his wife, to hear what his son might say. But Louis had decided not to preach. When he went to the pulpit he affixed a big crucifix to it. Then, with the cross Pope Clement had so richly indulgenced, he went slowly through the congregation, allowing everyone to kiss it, saying: "Behold your Savior! Aren't you sorry you offended Him?"

"Tears," says Father Bolger, "came to eyes that rarely wept. Hearts, hardened by a quest for 'the good things of life' were strangely moved and softened."

It was Christ who preached that sermon. And Him crucified!

In the parish of St. Jean, Louis conducted a retreat for the unmarried women; and on the last day he led them in procession to the church of St. Nicholas, to honor Our Lady of the Rosary. After a short sermon he looked at each of the young ladies in turn. To one he said: "You will be the guardian of Our Lady of Wisdom in St. Lazare."

He didn't know her name, nor anything about her. But he was right. She was Mlle Guillemette Rousell, a third order Franciscan. She was like the duckling the mysterious mother duck left at the altar—a gift to the Lord. After Louis said farewell to the restored chapel, Guillemette took charge of it so long as she lived.

During the week or ten days he spent in his old home town, Louis decided to build a Calvary scene on the slope near the castle. He also thought of building a number of small chapels between the Calvary and the castle, so that he could show scenes of the Lord's passion on the "via dolorosa." Almost everybody in Montfort thought this was a wonderful idea. Even the merchants were in favor of it. It would advertise the town and bring much needed trade. With the help of many, he began to dig trenches, heaping the dug-up earth on high to add to the height of the hilltop. He wanted the cross of Jesus to stand where it could be seen from afar.

The work had scarce begun when somebody made it his business to tell the Duke de la Trémouille, the lord of Montfort, what was going on "underneath his nose." The duke promptly put a stop to it.

133

Louis looked at the big crucifix that never would be planted on the hill, and sighed. He looked at those around him, who included the Jansenist priests and laymen—and perhaps the duke himself.

"You do not wish this place to be sanctified," he said. "Yet one day it will be a place of prayer."

Today a church stands there, its cross reaching into the sky. And there is a statue of Louis, looking down in benediction.

He returned to St. Lazare, suspecting it wouldn't be long until Bishop Desmarets, a noted Jansenist prelate, would boot him out of the diocese. He hoped he could finish the repairs while he had time.

The crowds returned, to give, and to take, to help and to be helped. One day no one remembered to bring him and his two lay brothers any food. The three met at noon, as was their custom, and sat down to dinner. There was nothing to eat. Louis said grace, however, and read from a spiritual book. He said "grace after meals," and led his disciples to the chapel, for the Angelus.

"Have confidence," he bade the two. "God and Our Lady will provide."

The table was bare when they met for supper. The brothers complained. They had trusted God. Where was the food? Louis replied that, if God did not want them to fast this day, He would still find them something to eat. He had hardly finished talking when a nearby farmer came walking in with a big pot of soup, some home-made bread, and a few other dishes cooked by his wife.

When the chapel was finished, and the altar had been installed, Louis decorated the place to show the people the love of God and Mary. Above the altar he painted a dove, the symbol of the Holy Spirit, the Spirit of Wisdom, the Spirit of love. Beneath it he wrote the name of Jesus—Incarnate Wisdom. On the altar he placed the statue of our Lady of Wisdom, which he is believed to have carved during the nights he spent at St. Lazare. She is standing on the crescent moon, and showering gold and silver rays—torrents of graces and streams of wisdom—upon the arid earth.

When, in August, 1708, Bishop Desmarets came to Montfort, a large delegation of Mary-haters waited on him, and complained about de Montfort. The man was not only "committing miracles," they said, but he was preaching the love of Mary. He was forcing people to say the Rosary three times a day. He was making many of them her slaves. They wore her chains, openly, in token of their slavery to her, and in defiance of the order that nobody should be worshipped except Christ,

(Who died, "as you know," only for the few, not for the many). He was actually demanding people to pray to Mary, as they would talk to their own mothers!

The bishop was shocked. He summoned Louis at once. He was at dinner with his vicar-general and others of his clergy, when the shabby priest was admitted. The bishop scolded and scalded him, with a tongue used to scolding and scalding; and forbade him to preach or hear confessions so long as he remained in the diocese of St. Malo. Louis bowed his head and left. But before he had shaken the dust of the house off his feet, Father Henry Hindré, parish priest of Bréal—and possibly a relative of Father Pierre Hindré, who had baptized Louis—entered the house and saw him. He immediately went into the dining room, and asked the bishop to permit Louis to give a mission in his parish.

Whether from indecision of character, or a feeling of guilt in dismissing de Montfort without letting him say a word in his defense, or to show the vicar-general and the others how liberal and forgiving he was, or for some reason known only to God, the bishop revoked his ban and granted Father Hindré's request.

Before he left his native town, Louis, according to one biographer, took his last look at the beautiful hills and fields and streams and trees, at the old castle and fortress, at the walls where he had spent so many spell-bound hours, and at the houses with their roofs of tile or slate.

And he wept over it, as Jesus wept over Jerusalem. He told his lay brothers that misfortune would visit it because it would cease to love Our Lady. (In 1724, eight years after his death, a third of the houses in Montfort were deserted and falling in ruins.)

One of the first tasks Louis had at Bréal was to preach to the soldiers in the garrison. He established a confraternity among them, which he called "The Soldiers of St. Michael." He managed to have medals manufactured for each of them—and for hundreds of others. And he gave the soldiers "an easy way of life," to keep them out of mischief.

It was in Bréal that he encountered the man with the axe—the incident that so interested and intrigued the citizens of Roussay when they heard he had been sent to preach a mission to them.

He heard a woman screaming for help. He rushed into a house and saw a man beating his wife. He separated the pair and tried to reason with the husband. The enraged man seized an axe and attacked him.

135

But before he could do any harm, the muscles of his arm stiffened, and he dropped the weapon.

A Father Dardeux, curé of a nearby town, testified, years later, that he knew this man. "His name was Salmon. He was no good. He did not repent. At the end of the mission, Father de Montfort predicted that God's blessing would abandon him and he would die a poor and miserable death. The prediction was fulfilled. Salmon lost all his property, which was by no means inconsiderable. During the last years of his life he was seen to beg his bread from door to door. I have myself given him alms many times. From my hands he received the last Sacraments. He died lying stretched on a little straw in a house where he had been allowed to lodge out of charity."

Louis went to many places after Breál. Sometimes he was too occupied with other works to give a parish his whole attention. Often he sent Brother Mathurin ahead, to say the Rosary in public, to start the hymn-singing, or to distribute the crosses of St. Michael among the local soldiery.

Louis was giving a mission in Romillé when Bishop Desmarets again visited Montfort. This time a larger delegation than before awaited him, demanding Montfort's head. He gave it to them, on a Jansenist platter.

Louis was exiled from his home—even as Jesus was exiled from his home in Nazareth.

How could any follower of Jesus be so fortunate?

He was happy, too, for the results of all his missions.

"I have walked more than six thousand kilometers," he said, "asking God for the grace to touch men's hearts; and He has listened to my prayer."

17 The Enemy of Jansenism

Louis was prepared to leave the diocese of St. Malo long before its bishop banned him. His friend, Father Barrin, vicar-general of the diocese of Nantes, had invited him to come and help fight Jansenism and Louis was eager to go.

"The diocese of Nantes at that time," says Father Bolger, "can be compared to a battle ground on which the Jesuits and the Jansenists fought for mastery."

Another biographer says, "The Nantais, or southern division of Brittany . . . of which La Vendée was a part . . . was not then distinguished by the religious spirit of their people . . . not that the faith had died out . . . but there were many places where it only lay smouldering . . . anything more deplorable than the state of some of these provinces is hardly possible to conceive. To the troubles caused by the Huguenots, there had succeeded an indifference to all religion, which, in turn, fostered ignorance, superstition, blasphemy, immorality, and drunkenness . . . the errors of Jansenism . . . and Gallicanism."

Without going into details, he summarizes the perils Louis faced:

"We shall see the doors of churches closed in his face . . . godless libertines or emissaries of the Jansenists (who hated him and the devotion to the Mother of God which he taught everywhere) thronging the public squares and the streets and the taverns, doing their best to drown the voice of the preacher in their blasphemous and profane songs. In some places a whole population will greet him with groans and hisses, and take up stones to stone him; in others he will be led off to prison, or smitten on the face, or beaten, or threatened with the dagger or the sword, and this even in the sanctuary of God. Yet . . . he will leave behind him a people rooted in Christ . . ."

A tough mission? Louis was a tough missionary.

Another chronicler states that Louis—"too blunt to hide truths that

137

should be shouted from the housetops"—was doomed to be a whipping boy in this diocese, and under this bishop, M. Gilles de Bauveau, who was "touched with Gallicanism."

Louis gave his first mission, with a Jesuit, in the parish of St. Similien —and immediately got himself into the bad grace of a group of University students. These young bravos, who strutted through the streets with daggers and swords—and a fine brave air of superiority and worldly wisdom—didn't like the way he spoke to them. They didn't like the way he sometimes charged into a group of licentious dancers, and forced them to kneel and say an *Ave,* or even a whole decade of the Rosary. And they didn't like it when they heard him praying aloud, in some bagnio in which they happened to be. The man was a menace to their sophisticated way of life. He had actually taken some of their pals, and made church-going Christians out of them! He needed a serious man-to-man thrashing. He needed to be killed.

Louis heard from many people, and often from his little friend, Father des Bastières, that these students were going to waylay him some night and "finish him." He didn't believe it. Father des Bastières was a timid soul. He saw danger everywhere, and fled before it came too close. The others were merely "imagining things." But, as he walked out of the mission church one night, the band of intellectuals came at him, kicking and punching.

Louis had always wanted to be a martyr to the Faith. He had often dreamed of dying gladly, for Christ, from an Iroquois tomahawk, or a Zulu spear. Now he had important things to do for God; and the sight of these puppy assassins infuriated him. He let his fury snap its leash. He exploded. He fell on the dozen or so like a destroying angel. He had no wings. He didn't need them. His feet and his fists were better than wings for offense and defense.

He and his opponents—those still on their feet—made so much noise that men and women and children came running from everywhere. The young men among these pitched into the mêlée, on de Montfort's side. Then de Montfort had to save the students from the savagery of his friends.

From that date, all the Nantais knew they had a missionary they could respect. If he couldn't send you back to church, he could send you to a hospital. If he couldn't break your pagan spirit he could break your pagan bones. Listen to him, if you want to. If you don't like what he says, let him alone. Don't talk back to him. Don't provoke him. Run, don't walk.

Some of the people didn't heed these words of wisdom. A platoon of soldiers, for instance.

"I was passing by the Motte-St. Pierre," Louis told Father des Bastières. "I saw a party of soldiers fighting with some workmen, all of them horribly blaspheming. I rushed into the crowd of them and knelt down to pray for the blasphemers. Then I got up and threw myself headlong into the madmen; and, with some difficulty, I succeeded in parting them.

"The workmen hurried away, though they were the stronger party. The soldiers remained. I was going away too, when I noticed a table with black and white marks on it. They told me it was a gambling table. That was the cause of all the trouble, all the blasphemies and oaths! I threw it down and broke it to pieces with my feet.

"The soldiers were angry. They owned that table. They tore my coat, threatened me with their swords, and demanded fifty livres. I told them I would give them a million times as much, and all the blood in my veins, if I could destroy all the other gambling tables in the diocese. Then they put me under arrest and were taking me to the governor, who would get the money out of my hide."

Father des Bastières happened along as Montfort was being led away —followed by an ever-growing crowd. He was shocked, but he couldn't think of anything to do. He followed, with the crowd, until he saw one of Louis' friends, probably Father Barrin, talking to the soldiers. Louis walked away, free, with his friend—and, before many weeks had passed, all the soldiers were wearing medals of St. Michael.

The historians tend to make general statements about Louis' mission in Nantes, rather than recount specific instances. "La Vendée, especially, owed everything to him; it was through his teachings that the people of La Vendée marched to battle"—(for the Faith).

"What St. Dominic and his Rosary had been to the south of France, Louis with his Rosary was to the western province."

"As St. Patrick and St. Hyacinth rooted the faith in Ireland and Poland, so did St. Louis in Vendée."

"The very land seemed to mourn its spiritual desolation until the advent of the holy missionary."

As Father Grandet wrote; "He brought about numberless reconciliations, restitutions, and conversions . . . money and food came to him . . . so that he was able to make soup for the poor every day . . ."

"There was," says Rigault, "no lack of work in the Nantes district. Since the wars of religion, many souls had lain fallow and many churches in ruins. The miracle of Father de Montfort was to clear away the undergrowth so thoroughly, and to lay such a solid foundation, that the soil was able to bring forth a series of spiritual harvests, and to have churches which the devout generosity of the faithful revived."

They do, now and then, tell us stories of the saint. In St. Similien, many people stood in line, or in a crowd, waiting for him to preach. Many were fasting, expecting to go to Communion at his Mass. Among these was a Mlle. Guihoneux—who later became the head of a hospital. She had forgotten to take any food with her, and she had no money. She was weak with hunger late in the afternoon.

"Almost in tears," says Father Bolger, "she sat on a stone in front of the church, wondering how she could manage the long journey home. Suddenly there appeared a beautiful lady who, with an indescribably graceful gesture, offered her a piece of bread, saying gently, 'Take and eat.' A moment later she had disappeared." The morsel of bread, another commentator asserts, was "such as she had never before tasted in her life."

At Vallet, Louis had to advertize his mission. He sent Brother Mathurin through the streets, ringing a hand bell, and singing hymns and announcements as loudly as he could. Only one man in this village refused to come to the mission. While Louis was preaching to the others, a storm rose, and lightning killed the man in his home.

Vallet was devoted to Mary when Louis left it. Five years later, coming from Roussay, he headed toward the town. But, learning that the people had relapsed, he refused to go near them. When the townsmen heard this they felt like orphans. They were converted all over again.

In the parish of La Chaise which, for some reason or other, was also called Chevrolière, Louis met with the ferocious opposition of the pastor. On the first day of the Mission, Louis talking about Our Lady, had the congregation weeping—when, one might say, "up popped the devil." The pastor, in his choicest surplice and his newest stole, solemnly presented himself before the main altar, and told his people they were wasting their time. He advised them all to go home at once, and stay away from the mission.

Louis listened politely until the tirade was over. He came down out of the pulpit, bowed to his holy adversary, and went to Father des Bastières, saying; "Let us sing a *Te Deum* for this most welcome cross." Most of the congregation joined in the singing. Only a few gave any heed to the pastor.

Louis spent fifteen days in that parish, and, according to Father des

140

Bastières, suffered continuously from "colic and violent fever." When the time came to burn all the bad books and pictures and to plant the cross, it was raining; and the route marked for the procession was under water. De Montfort, burning with fever, took off his shoes—in honor of the cross—and led the march. When the cross had been blessed, and raised in its rightful place, the fever and the colic left him. He never felt better in his life, he told the little priest.

At Vertou he spent a month, and complained that everything was going too smoothly. Something must be wrong. The devil seemed to raise no trouble at all. "We are loved too much here," he said. "I suffer. No crosses! What a cross that is!"

It was at Vertou that Louis found another helper, Brother Pierre. The boy was felled by some mysterious disease, and lay in bed two weeks, unable to talk, unable to move. Father des Bastières felt he should anoint Pierre, for surely he was going to die. He asked Louis' opinion. Louis visited the sick bed, and told Pierre to get up and cook his dinner in an hour's time. In an hour, dinner was ready and Pierre was serving it.

He found Pierre and lost Brother John. That young man got tired of living like a beggar and looking like a tramp, and probably, also, of making such intense preparations for the Masses, the processions, the Calvaries, and the burning of lewd books and pictures.

At the same time Father des Bastières went away without a word of warning or goodbye. Louis noted his loss in a poignant verse:

> *A friend is unfaithful to me.*
> *God be praised. God be praised.*
> *A servant resists and deserts me.*
> *God be praised. God be praised.*
> *God does all; or lets it happen.*
> *Therefore, all things satisfy me.*

Evidently the little priest didn't think Nantes too healthy a place to live. He was worrying himself to death about de Montfort. He always saw vicious-looking men waiting just outside the house or the church. One night three of them made their way into the house, intent on mayhem or murder. But St. Louis talked them out of it and sent them on their way. Father des Bastières almost collapsed, when they were gone.

He had seen the big missionary fighting, actually fighting, he had seen him in the captivity of the soldiers. And he was present when

141

Louis charged a gathering of young men and women, who were dancing in the public square to the music of one of his hymns, and came near to being spitted on two swords.

His giant friend had sent the dancers sprawling. He had snatched the instruments from the musicians. He had held up his special crucifix and demanded that everybody immediately kneel and ask God's pardon for their blasphemous mockery of Him. The little priest watched, breathing with difficulty, his heart beating loudly and fast. He had seen this sort of thing before. He was not astonished when everybody—everybody but two—dropped to their knees and prayed.

But those two were still standing. Father des Bastières almost died looking at them. They had drawn their swords and were advancing on the saint, cold murder in their eyes. Then he saw his friend armed only with his crucifix—striding toward the swordsmen. There was such a holy anger in his face that the rebels could not stand it. They dropped their swords and ran! Father des Bastières recovered slowly, painfully.

He couldn't take much more of this. He would drop dead with fright the next time it happened. Better to go away right now. But he would come back. He could not stay away.

On Ash Wednesday, Feb. 13th, 1709, Louis was sent on a mission far away from the City of Nantes. He took the road to Vannes, one historian says, and passed near Savenay . . . "celebrated in after years for the last heroic stand made by all that was left of the peasant army of La Vendée." He opened the mission at Cambon, (also spelled Campbon). And crosses were showered on him.

In the church there, as in the church in Crossac, the peasants had, for uncounted years, been burying their relatives according to their own traditions. The bodies were interred inside the church, not outside. In Cambon slabs and headstones covered the graves. Many local priests had tried to stop the practice. The bishop of Nantes had issued an edict, forbidding it. But the people had gone to law, and the courts had sustained them.

The interior of the church in Cambon looked more like a graveyard than a church. In fact it was more of a graveyard than a church, for the nave was full of monuments and crosses and tombstones of various kinds, and broken and crumbling slabs.

Louis staggered out of the place—it smelled like a stable and a glue factory—and summoned the men of the parish. He told them, gently, that only the bodies of saints belonged in the House of God—and that these long dead bodies were keeping many living bodies out of this holy place. There was room here only for the dead. These must be taken up, and placed in the graveyard outside the church.

The men were hard to convince, but they finally agreed that the missionary was right. They took away their dead, and the slabs and the angels and the crosses and the headstones—on one of which, incidentally, St. Louis saw the name of his great uncle Peter Grignion.

After this was done, Louis inspected the church itself, with disgust, indignation, and holy horror. The walls and the ceiling were foul with dirt, and with neglect. Everything in it was covered with grime except the armorial crest of the House of Coislin, which had been painted above the altar.

Men and women helped him repair, scour, pave, plaster, whitewash and paint. Louis provided new pictures and statues. When he didn't have time to paint or carve he enlisted the talent of experts. Everybody worked in a fever of enthusiasm. And everybody rejoiced when the work was finished. Everybody but the Duke of Coislin, the man who had emblazoned his arms in the House of God.

When he was told that the missionary had dared to efface his ducal family's emblem, and had refused to have it repainted anywhere in the church, he swore he would have revenge. He would have imprisoned de Montfort, had it not been for his brother, Cardinal de Coislin, Bishop of Metz, who thought that Louis had acted correctly.

De Montfort revealed his feelings in a long poem:

Let us sigh, let us lament, let us bitterly weep.
One forsakes Jesus in the Blessed Sacrament!
One forgets Him! One insults Him in His extreme love!
One attacks Him! One outrages Him in His own house!
Everything shines at Monsieur's house; it is well furnished.
The church is forgotten, the altar laid bare.
The pavement is all broken, the roof uncovered.
The walls are crumbling, and covered with filth.
The ciborium is broken; the chalice is black.
The monstrance is a vessel of cheap molded brass.
The crucifix has been severed; the lamps have no light.
Everything is chaos; everywhere is dust.
Altar cloths have rotted; ornaments are soiled.
The statues are maimed and the paintings are marred.
Alas, from the fonts to the sacristy, all is dishonor,
All is neglect.

143

Some come, at times, at night, or at daylight,
To see, to be seen, as they make their way
To hear a sermon prepared by an abbot—
But for Jesus alone? Perhaps; oh how rare!
Behold, O tearfully behold!
Lady Pompous comes, ballooning from her richest brocades,
In her dainty shoes, in her three-storey hairdo,
Into our holy places, playing her role.
Often we see her, the lovely balloon,
Settling herself softly near our altars,
Near our living God.
And one no longer looks at the tabernacle.
This devil's helper becomes the spectacle itself!
And one sees, instead of the name of our immortal Lord,
The coat of arms of Monsieur above the center of the altar!
The priest and the donkey wear his insignia.
One honors him at the altar, the other in his stall.
What! Are our altars worldly theatres?
Are our sacred mysteries the tricks of troubadours?
Is Mass a pastime, and the gospel just a fairy tale?
Is Jesus Christ an idol, and the church a stable for an ass?
Friends of the Sacred Heart and the Blessed Sacrament,
Let us lament in concert; let us bitterly cry.
Bare-foot, bright torches in hand, and ropes at the neck,
Let us cry out, 'Lord, forgive, forgive! Have mercy!

None of the books written about St. Louis mentions that a donkey was kept in the church. But, if there was, Louis was less concerned about it than about that blimp, brunette or blonde, whose vanity far outweighed her virtue. After all, there was an ass and an ox in the cave of Bethlehem, when the Lord was born.

There was no graveyard in the church at Crossac; only the graves. The nave was an open field, "broken into furrows." And it was probably full of dandelions and weeds. The people of this parish were more difficult to deal with, but de Montfort won them over. The bodies were removed, the ground was smoothed, and covered with a pavement of flat stones, and the edifice soon became, once more, the House of God.

Now Louis could proceed to Pontchateau. He had at least two powerful enemies there. The duke of Coislin, and his chief bully boy, the

144

seneschal of Pontchateau. He had seen the seneschal. The duke had sent him, with a band of soldiers, to arrest him, shackle him, and throw him into a dungeon until such time as his lordship should see fit to try him. The seneschal arrived, all right; but too late. The Cardinal Bishop was there to frustrate him.

Before he left for his new mission, Louis asked for help:

> *O great God, give me Your weapons*
> *To vanquish the world and its wiles*
> *And those who despise Your laws.*
>
> *Place, in my soul, sanctity;*
> *In my spirit, truth;*
> *And in my heart, pure flames,*
> *That I may convert souls.*
>
> *O Mary, O my good Mother Mary,*
> *Strong as an army in battle arrayed,*
> *Hasten to rescue me . . .*
> *That I may grow in sanctity,*
> *So that my God will glorify me,*
> *God alone!*

He went boldly on his way. The closer one comes to Jesus and Mary the closer he comes to Wisdom, the closer he comes to Power.

18   Enemies of the Cross

"**T**he whole country between the Loire and the Vilaine had been made fragrant with the memory of St. Louis," one of his biographers has written, "but it is around Pontchateau, some thirty miles from Nantes . . . in the wasteland of the Magdalene, all covered with heather and fern and broom . . . that traditions relating to him and his works cluster richer in glory than around any other place visited by him in his missions . . . or, perhaps, even during his entire missionary life."

Biographers differ as to the time he came to this "wasteland of the Magdalene." One says it was in May. Another swears it was in July. Another is content to say that it was in the summer of 1709. He was welcomed by the people. They were, he thought, the most wonderful Catholics he had met in all his travels. And he became certain, during his Mission, that these were the people to help him build such a Calvary as he had in his mind . . . an enduring reminder of the passion and suffering of Jesus, and the sorrows of His virgin mother. Was it not most fitting that it should be erected on the wasteland of the Magdalene?

The people of Pontchateau, and some of the clergy, received the news with joy and enthusiasm; and immediately got ready to dig. De Montfort chose a site, near a chapel, but at a considerable distance from the town. He worked with spade and pick, like the others, but he was troubled. The hill wasn't high enough. It was inconvenient. Surely there must be a better place. He spent a night in prayer. When the workers gathered in the morning, he led them into the chapel and asked them to pray. They asked Our Lady for guidance, putting everything in her care.

When they went back to work they watched two white doves come down from the blue skies. Strange doves. They were not looking for worms. They filled their bills with earth and flew away. They came back perhaps ten or a dozen times. Then Louis led the workers to their landing place. There they found a "hive-shaped" mound of fresh earth. It happened to be on top of the highest point in the Magdalene's wasteland. You could plant a tall cross there, and it could be seen from thirty or forty miles around. This was the place to build the Calvary!

As soon as he had decided this was the site Our Lady wanted, he began to hear stories from many old inhabitants. Thirty-six years before, they said, they had seen crosses, with banners flying from them, come down at mid-day, out of a clear sky, and hover over this exact spot. A strange noise was heard, a noise so loud it scattered cattle and dogs and sheep in panic. And there were voices singing, some said, between the heavens and the earth. There were a few who claimed they remembered the exact day this happened. It was, they said, January 31, 1673 —the day St. Louis was born in Montfort-la-Cane!

At first, only the citizens of Pontchateau were concerned, but in a short time men and women came from nearby towns, carrying their lunches and their tools. Within a few weeks, workers were coming from as far away as Paris, and some from various parts of Spain and Belgium. Some were the poorest of the poor. Some were the richest of the rich. Every one was happy to dig the ditches, and to take the dirt to the top of the hill in baskets, bags, hods, or clumsy wheelbarrows. The little town on the banks of the Brivet, which had hitherto given itself almost entirely to trade—its square was always filled with hand carts, and with beasts waiting to be bought and sold—devoted itself to the job. Even the children worked, after school hours. Everybody worked in silence—as though they were in a great cathedral. Yet, now and then, they could not help but say the Rosary aloud, or sing one of the hymns Louis had written for the occasion.

> *Oh what unequaled marvels we will see, in this Calvary!*
> *What conversions, what healings, what ocean tides of graces!*
> *Let us make a Calvary here.*
> *Let us make a Calvary.*

Or it might be the words he attributed to Jesus.

> *Yes, I want it. My glory depends upon it.*
> *From the light of the cross*
> *I will sing victory in this holy place.*
> *Make my Calvary here.*
> *Make my Calvary.*

148

Sometimes there would be five hundred or six hundred men and women singing these verses—and later a hundred ox-cart drivers singing with them as they drove their teams up and down the mount.

The work grew; and de Montfort's plans for it grew. And the crowds of visitors kept pace with the increase in the numbers of the workmen. Among these visitors, of course, were those Jansenist priests of St. Clement—"in their velvet coats and gold buttons"—and the jovial seneschal of the town, M. Gueschard de la Chauvelière. He was jovial for reasons of his own.

"The seneschal," Father Bolger reports, "was not a man who forgave injuries, and he bitterly resented this beggarly priest's triumph in the matter of the armorial bearings in the church at Campbon. In that adventure he had been deeply humiliated by the refusal of the Bishop of Metz to take action. After arriving on the scene, full of self-importance, and solemnly arresting Montfort, he had been obliged to release the prisoner; and it cannot be doubted that the peasants of the district chuckled openly at his discomfiture. With the intensity of a small mind, he awaited the opportunity for revenge."

De Montfort had erased the coat-of-arms of his lord, the duke, and made a fool of Guischard himself. So why should not he, and the duke, and those priests with the gold buttons, erase this Calvary? What a sweet, what an exquisite, what a complete revenge!

The calvary was a gigantic undertaking. The mount must be terraced. It must have a winding path to the top, where the great cross would stand. There would be the crosses of the thieves on either side. And, at the foot of the crosses, there would be life-sized statues of Our Lady, the Magdalene, and St. John, the Beloved. Other statues would be placed along the winding path. One hundred and fifty trees would be planted, for the *Aves* in the fifteen mysteries of the Rosary. And taller trees would serve for the *Pater Nosters*.

The workmen must dig three great ditches, and bring the dirt to the top—in bags or pouches carried on their backs, or in carts or barrows. Something like 300,000 cubic feet of clay and stone had to be extracted and transported. Always, even in the winter, there were anywhere from two hundred to six hundred men, women, and children, working through the day in honor of the crucifixion of the Lord. And always, day and night, anywhere from 200 to 600—or even 6,000—worked on the side of the devil.

France was in a desperate condition at this time. The crops had been poor in the harvest, and the winter of 1709 had been the worst in more than a hundred years. There was famine everywhere.

All through the country livestock had starved or been frozen to death. In January there was a solid freeze that lasted for more than two weeks. Then a thaw came and rotted whatever had been planted in the Fall. People made flour out of bracken. Others grazed on the dead grass on their hands and knees, like so many sheep, or they dug up roots. Wolf-packs of hungry children were everywhere, breaking and entering, pilfering whatever food they could find. Soldiers died of exhaustion, or cold, at their posts. These were mostly untrained men, undernourished men, tired men and boys. France's mighty army had been defeated at Blenheim in 1704, and disorganized at Ramillies in 1706; and in 1709 the king, and all his nobles, and all his countrymen, were crying for "peace at any price." And there was no peace in sight.

It was not strange, then, that hordes of beggars came to offer themselves to Louis in Pontchateau. He took them all into his care, and begged food for them. There was no "grass soup" in Pontchateau. Many stories are told of how the saint begged.

"He would knock at some cottage door and ask for food, although, while at a distance he had heard the goodman tell his wife that, since he had given his all, and had no more to give, he would hide himself when Father de Montfort came to beg . . . so the man of God stood before the goodman's wife, and the goodman came out from hiding."

Louis knew the couple was destitute, but he wanted an offering. When it came, he blessed them and their children and their houses, and their empty cupboards. And he promised that they and theirs would never starve. Sometimes he blessed their fields, and assured them they would always have abundant crops.

A widow named Jeanne Guégan, living near La Viotterie, told him she had not even a crust of bread to give him. He bade her look in her cold oven. There she found a loaf of fresh-baked bread. She cut off a big slice for him; and still had the loaf. Thereafter she frequented the well, around which the very poor gathered. She cut slice after slice after slice—and took the loaf home with her. When he had to go away from Pontchateau, Louis put Jeanne in charge of feeding the poor. And her supplies of food never diminished.

The work continued for fifteen months or more. Louis had organized it so well that he could go away for a week or more, to give missions, to beg, to heal the sick, and to carry his Lady's name far and wide. The work went on as well, when he was absent, as when he was in charge.

150

The year 1710 was a miserable one for France. Its armies had been shattered and scattered. It still begged for peace; but its enemies demanded an intolerable price. Its people, suffering from famine, were called upon to give the king new recruits and new taxes. France was a graveyard. Its people were ghosts. And there was smallpox everywhere, and typhoid—and scandals.

In the spring of 1710, the army of beggar workmen increased; and men came from various parts of the country with ox-carts. It was no longer necessary for a man to strap a bag of dirt onto his back and climb up to the top where the soil was needed. Now they simply filled the carts. The oxen carried it on high. The work speeded up.

In the first week of September 1710 the task was completed. The cross, 50-foot high, made of a chestnut tree, towered over the land of the Magdalene, inviting all those within twelve hundred or more square miles to come and be forgiven. The trees and the statues were in place. The little chapels of the Rosary mysteries were ready. There were two gardens, one representing Eden—where Adam and Eve were led into sin—the other representing Gethsemane, where the New Adam sweat blood because of sin, and in redemption for sin. They were ready for the pilgrims.

The bishop of Nantes promised to give this Calvary his most solemn blessing, and the day set for this was the Feast of the Exaltation of the Holy Cross. Twenty or thirty thousand people had come for the ceremony, and Louis had made many preparations. Four preachers were to address the crowds, from different parts of the Calvary. There would be a tremendous procession. Many choirs would sing. Many souls might be converted.

Exactly how Louis felt at this time nobody knows. He had often predicted during the long months of labor that the calvary would be twice destroyed, and twice restored. Many witnesses swore they had seen him, several times, talking to "a woman of unearthly beauty," who suddenly appeared and suddenly disappeared. Some think this lady told him to beware.

Others are of the opinion that he was aware of the efforts of the seneschal, his master, the duke, and of various priests and government officials to undermine his work. They recall that when the duke died, in May, 1710, and his brother, the Bishop of Metz succeeded him, Louis asked and received permission to go on with the work, "without fear of interruption or annoyance." The fact that the bishop owned the wasteland of the Magdalene helped immeasurably; but it did not insure a victory.

151

The seneschal raged when the bishop acted. He felt suddenly power-less. But then he laughed. He was even glad that the work was going on. He began to realize that the time to strike was not just then. Oh no, no, no! The right time, the most delightful time, would be when the calvary was finished—but not yet blessed. How nice to wait for that fulfilling time!

He talked to the commander of the king's forces in Brittany. He told him how this fool of a priest was drawing hundreds and hundreds of beggars from all over France. The town of Pontchateau was overrun with them. They were worse than a plague of rats. Also he was "throwing up earthworks and making underground passages." Suppose the English came here! The calvary would be an ideal fortress for them. (The English—a happy thought!) England was at war with France, and her naval vessels were everywhere. They had even come into the mouth of the Loire and attacked some French frigates.

The commander reported these distressing matters to the Marquis de Torcy, Minister of Foreign Affairs. The Marquis asked M. Ferrand, the king's commissioner for Brittany to investigate this danger to the throne. M. Ferrand came not from Brittany but from Versailles—where people were still eating cake. He brought "some fine ladies" with him. The attitude of these people toward the workmen, and toward the idea behind the calvary, annoyed de Montfort. His attitude annoyed M. Ferrand and his friends. Before he left Pontchateau, M. Ferrand wrote to a friend in Nantes: "If you wish to be amused, wait for what happens here; but don't say I told you so."

The blow fell at the precise time desired by the seneschal—like a knife in the back. On the eve of the ceremony, de Montfort was hand-ed a message from the bishop. It informed him that the blessing of the calvary was forbidden. It was short and tough, and without any details.

"It was 4 o'clock in the afternoon," says Father Bolger, "when the messenger arrived. In the midst of universal consternation, Montfort, the one most affected by the order, was the only one unmoved. How-ever he was not going to take this without question; he found the man-ner of proceeding very strange and appears to have had doubts about the authenticity of the letter. Without delay he set off to ask the bishop if it were really true. Nantes was thirty miles distant, but he would not borrow a horse, and walked throughout the night.

"Next morning he sought an interview with M. de Bauveau, the bish-op. It was brief and to the point. No reasons were given, but the prohi-bition was confirmed—the calvary was not to be blessed. On the following day, Montfort returned to Pontchateau, to find that, with the exception of the blessing, the ceremonies had been carried out. There had been sermons, Masses, acclamations, so that for one day at least the builders had been able to rejoice in the finished work. That was to be their only earthly reward." None of them, it seems, had asked for, or been given, even half a sou for all their toil.

De Montfort told the people about the bishop's opposition, and sent them home, some weeping, some shouting angry curses, some too stunned to say a word.

Louis, though he must have been somewhat tired after walking sixty miles or more in twenty-four hours—only a saint could do it—and somewhat astonished and pained at the terrible cross that had been given him, was, says one commentator, "as contented and cheerful as if all his dearest wishes had been fulfilled."

Well, he could look back through those fifteen wearing months and see all the good the calvary had done—how many thousands of people had worked for the honor of God, and so endeared themselves to Him—how many hundreds had come back to the Faith—how many poor beggars had been fed and nurtured.

On the following Sunday he went to St. Molf to open a mission. He was there only a few days when he was given another message from the bishop. He was to turn over his mission to another priest, and return, in haste, to Nantes.

He read it, we are told, "with tears in his eyes."

If this be true, he was not weeping for himself. He may have been aware that the bishop was not only recalling him but was also about to demolish the work so lovingly accomplished in the past fifteen months. He may have been weeping for the grief this would bring to all the people who had helped him. He may have been weeping because so many many souls would be lost before the calvary would be restored. He may have been weeping because, after 1700 years of Christianity, and here in this most Catholic country, men still hated Jesus and spurned His love. He may have been weeping for the bishop, who, to obey his king, and the royal sycophants, would shut out the Light of the Cross on top of the hill in Pontchateau—and slight the King of Kings. He may have been weeping for France which was in such desperate need of God's help.

He set out at once for Nantes, serene in mind and heart. The devil must have been badly hurt, to contrive such a thing as this. But the calvary would, in time, be restored. And the light of the Lord would shine there more gloriously than before.

153

Undoubtedly the bishop expected Louis to come raging into his presence, demanding explanations, and thundering reproaches. He was evidently shocked at the man's dignity, and meekness, and his air of humble obedience. How do you talk to a man like that? He told him the calvary was to be "totally destroyed." De Montfort bowed his head, and cried out—grateful for this cross of crosses—"Blessed be God! It was His glory I sought, not mine. I hope He will accept the gift I intended for Him, as though I had had it to give."

He bowed again, in farewell, and went to his friends, the Jesuits, to make a long retreat. God had willed the calvary to be built. He had also willed it to be destroyed. Blessed be His holy name!

The work of destruction was entrusted to M. d'Espinose, commandant of the Pontchateau militia. This gentleman at once picked out 500 of the men who had worked most efficiently on the project, and ordered them to undo it. He surrounded them with his militia to enforce his orders; but the men refused to obey. They were Frenchmen, they claimed, not slaves. And they were Catholics, not heretics or atheists. M. d'Espinose took full advantage of their faith.

"Get to work at once," he shouted, "or I'll cut that big cross down, and let it fall."

Let it fall? If it fell, that beautiful figure of Christ—so dear to Father de Montfort, and to every one who had helped to raise it—would be smashed. The statue was made of Breton oak—the trees that grew so plentifully in and around Montfort-la-Cane—and Louis had either carved it himself, or directed its carving. If anything happened to that figure of Jesus, it would be a terrible sacrilege.

"Let us take Him down first," a man implored the commandant. "than we will work."

The commandant was proud of himself. His trick had worked better than he had expected. He gave his permission to remove the statue.

"Lovingly, reverently," says Father Bolger, "they took down the figure from the cross; d'Espinose himself stated later that not even the true Descent from the Cross at Jerusalem could have been more touching. Around the hill knelt thousands of people; and as the image of their crucified Lord was lowered gently to the earth, even the hardest among them sobbed."

The men, true to their word, went to work, but listlessly, sullenly, taking their own time to level the hill and fill the ditches. There was only desolation in the wasteland of the Magdalene.

In 1747, some of de Montfort's spiritual sons began to restore the calvary. Before they could finish it, the commandant of the local garrison claimed that the land of the Magdalene was his, and he had not given anybody permission to turn the hill into "an ideal refuge for robbers." The place was blessed, though it could not be completed.

In 1793, during "the Terror," the haters of religion did their best to destroy and efface all that had been done by the priests. But in 1821, the people of God began to rebuild it. Today it is a shrine; and pilgrims come there from all over France, and all over the world, to adore God and to revere His mother.

The biographer who signs himself only as "a secular priest," could not close his chapter on Pontchateau without making these remarks:

"One last triumphal fulfillment up to the time these words are written; on the 24th of June, 1891, as if still more solemnly to redeem the promise of the Servant of God—now declared Blessed by the Sovereign Pontiff—that it would one day come back to his calvary with all the greater glory when the chapel should be built, the Christ of Blessed Louis was carried in royal triumph by five hundred men chosen from twenty-two parishes, up and around the calvary, in the presence of many thousands of people, with banners waving and crosses flashing in the light; while, at the close, the Blessed Sacrament, uplifted by their bishop, blessed the mighty multitude. Then, like the sound of many waters went up to heaven the triumphant song which the prophet-poet had once placed on the lips of the Redeemer of the world: 'I will sing victory in this holy place.' "

19 Attempt on His Life

The last years of Louis de Montfort's life were filled with the mystical and the miraculous—and with the ordinary joy of seeing God's love and God's mercy all around, and God's will directing him in everything. The whole world, it seems, spoke to him of God—especially when he travelled. He reveals this in one of his hymns.

As I was walking, the other day,
I heard my Love's voice talking to me
And my own voice replying.
O Charity Sublime, Supreme!
Always and a thousand times my Love,
I love You!

I was inflamed that day.
Everything spoke to me of Love.
Even the countryside around me,
Understood me and rejoiced in me.
We talked to each other. We talked in concert.
'Let us love God more!'

The birds that sang to me,
The streams that chattered,
The wind and the rain that came to me from You,
All fanned the flame within me.
Even the dull roads understood
The Love consuming me.

I thanked the birds, the woods, the streams,
Your messengers, for bringing Love Supreme to me;
And bade them take back to You
The fire in my heart and soul.

> *I shouted among the knolls;*
> *Is He there, my Love, Sublime, Supreme?*
> *Do you have him, woods and streams?*
> *Seek Him out for me, little birds,*
> *And bring Him here to end my woes.*

Can anyone, reading those lines, believe that Louis was ever a clod who walked alone, watching only his thick shoes—or his bare and blistered and bleeding feet—as they kicked up the dust of the road—never lifting his eyes to look at birds, or men, or—God help us—women or girls?

Louis did not feel crushed at the destruction of his work. He continued his apostolic missions as though nothing had happened. His friends, who sought to comfort him in his new disgrace, found, to their amazement, that he was content and cheerful. He was not living in the past, but in the present and the future.

He lived as always on the charity of the very poor, in rags and tatters and broken shoes and on his love for God.

He remained at Nantes through the winter. The bishop had forbidden him to preach, being afraid he might stir up another storm—and Versailles might not like it. But that did not prevent Louis from teaching the catechism to children and adults, or forming such lay organizations as the Friends of the Cross. And, evidently, he began to write some of his books, notably *The Secret of Mary*, which he later expanded into *True Devotion of Mary*. He rebuilt the ruined chapel attached to the decrepit house in which he lived, and there he said his daily Mass. He managed somehow to start a hospital for incurables. He became a Tertiary in the Order of Preachers, although, through spreading everywhere the aroma of the Rosary, he had long been one of St. Dominic's most stalwart sons.

To many in the city he was a "nice old man"—though he was only 38 years old—a frail tall saint.

Then, early in 1711, the Loire overflowed its banks; and the Biesse section, across the stream, was in grave danger. Only the roofs and the chimneys of the houses were above water there; and many people were clinging to precarious holds.

Louis went swiftly here, there, next door, and the next door, and the next, collecting all the food and dry clothing his neighbors had. He found a boat, and stocked it with his provisions. He had enough for several boats. Boatmen gathered at the river's edge tried to stop him. Was he mad? Didn't he know that no boat could live in that stream?

158

Look at it! It was a torrent! It was filled with driftwood, with logs, with great chunks of ice, with houses and barns and sheds. What was the poor old man trying to do? Kill himself?

"Come on," he said to them, "follow me. You will be safe. Trust in God, and come. The people need you." He began to fill their boats.

Before they half-realized what they were doing, they were—as crazy as he was—following him through the flood. They gained their objective safely, left their supplies—throwing them into the garrets, or openings in the roofs. Then they came safely back.

"His heroism," Father Bolger remarks "caused no softening upon the part of the bishop." Louis still remained a nuisance.

But in March of that year, 1711, Bishop de Champflour asked Louis to work in his diocese of La Rochelle. It was a bugle call. Louis left at once with the most gracious consent of the bishop of Nantes.

He stopped in La Garnache, remembering he had promised to give a mission there. The parish priest, Father Dorion, received him gladly, and opened the rectory to him. The people loved him and followed him wherever he went. Beggars swarmed to him. He persuaded some of the citizens to take them into their homes. He kept "two of the most repulsive" for himself, and saw to it that they ate at his table. It is recorded that he went into the rectory garden one evening, before dinner, to say his office. A boy who had been sent to tell him that dinner was ready, reported that he couldn't talk to the missionary because he was conversing with "a beautiful lady who floated in the air above him."

Louis stopped also at St. Hilary de Loulay. He had promised to preach a mission there too. He arrived late at night, with Brother Mathurin. It was raining furiously, and it was extremely cold. He woke the parish priest. But that man had heard stories about Father de Montfort; and he wanted nothing to do with him. He shoved him back into the icy rain.

Louis went to an inn, and was again forced into the street. He didn't look respectable enough. He was walking out of town, with Brother Mathurin, his heart singing, when an old woman saw him and brought him and his companion into her home—the poorest in the area.

He stopped also in Luçon, to pay a short visit to Bishop de Lescure, a close friend of the bishop of La Rochelle, and to make a retreat with the Jesuits, friends who never failed him. While saying Mass the next morning, the Jesuits report, Louis "went into an ecstasy that held him half an hour." Here, most unexpectedly Father des Bastières came to see him.

159

Louis, with Brother Mathurin, arrived in La Rochelle in May, and found an innkeeper willing to shelter and feed him—and, also, willing to trust him. Neither of the two had any money, but Louis acted as if that didn't matter. After breakfast he left his staff with the landlord, as a pledge, and went out to see the town—which, in his language, meant visiting the hospitals and the slums. The staff was extremely valuable to him because it contained the crucifix indulgenced by the Pope.

Before he returned, he met a woman who insisted on giving him enough money to satisfy the innkeeper, and on making herself his hostess. Through this woman he met a priest who introduced him to Bishop de Champflour. The bishop welcomed him, and asked him to preach a general mission for the city. La Rochelle at that time was the headquarters of the Calvinist heresy—which stressed predestination, a strict moral code, and the idea that God makes the just man rich. It was also the capital of the Huguenots.

Father de Montfort was placed in charge of a number of priests—including his own brother, Gabriel Francis, the rector of St. Léger's church—and the mission was preached in the church of the Dominicans, an immense edifice. There was a mission for men, another for women, and a third for the soldiers in the garrison.

If La Rochelle expected him to call down fire from heaven on all the heretics, they were disappointed. He told his congregation about the Rosary, and about God's love, and about the joy of finding their Mother Mary—the Mother of their brother Jesus, the Mother of their God. He explained that the Rosary was not only a sovereign prayer, it was also an exposition of the Faith. He ended all his sermons by asking his hearers to renew their Baptismal vows.

He was especially successful with the soldiers. Many of these, says Father Bolger, could not read. Louis told them "easily absorbed rhymes."

"Reading his verses today," he adds, "you can hear the tramp of marching feet . . . to quote only two lines . . . 'Women and wine I now detest, the pair are just a deadly pest.' " Before de Montfort had finished with them, they were walking barefooted, in solemn procession down the main street, a crucifix in one hand, a Rosary in the other, and they were singing to Our Lady."

Louis was happy that Father des Bastières was with him again. Perhaps he enjoyed ushering the timid little man into, and out of, desperate situations. Also, perhaps, he knew the priest was holy.

"We often started out together," Father des Bastières wrote, "without my having any idea where we were headed. He knew that if he told

160

me, I would refuse to go. We went, many times, to some accursed house of women. He would preach in a loud voice. He would kneel and say the Rosary aloud; and always there was clamor, and outcry, and threats of violence. But sometimes the women went to confession to us.

"Once a man drew his sword and threatened to kill Father de Montfort if he didn't get up and leave the place. Father, kneeling on the floor, not budging an inch, said he would be glad to die if that would make the swordsman change his evil ways. The fellow was so overcome by this that his hands shook. He sheathed his sword clumsily, as though he were drunk. And he groped his way to the door, as if he were suddenly taken ill."

De Montfort's critics had predicted he would have a hard time in La Rochelle. Hitherto, they said, all he had had to contend with were poor, ignorant, lapsed, indifferent, or apathetic Catholics—people who could be emotionally stirred only by de Montfort's particular outlandish ideas—hymn-singing, long processions, hysterical sermons, and fanatic carrying of gigantic crosses. How was he going to handle the Calvinist and Huguenot heretics of La Rochelle—especially the educated ones, "the intelligentsia?"

The Protestants in the city didn't try to resist de Montfort, at first. They contented themselves with jeering at him—from safe distances—on the streets. They sometimes sang lewd songs as he passed. And now and then someone, usually a boy, dared to throw a stone at him. But they considered him "harmless" until he began converting some of their most prominent men and women. Then they thought of poison, bludgeons, knives, firearms.

It was shortly after he brought Mme. de Mailly into the Church that someone sneaked into the kitchen of the house in which he dwelled, and placed a powerful dose of poison in the soup that was meant for him.

Mme. de Mailly, we are told, was "a staunch and most intelligent Huguenot . . . who was endeared to her sect not only by the brilliant qualities of her mind, but also by her high birth, and her firm attachment to her faith."

For a long time the lady had been troubled with certain doubts concerning her religion; and her ministers had been unable to help her. She had heard that this strange Father de Montfort had been endowed with great wisdom. Hence it was imperative that she go to him. She couldn't afford to be seen with him anywhere in La Rochelle, where she was so well known. Heavens, what a scandal—to be found, by some of her friends, actually talking to a Catholic priest! And such a priest! Nor could she dare be seen in any Catholic church. A Catholic friend arranged for her to see Father de Montfort in a nearby village. And, there Mme. de Mailly began "to take instructions."

Had de Montfort been the rigid stick that Canon Blain and others have made him he might never have been able to "handle" this particular lady. But he had learned about women from experts—beginning with his sisters, and continuing on through Mme. de Montespan and other friends, to Marie Louise and Catherine Brunet.

Perhaps Mlle. Brunet was his best teacher, for he could relax in her presence; laugh at her levity and her seeming hardness, and enjoy her teasing. Catherine was introduced to Louis by her sister, who complained that the girl was always too merry, too ready to laugh at everything. She enjoyed life too much. She could not be solemn. She just simply had to be happy all the time.

Louis knew that it takes purity of heart to make a man or woman happy "all the time." He suspected that Catherine was a soul chosen by God and Our Lady to make others happy. He was sure her seeming "hardness" was a fake; and that her levity covered depths unplumbed. He began to study her, to enjoy her conversation, her "secular ways, and her little vanities." She flirted with him, mildly. But he knew what was in her mind—and he did not chide her or criticize her in any way. Catherine, in her own way, loved this poor underrated priest—and delighted to contradict him and annoy him.

"I am crazy about that hymn," she once said, discussing one de Montfort had written. "It sets me dancing. Of course the words are nothing; nothing at all. It's the music." She knew very well that the words were de Montfort's, and the music had been borrowed. "How would it be if I put different words to it—made it a real song?"

Louis smiled. He said; "Suppose you write a song—a hymn, rather—and let me put it to music."

Catherine laughed and got up and danced a few steps to show how she liked the idea. She did write the hymn, Louis supplied the melody. And Catherine sang it with rapture.

All the time, of course, while the girl was working on him, he was turning her thoughts and ambitions more and more toward heaven. Eventually he thought she was good enough to join the twenty women in the general hospital at Poitiers, whom he had placed under obedience to a blind woman.

Eventually she became sister Conception, the second Daughter of

Wisdom. Before she went to the convent, one writer wants us to know, she knitted a woolen cassock for de Montfort—"a seamless robe." It was kept as a priceless relic. And some people were said to have been miraculously healed by touching it.

Louis was quite prepared to talk to Mme. de Mailly. And he had no trouble in settling her problems and teaching her to love Our Lady, and to wear the chains. When she was ready to profess her new Faith, she did so in public, to the horror and consternation and violent anger of all her friends and relatives.

"Kill the anti-Christ!" people cried. "Kill de Montfort!"

Years later, in Paris, Mme. de Mailly was a witness to one of de Montfort's miracles. He had just come from the church, where he had said Mass, and was standing with a number of friends, when a peasant woman approached. She had a child in her arms. She asked for his help. The child's head was covered by masses of ugly, ill-smelling scabs, or scalls." And her body was pathetically thin.

"Help me, in the holy name of Jesus," the woman begged.

"Do you believe in prayer?" the priest asked. "Do you believe in the power of the name of Jesus?"

"Yes, Father."

Louis, Mme. de Mailly reports, put his hand on the little head and said a prayer: "May the Lord Jesus heal you, little girl, if only to reward your mother's faith." Instantly the scabs, or scalls, dropped off. The sores healed. The child was well. Her mother wept with joy; the child laughed and clapped her hands.

The historians tell us about the poison. But whether it was administered after the conversion of Mme. de Mailly, or that of Mlle. Bénigne Page, is uncertain.

Bénigne was young, frivolous, bored, rich. She was the daughter of one of the Treasurers of France; and we would say, today, in America, that she was "definitely of the 'in' set." When she heard that the clowning priest everybody was talking about had been appointed to give a retreat in the chapel of the general hospital, she decided to amuse herself and her friends by attending it.

She put on as little as she could in the way of costume. But that little was rich, and it sparkled with gems. No preacher on earth could miss seeing her, or be mistaken in her purpose. No holy priest could keep from breaking into flames and raucous screams. No missionary could help shouting abuse. It was going to be the fun riot of the day! Her set would talk of it for weeks!

163

The chapel was packed, but Bénigne didn't mind. Someone always made way for her and her friends. She picked a spot down front and people scattered, leaving plenty of seats for herself and her friends.

De Montfort saw her as she came down the aisle, and as she plumped herself into a choice seat—without, of course, bothering to thank any of those who made the space available.

Something about her appealed to him. She was young and lovely, like Catherine Brunet. And there were depths to her that she herself never dreamed of. She had come here to have a queer sort of fun. How lonely she must be! How empty her life must be! How hungry she must be for the love of God! She didn't know she was seeking God, of course. But most certainly she was. Only God could make this woman happy.

He gave Bénigne such a look of pity that she was outraged. Pity! That was the last thing she had expected. Pity from a rag-bag ruffian priest! Who did he think he was, pitying Bénigne Pagé? She was so angered that she forgot she had come here to laugh. For some little time she heard nothing de Montfort said. But people were weeping all around her, and, eventually she had to listen. He was talking about Mary, the mother of God and the mother of men and women. How empty life would be without Mary, without a mother's love, without a mother's wisdom, without a mother's comfort and consolation.

In spite of herself Bénigne began crying too. And she couldn't stop. Some of her giddy friends were sobbing, but most of them were just looking foolish and—and "sort of lost."

Bénigne stayed in her seat a long time after the sermon was finished, letting her friends go, one by one, away without her. She demanded to see Father de Montfort. The saint listened to her for two hours, and talked to her as he had talked, so many times, to Catherine Brunet and Marie Louise Trichet.

Late that night a happy Bénigne Pagé "put her affairs in order." And, early the next morning, she walked to the Convent of the Poor Clares, and begged that she might wear their habit. She asked only two favors of the abbess—that she might never be given any office, and that she should never be sent to the parlor to meet anyone, unless it were absolutely necessary.

The woman became, overnight, a heroine to many young Catholic women; and a scandal and an aching wound to all the people of her world.

Catholics and Protestants both threatened to kill de Montfort, to burn the convent, and to drag Bénigne out of her cell even if they had to walk over the dead bodies of the abbess and all the nuns. But nothing came of it all. Nothing but the poison. Mlle. Pagé, in due time, made her vows as a Poor Clare, and took the name of Louise, the feminine form of Louis.

De Montfort wrote a few lines of verse for her—an epitaph not written on stone.

> *Glory to the Lord!*
> *The world has lost you, my Bénigne.*
> *Glory to the Lord!*
> *Cry always, 'All or nothing.'*
> *The world, or the convent of St. Clare?*
> *Either all or nothing!*
> *A great heart chooses the greatest good;*
> *Of all convents the one most strict;*
> *Of all victories, the one most perfect.*
> *Either all or nothing!*

"My Bénigne!" A stick? Louis Marie de Montfort was a truly human saint.

If he had swallowed the poison, he would not have regretted that he died for Bénigne Pagé—or for Mme. de Mailly—But he swallowed only a little of it. He spat most of it out of his mouth, then took an emetic. That saved his life, but his health was shattered.

"Never again," says a biographer, "would he have those giant reserves of strength to call upon in time of stress. And his early death must undoubtedly be attributed, in part, to the poisoned broth of La Rochelle."

20   Island Mission

Father des Bastières, though still fearful of his life, attached himself more closely than ever to St. Louis. He was sure that all the heretics in La Rochelle were spying on his friend. They knew, he believed, everything that Louis was going to do, and they took measures to prevent his doing it. He tells a strange story to prove it. It begins with a trio of well-dressed thugs marching into a church in La Rochelle, meaning to heckle Louis with silly questions. Louis saw them first. "Out," he shouted. "Out of this holy place, you devils in powdered wigs! Out, before I come down from the pulpit and throw you out." They went. But they were not done with Louis.

Late that night, says the little priest, Louis was going to visit a sculptor named Adam, who lived in the rue de La Rochelle. Suddenly he stopped. He would go no further. He turned and went back to his lodgings, unable to explain why he did so. Years later, Father des Bastières, traveling from Nantes to La Rochelle, met "seven gentlemen on horseback," who were talking about Father de Montfort as though he had been some sort of friend. Among them were three who acknowledged Louis had driven them out of the church. They had waited in ambush for him, they said, outside the house of a sculptor named Adam—knowing he was going to see Adam, that night, about some statues. They waited all night, but he did not come. They waited for him on other nights, and in other places, but "by the devil's luck," he always escaped them.

Sometime after the poison had wrecked de Montfort's strength, the bishop of Luçon asked him to preach a mission on the Island of Yeu. This required a voyage by sea, and Father des Bastières begged to be excused. And he pleaded with de Montfort to stay ashore . . . far away from the English.

England and France were at war at this time, and the English ships were perilously close to the city. He warned Louis that the heretics would find out all about his plans; and they would sell him to the English navy.

"Why should that bother us?" Louis asked.

The little priest turned pale. "The English are pirates," he said. "They'll catch us. I tell you they know the boat we must take. They will be waiting for us. And they will feed us to the sharks."

"Then, by all means, let us go," de Montfort said. "If the martyrs had been as timid as we are, they never would have received their palms."

Father des Bastières looked as though he were already seasick, but Louis laughed, and told him not to worry. The boat, on which he was supposed to embark, would sail without him. He and Father des Bastières would take a later boat.

The ship on which the priests were scheduled to sail for the island was overtaken by a British corsair. Her captain was so angry when he learned that the two priests were not on board that he kept the French craft as a prize.

When the other boat was . . . "nine or ten miles out to sea," Fr. des Bastières wrote, "we saw two Guernsey corsairs coming toward us, with all sails spread. The wind was with the pirates, and against us. We knew we were lost. That is, I knew it, and everybody else but Father de Montfort knew it. And all of us were in mortal fear. Father de Montfort, though, began to sing to Mary, and asked us to sing with him. We didn't feel at all like singing—with that awful ship coming closer and closer toward us—but we sang. Then he asked us to recite the Rosary. He promised us that Our Lady would take care of us, her children. How many believed him? One of the corsairs came close enough to fire at us, but a puff of wind blew it out of our way, and we escaped unharmed."

He says that St. Louis spent two months on the island, and that Louis performed something of a miracle at one of the three chapels where he preached. There was a great rock on the site where he wanted to plant a cross. A number of men had tried to move it. St. Louis touched it gently and it rolled down the hillside with the docility of a pebble.

Louis carved the initials I.H.S. on the door of a hut he occupied. In time, the door decayed, we are told, but the plank with the letters carved by Louis Marie did not age. It is now in the possession of the Montfort Missionaries.

"We were well received by the inhabitants of the island," Father des

168

Bastières said; "but very badly by the governor and all his friends, who persecuted Father de Montfort all during the mission."

There were crosses. Louis was happy.

> *Here is my everyday word—*
> *'Blessed be God!'*
> *Whatever befalls me on this earth—*
> *'Blessed be God!'*
> *One offends me, one caresses me—*
> *'Blessed be God!'*
> *One heals me; another wounds me—*
> *'Blessed be God!'*

When he had finished the mission on the Island of Yeu, Louis went to La Garnache to bless the chapel of Our Lady of Victories. He tarried long enough on the way to look after the sick in his hospital in Nantes and to speak to the Friends of the Cross and the members of other lay organizations he had started.

He arrived in La Garnache two days ahead of schedule, and gave a short retreat to the parishioners. On the appointed day, May 12, so many people came for the ceremonies that the church could not hold them all. He took them out to a field some distance away. He was used to preaching in the open. Several times he had had such a crowd waiting for his words that he had to climb a tree to make sure he could be seen and heard. This day he had scarce begun his sermon when a heavy shower fell. Nobody ran for shelter. No man covered his head.

"Please put on your hats," Louis begged them.

No one obeyed.

"Put on your hats or I will finish talking immediately," he said.

Every man put on his hat. The sermon continued in the rain.

When he left that evening, to preach a mission in Sallertaine, half the congregation went with him, weeping, singing hymns, saying the Rosary. The parish priest came along too. He intended to go only to the place where the delegation from Sallertaine would meet them. But there were so few people there that the priest was distressed. He, and his flock decided to go all the way with the missionary.

At the cross outside the village of Sallertaine many people were gathered, singing profane songs, shouting filthy words, and pitching sharp stones, some of which hit de Montfort and hurt him.

Secretly de Montfort was pleased. The devil didn't want him here. For the moment the fiend was in control, but only for a moment. De

169

Montfort summoned St. Michael the Archangel to his side, and Our Lady, and her Son, Incarnate Wisdom. Then he went straight to the door of the church.

The crowd on that side of the cross hooted in derision. The doors had all been locked. The crowd on the far side of the cross knelt in prayer. Louis put his hand out to open the door, but it opened itself. The hooting stopped. The people from La Garnache began the Rosary.

Somebody told Louis that a certain fat bourgeois merchant had stirred up this mob in order to prevent him from preaching the mission. Louis went to his home with a bucket of holy water. He walked in without being invited. The entire family was in the living room. He sprinkled them with the holy water. He sprinkled the room. He sprinkled the other rooms. He placed a crucifix and a statue of Our Lady in the dining room, then knelt, blessed himself, and prayed.

When he had finished praying, he rose and addressed the merchant and his family, "I did not come alone."

They looked around him, but could see no companions of his.

"Jesus and Mary sent me," he said. "I am their ambassador. The Archangel Michael escorted me. Will you not receive us as Christians should?"

The merchant found his voice. "Welcome," he said weakly.

The man's wife and children smiled.

The merchant hesitated, scowled, then shrugged his shoulders.

"All right," he said. "Why not?"

Father des Bastières who had been waiting outside, sweating horribly and praying hard, almost sang a *Te Deum* when Louis came out of the house, not only alive and unmutilated, but with a train of friends behind him. He was, the little priest thought, like that fabulous duck of Montfort-la-Cane, leading her flock to the altar.

It was good that Father des Bastières could once in a while have a respite from his constant dread. It helped repay him for all the terrors that came to him through Louis. He "almost died of fright"—again— some years later, because of Louis and his idea of preaching a mission. It happened in Fontenay-le-Comte, in 1715.

The commandant of the garrison there, a Colonel du Mesnil, had been greatly impressed by the missionary's work with the soldiers in La Rochelle. He had seen those tamed wolves walk in procession through the streets, singing, "Holy Virgin obtain for us the holy love of Your Son," and holding up their crucifixes and their beads, while many people wept as they watched. He wanted the saint to transform his warriors into just such gentle lambs.

170

He did not want them to wait for a special mission, however. He sent them to the church of St. Jean at once. It happened to be a mission for women. The soldiers were admitted, but there was little space for them. Louis' attendants, Brother Mathurin and others, packed them into a transept of the church. They came every day for two weeks.

One afternoon Louis found a strange man talking to someone near the holy water font. He was a personage! And evidently had no business here. Certainly he had little respect for the house of God. He had not bothered to take off his hat, and he was sniffing snuff from a jewelled box! As de Montfort approached, the man began to laugh aloud.

De Montfort was outraged. He told the stranger to leave the church at once. The man was even more furious than de Montfort. He drew his sword. He claimed as much right to be in the church as the priest himself, and dared him to do anything about it.

"A gentleman," de Montfort said, "should know how to behave in the House of God. I ask you again to leave. This is a mission for women, not for men."

Thereupon, say the chroniclers, the gentleman began to curse the priest, in the language of the barracks yards. Several women rushed up to eject him. The man, Colonel du Mesnil himself, called for the help of his troops. There was plenty of action for some little time.

Amazons and soldiers fought it out, overturning and splintering benches and chairs, the women screaming, the soldiers shouting, du Mesnil and de Montfort breathless and disheveled. Louis was punched and nearly choked. The Colonel was most thoroughly scratched and battered.

Father des Bastières was in the confessional at the time, with a soldier on either side of him. He stayed there all through the little riot; and he kept the soldiers frozen there with him. Nobody suffered as much as he did. He admits he "almost fainted."

Peace came when more women joined the attack. Among them were the wives, daughters, and sisters of the soldiers; and a sprinkling of their sweethearts. The heroes of the king, surrounded, outnumbered, and overwhelmed with terror, fled into the peaceful street, carrying their leader with them.

Louis went calmly into his pulpit. But it was three days before Father des Bastières quit shaking.

Friends who wanted the saint to stay near them in La Rochelle bought him a small cottage in the parish of St. Eloi. It became another hermitage. He spent much time there in solitude, and in prayer and

171

meditation. He had to be alone with God every so often, in order that he could be strengthened to renew his missions.

It was in this house, biographers say, that he wrote the Constitutions of the Daughters of Wisdom and the rules for the nuns. He stayed there until after the harvest, until the beginning of winter. Missions were meant to be held in winter, when the peasants had no crops to bother them, and only a few chores to keep them busy. On the first really cold day, he set forth, with his lay-brothers, his staff, his statues and religious goods, and his sturdy burro, which carried his books and the Rosaries he would give away.

And again he performed miracles, rebuilt ruined chapels and churches, founded hospitals, organized various lay apostolates, converted thousands of people, Catholics and Protestants alike, led processions, and left behind him huge crosses—and sometimes little Calvaries too—to remind the people of the truths they had learned in the Missions.

He grew weaker with the days and the weeks and the months and the years; but his weakness was often discounted by his holy wrath. When he heard someone blaspheme, he became something of a one-man cyclone, no matter how feeble he might be. The incident at Esnandes is typical.

He and "his flock" were about to erect the cross, after the mission, when some people "in a large inn kept by a wealthy landlord named Morcant" broke up the solemn proceedings by singing loud and bawdy songs. They were all drunk, it seems, and uninhibited in speech, song, dance, or acts of violence. De Montfort tried to talk to them. They would not listen. They swore at him. They blasphemed. And the saint, it appears, took appropriate action.

Just what that action was, we are not told. We can only imagine what happened. Maybe Louis shuffled the pack of them, as he did with the blaspheming wine bibbers of Roussay. Maybe he just talked to them—on his knees with his indulgenced crucifix in his hand. At any rate it is only the landlord who bore the consequences. Louis held him responsible for the blasphemies—whereupon the landlord blasphemed to show his contempt of the priest.

"Woe to you," Louis said. "You will perish miserably—you and all your family!"

A commentator has this to say: "Alas! the awful prophecy came only too true, and the God of all charity speedily avenged the affront to His grace by the terrors of His justice. A few days after the Mission, the

172

man was suddenly seized with a trembling of his whole body, for which no physician could find a remedy, and he was known until the day of his death by no other name than that of 'the trembler.' He died in the greatest misery. His wife, who had shared his fault, shared also his punishment. She became a notorious drunkard. His children all died young, with the exception of a daughter; and she was an idiot . . ."

It is possible Louis had this and similar incidents in mind when he wrote to his sister Louise, on Jan. 1, 1713 . . . "God takes pleasure, my dear sister, in seeing us both fight for Him . . . you in secret, myself in public. Your battles are fought in yourself. Mine are fought all over France . . . fighting the devils in hell, or making war on the world and the worldly enemies of all truth."

He fights and he suffers.

"You would doubtless be surprised," he tells his sister, "if you knew all the particulars of the beloved cross with which God favors me, through the intercession of our dear Mother. I beg you to thank my loving Jesus, and to ask your community . . . to obtain for me, from Jesus Crucified, the strength to bear the hardest and heaviest crosses as if they were straws, and to stand against the powers of hell with a front of brass . . ."

Louis, of course, didn't always fight with his hands. One of his most effective weapons was his humility, which, added to his love for all men and his compassion for them, gave him a frightful advantage over the average missionary.

Once, while he was raising a mission cross on a hilltop, a man and woman stepped in front of him and shouted insults. They kept this up for twenty minutes. Louis stood where he was, accepting the worst the pair could offer. Then he used that deadly weapon of throwing himself at their feet and begging their pardon for anything he might have said or done "to cause them such anguish that they had to express it thus, in public vituperation." They had no defense against such an attack. They looked at him, almost in fear, and hurried away.

Over and over again Louis resorted to this unique martial tactic— and always it won the fight for him.

Sometimes he let his friends battle in his name, as he did at St. Pompain. It was the custom, the tradition in that town, to keep the market open on Sunday—especially on Sunday. Traders came from all the villages within the radius of a hundred miles, bringing their livestock to sell; and their carts and wagons were piled high with vegetables and fruits and wines and wares of all kind.

173

During his mission, St. Louis told the people that the market must be closed on all Sundays thereafter. They obeyed his orders as though he were the king himself. But the traders who came driving into St. Pompain the next Sunday were stubborn.

They were determined not to leave without selling all their wares. A holy procession was organized in a few minutes. It made a "frontal attack" on the embattled traders, and put them to a panic rout. They never came back on Sunday. Why should they? The Sunday market had been permanently closed.

There were so many ways to fight, when one fought for God!

21 First Followers

Louis Marie knew his time was "getting short." Hence he lengthened his work and increased his austerities and his prayers. He gave Mathurin the task of scourging him. Mathurin protested that the Saint was doing too much penance. Louis smiled. "The cock never crows better," he said, "than when he has beaten himself with his wings. And a man must do penance when so many do not."

The beginning of the end might be placed in the country town of La Séguinière, in the latter part of June, 1713. Louis came close to exhaustion there, yet managed to complete the mission, form various lay organizations, arrange processions, rebuild a chapel, and put up a great cross, before he left the parish. He also acted out some of his sermons on death, enacting the role of the sinner dying after a good confession. Friends and enemies both said he was as good an actor as he was a preacher.

The pastor, an Irishman named Canty, begged him to stay in the parish until he was entirely well. But he would not listen. There were several important duties he must perform before he died. He must go immediately to Paris. He must settle his father's business while he could.

"But you are too ill to walk that distance," Father Canty objected.

"I will rest on the way," Louis said simply. "Our Lady will see to that."

Perhaps he remembered the time, when he was young and powerful, when he walked to Paris that he might become a priest. Now he was going there to get priests for the community he must establish soon, if he was to establish it at all. His old friend Claude François Poullart des Places, who must have opened his seminary years ago, had promised him the best priests he had.

He found the seminary when, on a hot, stifling, dusty day in July, he reached the city.

His friend had died, but Father Bouic, his successor, greeted Louis warmly. He explained that the seminary was poor, and most of the students were still too young to become priests, especially missionary priests; but Louis could talk to all of them and select those he desired. In time they would be sent to him. Louis looked at all the candidates for the altar, embraced the poorest of them, and took the hat of another, which he placed on his own head. He said. "He belongs to me." The young man's name was Le Valois. Three others promised to join Father de Montfort when they could. One of these was Adrien Vatel.

It seemed, for a time, that the bursar of the seminary, Father Caris, would return with Louis, and become the first of his sons in the congregation to be so singularly devoted to Mary. But Father Bouic could find nobody to replace him. So, eventually, Louis went alone back to La Rochelle.

Adrien Vatel became the first priest in the new order. After his ordination, he decided not to give himself to de Montfort, but to go to India. He arranged to go there on a frigate in which he could serve as chaplain. The skipper advanced him money for books, vestments, and altar linens. Aboard ship, Father Vatel examined the faculties he had obtained from the Archbishop of Paris and the bishop of Rouen, and began to wonder about their validity. How good would they be in India?

When the frigate put into the harbour of La Rochelle, in February 1715, Father Vatel decided to ask the bishop of that diocese for his opinion. On the way to see the bishop, he learned that Father de Montfort was giving an open retreat in a nearby church. He could not help himself; he went into the church and found a place not too far from the pulpit. He listened for a time, in some distress. Could this be the great preacher he had heard so much about? Why, he was not saying anything worth listening to! The young man was about to leave, in great disappointment, when de Montfort suddenly called out, "There is someone here who resists me. The word of God comes back to me empty . . . He is trying to get away from me. But he shall not escape."

"He's talking to me," Father Vatel thought. He waited, wondering at the change that came over the preacher after that outcry. Yes, this was de Montfort—the great de Montfort! When he went to visit him after the sermon, Adrien found him absorbed in a letter. It was from a priest who had promised to help in a distant town. He wrote to say he had changed his mind.

Louis looked up and saw Father Vatel. He welcomed him with a beaming countenance.

176

"One priest breaks his word," he said. "Another is sent me by the good God."

This embarrassed Father Vatel. He took a long time explaining how he had become entangled; and how he could not help Father de Montfort, as he had wished to do. He was committed! He owed too much money! One hundred crowns! The skipper would make trouble!

"Don't worry about the money," Louis said. "The bishop of La Rochelle will be glad to reimburse the captain. Now let me see those faculties you speak of."

He looked at the papers. They were no good, he said. Only the pope, who had jurisdiction over the whole world, could give any one the right to preach missions in India. He took the young man to the bishop's residence. The bishop confirmed everything Louis had said—even to the payment of the money.

Strangely enough Father Vatel began to feel as though he had just been released from some diabolical trap. Only Satan, he realized, could have made him think he was intended for India and not for the priest to whom he had promised himself. What a fool the devil was! He should never have let that frigate come anywhere near La Rochelle!

The captain of the ship raged when he heard the news. He wanted his chaplain back. Father de Montfort was a thief! He would run him through if he ever saw him.

Louis, when he heard this, boarded the ship and confronted the man. "You want my life?" he said. "Take it." The captain took his hand, instead.

Sometime after this, Father Vatel sent a portrait of Louis to Le Valois, who was still in the seminary.

Another student, who, says Father Bolger, was "definitely queer in the head," invaded Le Valois' room and ripped all his pictures to pieces—then went to find his victim to tell him he would see "something interesting" in the room. Le Valois found the shreds of his pictures; and the portrait of Father de Montfort. This, evidently, had been torn up too, but it had been mysteriously, or miraculously, patched up again. Only a few faint lines showed where it had been torn.

St. Louis was dead at this time; but he brought Le Valois into his Company all the same.

Two of de Montfort's relics are still venerated in the seminary. One is the crucifix he gave to Father Bouic—"a simple little thing worn away with kisses." The other is a statue of Our Lady sheltering a dozen priests under her cloak.

The weeks Louis spent in Paris were fruitful. They were also full of thorns and crosses. He mentions this, lightly, in a letter to his sister Louise, dated August 15, 1713:

"Vive Jésus! Vive sa Croix! If you knew my crosses and humiliations in detail, I doubt you would desire so ardently to see me; for I am never in any place without giving a splinter of my cross to my best friends, often against my will and theirs. No one can take up my cause or dare to declare himself for me without suffering for so doing, or without falling under the power of hell, which I am combatting, or of the world which I am opposing, or of the flesh which I am persecuting. The swarm of sins and sinners I attack leaves me no rest. I am kept always on the *qui-vive,* always on thorns or sharp flints. I am like a ball in a game of tennis. No sooner am I driven to one side than I am driven to the other, and rudely struck. It is the fate of a poor sinner. It is thus that I have been, without relaxation and without rest, during the thirteen years which have passed since I left St. Sulpice. Nevertheless, dear sister, bless God, for I am happy and content in the midst of all my suffering . . . I do not think there is anything sweeter than a most bitter cross, when it is steeped in the blood of Jesus Crucified and in the milk of His mother . . . I have never made more conversions than after the most cruel and unjust interdictions . . . Were we to shed tears, we would be like little children complaining because they had to carry a hundred pounds of gold . . . or a farmer who would despair because his field had been covered with gold pieces!"

He remained in Paris until he was sure he could do no more to assure the establishment of his company of priests. Then he turned his face toward Poitiers, approximately a hundred and ninety miles away. It was time he saw to the establishment of his Daughters of Wisdom.

Marie Louise and Catherine Brunet were still working in the hospital-poor house there, still waiting for him to keep his word that they would be nuns. Marie Louise had waited years for him. He had done little for her. He had written, yes. But he had given her no encouragement.

"The heroism of these two women—they were really little more than girls—is beyond all praise," writes Father Bolger. "Both wished ardently to live the religious life; yet, so far, only Marie Louise was permitted to wear a religious habit. Year after year they had worked as nurses in the hospital with, humanly speaking, no hope of ever being able to strike out for themselves and enlarge their scope of doing good. The totally unexpected appearance of their spiritual father was

178

like a visitation from heaven; for, holy though they undoubtedly were, they would not have been human if they had not occasionally yearned for some consolation, and an indication of what they might expect in the future. For once, Montfort could bring them good news. He told them he was thinking of taking them to La Rochelle, and delighted Catherine by telling her she would soon receive the habit—a promise he was able to redeem the following year."

Louis must have felt "at home" here—for just an hour or so. The place was full of memories, bitter and sweet. He had been, in a way, "baptized" in the priesthood here. Here he had been given the right to hear confessions, and to preach missions. Here he had assembled his first lay apostolate—twenty sick and dying women, headed by one who was blind. Here he had discovered the first of his spiritual children. And from this place he had gone to his first mission.

Just an hour or so! His enemies had seen him come into the hospital and had rushed to report this felony to the bishop. And the bishop—like the old fashioned sheriff in a Wild West movie, ordered Louis to get out of town before sunrise . . .

One cannot help but wonder how that prelate felt, years later, when he realized what he had done to Louis. He knew then that Louis was a saint, because he used him. Two girls in his diocese were suffering from a form of epilepsy. The bishop suggested they should be sprinkled with water in which a relic of St. Louis had been immersed. The girls were instantly cured. This was only five years after he had driven de Montfort out of his see.

Louis left immediately after receiving the bishop's word. He rested, during the night, with some Capuchin priests outside the town. In the morning, after Mass, he started walking the ninety—some miles to La Rochelle. He got as far as Mauzé, about thirty miles from Poitiers, where he was asked to preach a mission. Two Jesuit priests begged to help him, and he joyfully agreed. He could never get enough of the Jesuits.

During most of this mission he was suffering severe pain. Also he was burning with fever. But he joked about it. The Good Lord, he said, always let him have a share of His own suffering, on and around the Exaltation of the Cross.

When the mission was over, however, the Jesuits insisted on carrying him to La Rochelle and placing him in the hospital of St. John of God.

"The source of the trouble," we are told, "seems to have been an abscess; but that it was no ordinary one is clear from the testimony of

179

Peter Seignette, one of the greatest surgeons of his day. He states plainly that not one of a hundred men suffering the same complaint would have escaped. The wound had to be probed twice a day, yet never a complaint left the sufferer's lips; indeed, he often stupefied the attendants by finding something to laugh at . . . This went on for two months. When he rose at last he was no longer the man of iron . . . But . . . instead of convalescing for a while, he preached two retreats on death, one at Courçon and the other at St. Louis' hospital."

Louis liked Courçon. He had preached a mission there sometime before his illness. He had reconciled the parish priest and his flock—who had bitterly hated each other—and he had induced the people to forgive their enemies, and be reconciled to them. He had been able to settle many law suits out of court.

It must have pleased him to act the dying sinner for these people. He, who had been so close to death,—and who still looked like a dying man—was a better actor than ever. And, it may be, also a better preacher.

"In the pulpit," Father Bolger tells us, "Montfort was an irresistible figure. Henri Brémond says he must have been one of the most compelling orators the world has ever known. . . . Somehow a legend has grown up around him portraying him as stern and harsh; such a picture is completely false. True, he was exceptionally harsh with himself, for he tried to win back sinners by performing penances they should have been doing for themselves. This was shouldering their burdens for them, and surely this is not harshness. With Marie Louise of Jesus he was also severe, but this was inevitable; she was to be the foundation stone of a great religious congregation, and things that are to last are never built the easy way. Moreover it was her own wish that he should treat her as an adult in spiritual life.

"That he was not harsh is proved by the crowds that beseiged his confessional, even when there were other confessors in abundance . . ."

Louis was irresistible outside the pulpit too. And he could summon drama to his aid at any time. The Rev. T. M'Geoy, in his book published in 1913 in Ireland, gives us an instance of this.

"Upon one occasion, when preaching to some rich persons he had assembled in a room in the presbytery," Father M'Geoy says, "Louis began by calling for a needle and a thick cord, and then, having tried in vain to pass the cord through the needle's eye, he explained the obligation of the rich to make themselves poor and humble in order to enter the Kingdom of Heaven."

180

If you couldn't put an ordinary cord through a needle's eye, how could you drive a camel through it? "Then Jesus said to his disciples, I say to you that a rich man shall hardly enter into the kingdom of heaven. And again I say to you, it is easier for a camel to pass through the eye of a needle than for a rich man to enter the kingdom of heaven . . . With men this is impossible, but with God all things are possible . . ." Let his rich friends think about that!

"At another time he had a great fire lit near the church . . . a number of rough and vagabond children . . . warned them against the sin of theft and its punishment . . . pointing to the fire to make them understand that a far more searching fire was in store for thieves, that would burn for all eternity."

22 Daughters of Wisdom

While he was still struggling back to health—of a sort—Louis was asked, by the parish priest of Vanneau, to preach a mission in his parish. He obtained the necessary faculties for Louis from the bishop of that diocese. Louis went and earned another heavy cross.

"I do not think there is anything sweeter than the most bitter cross," he had written his sister, "when it is steeped in the blood of Jesus Crucified, and in the milk of His mother . . . I have never made more conversions than after the most cruel and unjust interdictions."

It was just such a cruel and unjust interdiction that was presented to him in Vanneau. The bishop abruptly cancelled the priestly authority he had given Louis—and the powers of all the priests working with him!

"We had heard all the general confessions," Father des Bastières said in his memoirs, "and intended, on the following day, to give absolution to those properly disposed, to prepare them for Holy Communion. The bishop's order came like a clap of thunder. Father was moved to tears. Never in his life, he told us, had he felt so bad."

This must have been a heavier cross than the one he shouldered at Pontchateau. It must have hurt more because it was so unreasonable, so senseless, so unexpected and so evidently the work of enemies—the enemies of God. It was a cross really steeped in the blood of Christ and the milk of His mother! How those enemies must hate the mother of God! How many souls would it buy?

Louis was about to walk back to La Rochelle, but the parish priest begged him to wait.

"Let us go see His Excellency," he said. "I think I can make him realize that people have lied about you. Wait until I come back. I will gallop all the way, even if I kill a horse or two."

183

The priest returned at 5 o'clock the next morning. He had been gone a little more than twelve hours. He had covered ninety miles or so on the round trip! And he had good news. The bishop had cancelled his cancellation.

"And," says Father des Bastières, "it is impossible to conceive how many extraordinary conversions were made during this mission."

Vanneau was still talking about that mission a hundred and thirty years later—telling to all what their grandfathers had told them—that the parish priest had gone to the bishop on no ordinary horse. That nag had wings!

It was shortly after this historic mission that Louis found himself in Roussay, fighting strong drink and sturdy drunkards. He had as great a success there as he had at Vanneau, not only because he had visited violence on the violent and vile, but also because of other incidents. A drunken man staggered into the church on the second or third night of the mission, and insulted him with loud and vulgar words. Louis, to the astonishment of all the congregation, came down from the pulpit and walked slowly toward the man. Every man, woman and child who watched him, expected he would use those great fists again. They shivered with excitement. Louis knelt at the man's feet, when he came close enough, and spoke to him gently, like an old friend. Then he signaled Brother Mathurin to help the man out of the church. The drunkard went "like a lamb." De Montfort went back into the pulpit, as though nothing had happened.

When the mission had ended, and it was time to plant the great cross as a memorial, an enormous crowd assembled. Workmen were raising it with long lengths of stout rope. Without warning one of the ropes broke, and the heavy cross—"the great mass of oak"—fell into the crowd. Only one man was hurt, and he sustained merely a slight scratch on one hand.

Roussay is still saying the Rosary, and still venerating the statue of the Virgin Louis left there.

Wherever he was, whatever he was doing—preaching, hearing confessions, leading processions, working miracles, writing songs or books or rules for congregations of priests and nuns—St. Louis constantly prayed for the starved, ragged, ignorant, wonderful children of La Rochelle. He had met most all of them. And he loved each one. They flocked around him, when he came to the city. They followed him. They needed him. They needed him badly.

He decided to build schools for them; one for the boys and another for the girls. These buildings must be large; for there were many children. They must be centrally located. And they must have the best teachers it was possible to get. Perhaps he could induce some priest friends of his to teach the boys. But for the girls—of course—he would use the Daughters of Wisdom.

The bishop gave his enthusiastic consent to Louis' plans. "Invite your nuns here," he said. "I'll find money somewhere for both schools. I will also find a house for your Daughters of Wisdom. Meanwhile, get your little congregation of nuns fully organized."

Sometime in the spring of 1714, Louis wrote Sister Marie Louise of Jesus to get ready to leave the hospital at Poitiers, and prepare for the trip to La Rochelle and the new life of teaching. She was to come, with Catherine Brunet, in six months' time.

The letter may have reached Poitiers, but it was not delivered to Marie Louise. The devil's aids were still at work in the city that hated St. Louis with such a deadly hate.

Louis returned to La Rochelle from an extensive mission journey, without having heard from Marie Louise. He went on with the work of the schools, confident that she would come. He wrote the rules for both the pupils and the teachers. The schools were to be free. No child was ever to be charged a sou. There were to be nine benches for the students to be named after the choirs of the angels. The children who had made their First Holy Communion and were more advanced than the others were to sit on the bench at the far end of the room; a bench a trifle higher than the others; a bench that was to be called "the bench of the Seraphim." Each classroom was a sort of amphitheatre.

"Surely," one of the early biographers comments, "it was a happy thought to associate these poor children with the angels who always behold the face of the Father in heaven."

The children were to be taught not only their religious duties, but also such worldly subjects as reading, writing, arithmetic, geography, history, music, and the arts. The priests in charge of the boys were not the kind he sought for his own.

He made it clear in the rules he wrote for his Congregation that he did not want them to teach. He wanted them to be missionaries. They must not be overburdened. They must devote all their time, all their energies, all their lives, to preaching the good news. It seems clear, however, that, at times, he did use some of his lay brothers as teachers. Brother Mathurin, we learn, "labored as a school teacher, with abundant blessings."

When Louis visited Roussay, he was on his way to Rouen, where he hoped to see his old friend, Canon Blain. The canon had been an intimate friend of St. John Baptiste de la Salle, who had pioneered in establishing free schools in France; and he might have many valuable hints on education and training. Also, perhaps, he might be able to help with the organizing of that "company of poor priests" Louis had in mind.

He started his journey in May of that year, 1714, but stopped many times on the road. He had many things to do. And he was neither so strong as he used to be, nor so tirelessly young.

When he had reached Rouen, sometime in September, and had had no word from sister Marie Louise, he was sure his letter had gone astray. He wrote then, not to her, but to the chaplain of the hospital, to make sure his message would be received.

This plan succeeded. And immediately Poitiers was in turmoil. Marie Louise, who until this time had been an unimportant but mysterious little fly-wheel in the machinery of the city, suddenly became its most important part! Why she was—she was indispensable! She was the one person the hospital could not possibly do without!

What was de Montfort trying to do? Wreck the institution? How dare he ask for Marie Louise—just like that? He had only to beckon and she would come to him? No! Name of a name! Poitiers would keep her. So said the authorities. So said the chaplain. So said the bishop, who had sent St. Louis into exile. So said Marie Louise's mother. Louise must never, never, never leave Poitiers!

But St. Louis was praying for her. So, again suddenly, everybody began to help her and Catherine pack. Even mama was resigned, after a fashion. Marie Louise had met a poor blind woman crossing a bridge near the hospital, and had asked her to pray for her intention. The next day mama began to soften.

It still wasn't easy for the two nuns to get away. One of Louis' biographers puts it this way:

"There was one, however, who remained strong in his opposition to their departure, and inconsolable at the thought of it. This was the chaplain, who knew, better than any one else, all that the hospital was losing, and who, both by reproaches and entreaties, endeavored to turn them from their purpose. Indeed, at the very last moment, as they were about to leave what with the earnest remonstrances of the chaplain, and the loud laments of Mme. Trichet, and the sobs and tears of the poor inmates, Sister Marie Louise, for a moment, gave way to human weakness, and would have delayed their departure.

186

"But then Catherine Brunet, now Sister Conception, (acting, as in truth she was, as the elder of the two, and as the mother rather than the daughter of Sister Marie Louise) took her and her mother by the arms, led them to the door, then placed her young mother superior in the carriage, took her place beside her, and gave the driver the signal to speed away."

Louis was "on the road," after returning from his visit to Canon Blain, when the two daughters of Wisdom arrived in La Rochelle. This was in March, 1715. The bishop welcomed them to his diocese; and apologized for neglecting to get them a suitable house. However he referred them to a lady, who took them into her own home. Subsequently the bishop rented a small house, and there the sisters opened their school.

Instructions came to them from Louis. He had written a long letter, and entrusted it to one of the brothers. He asked them to take the dean of the cathedral for their spiritual director and confessor, temporarily; go to communion every day, be models of modesty, recollection, and humility, and not "go about, seeing the town." They were to learn to write well . . . and to follow certain rules he had laid down for them. Marie Louise was to be the mother superior, for at least three years. This was "truly God's will."

Eventually Louis found a holiday from his missions, and met the pair at a country house of a friend, near La Rochelle. There, after he had said Mass, he went for a walk with Marie Louise. He showed her a hen with her little brood of chicks. "See how that mother hen loves and guides and protects her young ones," he said. "You must be like her, as the mother superior."

From this country house, the three walked to Louis' hermitage at St. Eloi. He kept talking to them, says one commentator, as the risen Lord talked to His disciples on the road to Emmaus. He talked of Marie Louise's sorrow, when he left Poitiers and she believed there would never be any foundation of nuns. She had no funds, then, no friend, no champion, no guide.

He reminded her of what he had said then: "If it takes ten years before the Daughters of Wisdom begin to function, the will of God will be accomplished and His designs carried into effect." That had been ten years ago.

"I know how you feel about leaving Poitiers," he told Marie Louise. "But take comfort. You will go back to the hospital there. They want you. They will invite you back. You will live there."

187

Louis returned to La Rochelle every time he could—when he was doing missionary work not too far away—and he often visited the two schools. He tested his daughters too. Once he sent a girl to apply for admission as a student. She was to offer the mother superior money. She was to insist that the money be received, because she wanted to pay her own way. Why should she ask to be taught for nothing?

Mother Marie told her to keep her money and to go to some other school. A few hours after the child had left—a most capable little actress—Louis arrived, beaming. "God be blessed for your fidelity," he greeted Mother Marie. "How happy I am to see you keep the rule! And this morning I heard children talking about the Daughters of Wisdom. How my heart rejoiced when I heard the name you bear. Daughters of Wisdom! What a glory for you if you realize all its significance!"

This was the last time he saw his favorite daughter, but he wrote her often, to direct her work.

"Do not be impatient at my absence," he wrote her, on Dec. 31, 1715. "My person, and my wholly devilish will, spoil everything . . . The less I have to do with your establishment, the more it will succeed . . . I carry you everywhere in my heart . . . in God alone . . . I wish you a year full of combats, victories, crosses, poverty, and contempt."

He had had his own full year of combat, victory, poverty, contempt, and crosses, and he was about to have another—or part of another.

On his way from Roussay to Rouen, Louis stopped in Nantes, to visit the "incurables" in the hospital he had started, and to see some of the Friends of the Cross. He did not linger, for the bishop was still hostile to him.

He started to Rennes, leading the donkey that carried his books and his banners and his stock of Rosaries, crucifixes, and medals.

On the road he met a young man who appealed to him because he was ragged and thin, and verminous, and evidently lonely and in need of a friend. He told a long sad story, took all the money Louis had begged. Then, awaiting his time, he stole Louis' donkey and rode away on it.

The bishop of Rennes, thanks to the missionary's Jansenist enemies, would not give Louis permission to preach in the city of Rennes—the city that was as dear to him as his birthplace. Therefore he did not preach. He made a long retreat, instead. It was on the last day of that retreat that he wrote his famous Letter to the Friends of the Cross.

"Today," he says, "I come out of the allurements of my thoughts, so to speak, to send you a few arrows, made of the Cross, with which to

188

pierce your hearts. Would to God I could sharpen them with the blood of my veins—but, alas, I am too great a criminal! . . . You are a group of crusaders united to fight against the world, not like those religious men and women who leave the world for fear of being overcome, but, like brave intrepid warriors on the battlefront, refusing to retreat or even yield an inch. Bind yourselves in that strong union of heart and mind which is far superior, far more terrifying, to the world and hell than the armed forces of a well-organized kingdom are to its enemies. Demons are united for your destruction . . . Unite for their overthrow.

" 'Friends of the Cross.' What a wonderful name! It charms and fascinates me. It is brighter than the sun . . . more imposing and resplendent than any title given king or emperor, it is the name of Christ Himself, true God and true Man. It is the unmistakable title of a Christian.

"A Friend of the Cross is one chosen by God from among ten thousand who have reason and sense for their only guides. He is raised above reason, and thoroughly opposed to the things of sense, for he lives in the light of true faith, and burns with love for the Cross . . . He is a king, a hero who triumphs over the devil, the world, and the flesh . . . a trophy which the crucified Christ won on Calvary, with His blessed mother . . . He can say, truthfully, (with St. Paul), 'I live now, not I, but Christ liveth in me.' "

He tells his friends that Christian perfection consists in willing to become a saint, in self-denial, in suffering, and in action. He is most explicit in writing about "suffering." A man must carry his cross, not drag it. He must not try to lighten it. He must not hide it.

"Let him root it in his heart, and there change it into a fiery bush, burning day and night with the pure love of God, without being consumed . . . The cross is our natural as well as supernatural philosophy. It is our divine mysterious theology. It is our philosopher stone, which, by dint of patience is able to transmute the grossest of metals into precious ones, the sharpest pain into delight, poverty into wealth, the deepest humiliation into glory. He who knows how to carry his cross, though he know not A from B, towers above all others in learning . . ."

He does not resist the impulse to add a verse, and a long song, to the letter. The verse is short, but profound.

> *Three crosses stand on Calvary's height.*
> *One must be chosen. So choose aright;*
> *Like Christ you must suffer; or like the good thief;*
> *Or like the reprobate, in eternal grief.*

189

He speaks to them as Christ might have spoken . . . "Will you also leave Me, fleeing from my cross? . . . I have many who call themselves My friends, but who really hate me, because they do not love My Cross . . . I have many friends at the table, very few at My Cross . . . If any man will come after Me, let him deny himself and take up his cross and follow Me . . ."

He speaks of Incarnate Wisdom, also, in this Letter. The death of Jesus, who is Incarnate Wisdom, he states, "has made the cross glorious, turned its poverty into wealth, changed its pain and agony into joy."

The Cross, he maintains, is Wisdom; and Wisdom is the Cross.

"Wisdom is so united to, and incorporated in, the Cross, that neither man nor angel can part them."

Hence true Friends of the Cross welcome all the upsets and trials and frustrations they encounter. Then their hearts will know "the sublime charm" born of the realization that the greatest proof of Divine Wisdom's love for us was his passion and his death on the cross. This "greatest secret of the king," this delight in the Wisdom of the Cross, can be attained only by a few—"if we knew how few, we would die of grief."

And Wisdom, he does not fail to proclaim, came to men through Mary.

23

Living the Gospel

Louis could not leave Rennes without saying farewell to a dear friend—and spiritual directee—the Marquis of Magnane. The distinguished soldier and courtier had radically changed his life since he met the saint. And, now that he was a widower, he wanted to become a priest. (He remained a layman however. After Louis' death, the marquis practically took charge of the saint's affairs, supporting the two congregations and helping them in many ways. He was buried, years later, beside his friend.)

The marquis, at this time, was a guest of M. and Mme d'Orville, who lived in one of the biggest homes in the city, and certainly one of the richest.

He was talking to Louis in the magnificent garden of this place when the d'Orville household became aware of Louis' presence. The priest had, long before this, gained the reputation of "high sanctity." People flocked about him wherever he was recognized, hoping to see him perform a miracle, hoping to get his blessing for themselves or their children, or perhaps for some sick and dying friend, hoping to get close enough to shake his hand.

Mme. d'Orville, possibly somewhat annoyed at not being able to find any of her servants, went into the garden to see what had happened to them. She listened for a time to Louis, thinking it strange that such a battered and tattered old man could talk so intelligently, so brilliantly, and at the same time so simply, about Jesus Christ. She asked him to dinner. He accepted, graciously.

"Father de Montfort," says Rigault, "with all his austerity and singularity, did not shock people of rank. He had his intellect, and, if he thought it necessary, could adapt himself to their milieu. This was a pleasant surprise for the young chatelaine . . . She was twenty-five . . . gay and amusing and not at all devout. She had made up her mind to laugh at the people's preacher. But she was amazed by the substance, wisdom, and depth of his sermons. She received him more than once at her residence, and later wrote that he was both amusing and edifying, so that his conversation was at once instructive and delightful. She was very frank with him, with a touch of malice. She put on a frivolous air on purpose and hummed light songs, but he took it all not too seriously, never lost his temper, and never seemed shocked. He smiled and spoke to her with great gentleness . . . Such accounts show that . . . Louis Marie Grignion, absolute master of himself, could come down out of his ecstasies to walk in the light of common day . . ."

Louis must have found the lady not too unlike Catherine Brunet, Bénigne Pagé, Mme. de Mailly, and other women who had verbally sparred with him. In this instance, though, it was not the lady who challenged the "magic" of the saint. It was the lady's husband.

At the dinner table Louis produced a small statue of the Virgin. This he placed in front of M. d'Orville, asking him if he did not love her very much, this lady who had been so good to him and his!

The host was embarrassed. He had never been devout to Mary or to God. He had never paid homage to anybody except King Louis and "his three queens." But something mysterious happened to him as Louis continued to talk about Our Lady. He listened with profound attention. And before he had bade his guest adieu, he had promised to say the Rosary every day!

On his way to Rouen, traveling from Rennes, Louis stopped overnight in Avranches, in Normandy, kneeling for hours in the cathedral, where Henry II of England went to make atonement for the murder of St. Thomas a Becket. The next morning, the feast of the Assumption of Our Lady, he visited the bishop, offered his services as a missionary, and begged permission to say Mass.

"The only favor you can do for me," said His Excellency, "is to get out of my diocese as speedily as you can."

Another cruel interdiction! Another tremendous cross! How many souls would this one buy?

Louis was elated in spirit but not in his body. He had to get away at once. He had to get to Villedieu, in the neighboring diocese. And he could not afford to walk. In his present weak condition he might never get there.

He would, for the first time since he was a boy on the farm, have to ride. Otherwise the feast day would end without his saying Mass. And such a feast day! He begged enough money to hire a fast horse from the livery stable. And he urged the beast to hurry.

192

When he arrived at the rectory in Villedieu, literally a beggar on horseback, he had trouble in obtaining the right to offer Mass. He was exhausted, He was in rags. He was so emaciated the pastor thought he might drop dead at any minute. Besides, he didn't look like a priest; he didn't act like a priest. He had papers tending to prove he really was a priest. But he could have stolen them.

Still, there was something so holy about this skeleton of a man, something so irrresistible, that at length the good priest gave his consent. After the Mass, he invited Louis to stay with him for a day or two.

Louis remained in the parish, one writer says, "only long enough to establish the recital of the Rosary." Then he pushed on, walking again, to St. Lo, twenty miles or so away, with a young man who afterwards became Brother Nicholas.

He no longer walked with his usual long stride. He no longer went swiftly over the earth, singing the praises of his Lady and his Lord. He was only a little over forty; but he was an old old man.

Night overtook him and his friend, when they had traveled no more than fifteen miles. They went to an inn, but were booted into the street. The landlord hated "tramps." They walked on a little way, then found a post, which was decorated with a hand holding a cross. There they sat down to rest. The boy slept, but Louis stayed awake most of the night writing a poem about the hand that held the cross—or the cross that held the hand—and thinking, perhaps, that it was the hand of the bishop, offering him a gift beyond all price.

In St. Lo, Louis was a sensation. "Men and women of all classes," one scribe reports, "flocked to hear him. Even priests and religious marveled as they said to one another, 'Who, then, is this stranger, who has just come into town, staff in hand, and who preaches with such power and persuasion that all the world runs after him?' "

With the permission of the bishop of this diocese, Louis held conferences for people of all religions, or none, at which they could ask questions, and make such comments as they pleased. Hundreds of converts, it is said, came into the Church through these conferences. And hundreds of Catholics changed their lives.

"His confessional," says M. Picot de Clorivière, "was always surrounded, and among the crowd were not a few young men whose dissolute life had been a scandal to the town, and who, even a day or two before, would have blushed to be seen performing even the commonest duties of religion."

And M. Le François adds, "It would be impossible to relate all the

193

good de Montfort accomplished at St. Lo, the conversions he brought about, the heroic acts of virtue he practiced . . ."

When he walked away from St. Lo, Louis was still elated spiritually, and somewhat elated physically; for he sang, to the tunes of a hunting song, as he walked along in the dust:

> *When I go traveling the road,*
> *I go barefoot, without trappings,*
> *With only my staff in hand.*
> *I go unburdened with worry or with sorrow,*
> *And I walk like a king in his court;*
> *With pomp and the sounds of trumpets.*
> *Tarantara! Tarantara! Tarantara!*
> *Like a king in his court all day.*

That day, leaving early in the morning, he walked eighteen miles to the next town. He arrived there as the bells of the mid-day Angelus were ringing. Tarantara! Tarantara! Tarantara! These were the trumpets of his Queen!

He had written Canon Blain to meet him at Caen, or at Bayeux, but the canon preferred to remain in his fat wide chair. Canon Blain had become an ecclesiastic of some prominence. He was canon of the cathedral of Rouen, pastor of St. Patrick's parish, inspector of seminaries, superior of the Out-Sisters of St. Francis, and superior of the Brothers of the Christian Schools in the absence of St. John Baptiste de la Salle. He was hardly prepared to welcome his old friend. He did not recognize Louis when he saw him.

When he did so, he began immediately to berate him for the kind of life he led. Why, he demanded, must Louis continue to antagonize bishops? Why must he look and act like a beggar? Why couldn't he look and act like other priests—himself included? Why must he fast so much? Why must he scourge himself so much? And why did he want to start a community of priests? Did he expect them to go hungry through life, to go ragged, to walk everywhere they went, to beg people to feed them, to give them a bed, to give them decent shoes and warm clothing?

Louis let his old friend go on, for a time. Then he opened his New Testament, and read a few lines to show that Jesus had lived that way. He walked usually. He begged alms. He had no place on which to lay His head. He told his disciples to be beggars, to walk, to be poor, to rely on heaven for their daily sustenance.

194

"If I am different than other priests," he said, "it is not because I try to be. And if my way of life brings me crosses, shall I complain?"

"The canon yielded at last," says Rigault. "He could not struggle against this impetuous genius, but he did understand and admire him. The more he looked at de Montfort, the more he was struck by something divine in his voice, his face, his gestures, his words. He was not the only one to feel a deep impression, a mingled sense of respect, amazement, and super-human joy, a foretaste of bliss, when face to face with Louis Marie Grignion. He took the holy missioner to a training college for teachers, and asked him to say something to the girls . . ."

Louis made it clear to the canon that there had to be a difference between priests who lived in communities, and those who roamed the world as missionaries. The ordinary priest had nothing to do on his own initiative. He followed the rules as best as he could, and everything was provided for him; whereas the missionary "had to procure the glory of God at the cost of his own glory . . . had to fight continually against the world and the devil and the flesh; had to endure persecutions, trials, outrages, and hardships of all kinds; and had to go everywhere, do everything, suffer everything, without guidance—except from above."

He also mentioned the fact that a missionary might plan something good, with the approval of superiors—then be thwarted by the superiors' going back on their word, because they were prejudiced, because somebody had lied to them, or because they thought, at the last minute, that the plans they had so readily approved, were now imprudent, and even politically dangerous. Yet the missionary priest must always obey those superiors.

Louis' biographers do not believe he came all the way to Rouen just to see his friend and ask for his help with the schools in La Rochelle. Some are sure he intended to ask the canon to become one of his "company of poor priests," or at least to ask his help in founding such a company. Blain, in his memoirs, is silent on this subject.

He admits that he asked Louis for advice. "I have been offered the charge of a parish in the city, and I don't know whether to take it or reject it," he said. Louis made a prophecy.

"You will take it," he said. "It will give you many crosses. And you will reject it."

"This," Blain wrote, "was the second prediction he made to me concerning matters which he could know about only through the light of

God. In this conversation he told me God had given him a very special grace, the abiding presence of Jesus and Mary in the depths of his soul. I had difficulty in understanding so high a favor; and did not ask him for an explanation. Maybe he could not have explained, for in the mystical life there are operations of grace which even the soul blessed with them cannot understand."

Blain may have been wrong. Possibly Louis could have explained that this grace came from his dedication, his consecration, to Jesus in Mary, his "true devotion," his holy slavery to Jesus through Mary.

"When the life of Mary is well established in the soul," he wrote in his book on true devotion, "it is, in some way, no longer the soul that lives; it is Mary who lives in the soul!

"The soul of Mary becomes, so to speak, our soul. But when, by an unspeakable but true grace, Mary becomes queen in a soul—what marvels does she not work! . . . She works them in secret, unknown to the soul itself; for, were the soul to know, it would destroy the beauty of Mary's work.

"Mary . . . will make a soul live . . . She becomes everything to that soul, with Jesus. She enlightens its spirit . . . deepens its heart . . . enlarges and inflames it . . . purifies it . . . ennobles it . . . When will souls breathe Mary as the bodies breathe the air? . . . When will souls, losing themselves in the abyss of her interior, become living copies of her, to love and glorify Jesus?"

The morning after his arrival at Rouen, Louis said Mass in the cathedral, then visited a nun in the convent of the Blessed Sacrament. She asked him to speak to the community. Before he left, to return to La Rochelle, he asked and received "Our Lady's portion," the food set aside daily by the nuns for the poorest of the poor.

He left on a boat, which Blain describes as "a perfect Noah's ark, filled with all kinds of animals." He had a large Rosary in his hands as he boarded this "ark." The last thing the canon saw, was that all the passengers were praying the Rosary with him.

How far he and Brother Nicholas went by boat nobody knows; but both were walking when they drew near Nantes. Both were weary. Both were covered with dust and wet with sweat. The boy who had walked something like six hundred miles in the last ninety days claimed that he could not possibly take another step. "It's not far now," Louis said. "Only a few miles. Let me carry you. I still have enough strength for that. You are not too heavy."

The boy wouldn't permit that.

196

"Then I'll carry your heavy coat," Louis said, taking it from him and throwing it over his shoulder. Then, with his free arm, he helped the young man walk.

"We look awful," Brother Nicholas said as they came close to the city. "What will people say?"

De Montfort smiled and shrugged.

"What will Jesus say?" he countered.

24   The Prophet

The only practical business de Montfort had in the city of Nantes was that of arranging to store six of his Pontchateau statues in his home for the "incurables," where, he knew they would be reverenced and kept safe. Some day they would go back to the new calvary at Pontchateau.

After he had talked to some people at the hospital, and blessed the sick, he hurried, with Brother Nicholas, to the little town of Laveau, near Pontchateau, where he had placed the statues four years earlier. The only safe way to get them to Nantes, he discovered, was to send them up the Loire by barge. He had money enough to hire a barge, but he and Brother Nicholas had to carry the statues from Laveau to the river front, and place each one gently aboard the barge.

On the bank of the Loire, Louis tried to get someone to help him. But no man lifted a hand. In fact, says one biographer, "the boatmen and the bystanders amused themselves at his expense. To see a priest throwing himself desperately into the mud and working as if he were the poorest of poor laborers, made them laugh; and they laughed the more, and the louder, when they saw him make any false step, and slip with a statue in his arms."

This was more manual work than Louis was accustomed to, and he was in sorry condition to perform any kind of work. The laughter and gibes of the men must have cut deeper welts into his spirit than the riding whip of that woman in Sallertaine had left on his body. (Louis had said a few words to a young lady there, whose dress and behavior did not belong in the church where he was preaching. The girl's mother waited until he came out to lead the procession to the place where he would plant the cross. Fifteen thousand people witnessed that whipping, and saw Louis submit meekly to the torment.) Whips of laughter cut more cruelly than other lashes—especially when the laughters are young and strong and they are laughing at a priest whom they should reverence because he is another Christ. But, thank God, what a lovely cross to carry! Jesus was lashed too. And how often was he laughed at!

When the last statue had been placed safely on the barge, Louis led Brother Nicholas to an inn. There he had the boy wash his dirty clothes. He put them on wet, and hurried on. He must be in Nantes when the barge arrived there. For he and Brother Nicholas must help unload them and bring them to the hospital.

When he had finished this business, he set out for Rennes to visit M. d'Orville who had written him several letters, asking him to be his spiritual director. He had two pleasant surprises in Rennes. He found his stolen donkey there, and managed to get it back from its new owner. (Possibly M. d'Orville supplied the money for this.) And he found his friend had become an ardent lover of the Queen of Heaven.

But there was a problem. The d'Orville home adjoined a public square, and many young people came there, at odd hours, to sing and dance, to drink, and to make love. These people were an infernal nuisance, a constant annoyance, and a serious distraction to those in the household who were saying the Rosary. What could be done about this?

"Make a niche in the façade overlooking the square," Louis said. "Put a statue of Our Lady there. And say the Rosary there."

"There? In the public square?"

"In the public square. Below the Lady's image."

M. d'Orville acted immediately. The next day his family and all the servants said the Rosary in the square. D'Orville let his wife "give out the mysteries," while he, with a whip in hand, stood guard to keep young hoodlums from getting too close.

While he was thus "standing guard" a long string of carriages went through the square, and many friends called out to him, inviting him and his wife to a party. At first he was tempted to hide the beads in his hand. But he conquered himself and held the Rosary high, so that all could see he was at prayer.

A strange thing happened. The square became an attraction to all classes. "The people came in crowds to pray, as if for some great church ceremony, and all disorders ceased. Truly it was a scene worthy of the first companions of St. Francis."

D'Orville accompanied Louis and Brother Nicholas, and the donkey, when they resumed their journey back to La Rochelle. He walked for several miles, and parted with tears. Louis was moved too, but did not weep. He blessed his friend. And three times he said, "Sir, I wish you many crosses!"

200

The lines of a poem were writing themselves in Louis' mind, and he trudged on: a lamentation for the city that he loved, a city he knew was waiting for disaster.

Farewell, Rennes, Rennes, Rennes.
One deplores your destiny;
One warns you of a thousand woes.
You will perish, in the end,
Unless you break the chains
You hide within yourself.

Everything is festal here.
The husband's in the cabaret,
The daughter's at a dance,
And Madame's in a gambling hall.
Each goes his own sweet way
Not believing it is wrong.

How many unhappy women
Wear masks of gayety!
How many scandalous young maidens
Wear the garb of piety!
How many an arrogant shoulder
Hides 'neath a borrowed cloak!
What do you see in the churches?
Often idlers, loafers, dogs,
Gossipy women in fine attire,
Libertines, pagans, who hold forth
Among a scattering of Christians.

To the one who points out your errors, Rennes,
You answer; 'God will be merciful.
He is good. Have no fear. He gives
Mercy to him who asks for it.
And besides, all men are sinners.'

Rennes, Rennes, Rennes, farewell.
I grieve for your dread fate.

He seemed to know, five years ahead of time, that a great fire would sweep through this city, raging for ten days and nights, and consume a great portion of it.

Did he look far enough into the future to see the great cities of America burning because of their sins against the Negro?

His journey from Rennes to La Rochelle was one of triumph, a strange and disturbing and pathetic ovation from the people who regarded him as a saint. Wherever he stopped, great crowds gathered to greet him, to kneel before him and ask his blessing. People knelt even in ditches as he passed by, calling to him, blessing him, holding up their children that he might make the sign of the cross over them, and heal them, and save them, and make them holy. Gentlemen sometimes got off their horses and knelt before him as he passed by on some dust-powdered road. And here and there, whole families waited for hours, just to look at him.

"In the towns and villages," one writer says, "they pressed around him in such numbers, and so frequently, that he was forced to pass on without stopping, contenting himself with saying to them; 'My dear children, I pray the Lord to bless you and make you saints.' The places where he stopped for the night he left early the next morning, in order to escape the eager greetings . . . but in vain. Many watched at his door all night, to be ready to accompany him on his way whenever he was ready to depart. They went as far as they might, and when they could go no further there was much weeping among them all. They felt, as they looked at his wasted form, and his eyes, which were already lit with the light of heaven, that he was ready to be sacrificed, and the hour of his dissolution was at hand . . . Like the ancients of Ephesus, when they took leave of St. Paul for the last time, they sorrowed that they should see his face no more."

But there were no ovations as Louis neared the big city that had become his headquarters. The roads were almost impassable here; and they were cold, and wet, and deserted. It was November. It was "mission time," once more. He and Brother Nicholas crept, almost crawled, into the city. No one Louis knew was there to welcome him. No one knew where he had been; nor when he would return. But as soon as he resumed his work to develop the schools, La Rochelle woke up and gave him a fond "Hello."

The schools didn't take all his time. He went "on the road again," preaching, healing, forming processions, organizing great redemptive mission drives, walking miles along frozen and rutted roads, sleeping where and when he could. Sometimes his bed would be covered with snow when he woke. Sometimes a chill rain, or a shower of sleet, leaking through a scabby roof, would wake him—and give him both a jolt of misery and a throb of holy joy.

He was more effective in his work than ever. On the isle of Aix, a few miles off the coast, he turned a garrison of soldiers into something like a monastery of monks. This within two weeks. The king's men, the forgotten ones, the neglected ones, the brutalized, half-savage, half-starved heroes of a hundred battle fields, resented Louis at first. They taunted him. They badgered him. They threatened to make life miserable for him.

Before he left they were saying the Rosary aloud with him, and wonder of wonders, they were scourging themselves, like him, in atonement for their sins. Louis and Brother Nicholas, in recent months, had learned they could dispose of many articles that could be used by repentant sinners for inflicting punishments on themselves. Some wanted disciplines of stout cord. Some wanted iron chains with little barbs in them, or wickedly sharp spikes. Louis found out he hadn't enough for his new friends. He had to go from house to house, begging cords with which to manufacture disciplinary whips.

It was so cold the day he left Aix, that the ship was a mass of ice and icicles. But he stood on the deck, spurning the warmth of the fireplace in the hold, letting the chill winds scourge him, doing penance along with his warrior friends.

On February 2, 1715—his last Candlemas day save one—the Lord was pleased to let the people of La Rochelle see His servant in a new light, the light of the radiance of heaven.

It was one of Our Lady's great feast days, and Louis was talking to a great audience about the wonder and the glory and the tenderness of Mary, the mother of God, when he was transfigured, somewhat in the way that Jesus was the day he took Peter and James and John up into the mountain with Him.

"It came to pass," the secular priest biographer relates, "that, as he was speaking, there shone down upon him, as of old on the face of St. Stephen, a reflection of the glory of his transfigured Lord. Of a sudden his worn and wasted face . . . became luminous. Rays of glory seemed to go forth from it . . . so that even they who were used to looking at him knew him only by his voice.

"He stood there before them all, this true-hearted herald of Mary's name, and they saw his glory, the glory given by the 'Father of lights' to them who love and serve the mother of his Son . . . So marvelous did this transfiguration seem to all the people . . . that they waited to attend his Mass, which he celebrated after the High Mass had ended."

In April, preaching at St. Amand-sur-Sèvre, Louis cured a woman

203

who was thought to have been possessed by the devil. This event brought hundreds of people to him, peasants and gentry, some of them carrying their sick or crippled relatives and friends.

Montfort didn't believe the woman was "possessed," but he said the prayers of the Church—and she answered in Latin—a language she did not know. He said Mass for her, and she went away "completely cured." So many people came to him for help after this that he was physically exhausted. Two women took pity on him and rescued him from the crowds. These were nieces of the bishop of Nantes—one of the seven who could not bear to have St. Louis in their sees. The two women shut him up in their chateau at La Séguinière; but the people invaded the chateau, and Louis worked as usual among them. After a little "rest," he was ready for the road again.

In June, in Mervent, he found a place he sorely needed, a shallow cave he could use as a hermitage. Mission time was over. Peasants were busy on their tiny patches of land, and at their various tasks. Nobody had time to spend going to church every day and listening to sermons. Nobody had time for religious processions, the repairing or rebuilding of old chapels, or the solemn planting of great crosses on the highest hill top. A tired missionary could crawl into a peaceful crevice, and be alone with God.

As soon as Louis moved into the cave, however, the village flocked to him. They did what they could to make him comfortable, for the cave was a wretched little hole on the side of a hill, and open to all the winds that blew. They built a rough wall in front of it, to cheat the winds of most of their force; but they didn't better it much. Louis stayed there until late in October; but not steadily. He was constantly called away on one errand of mercy or another. In October it was taken away from him.

"He was charged," says Fr. Bolger, "with having appropriated half an acre of the king's forest, and with having uprooted seven old chestnut stumps. The prosecution parties were willing to believe that he acted with the best of intentions and through ignorance of the existence of the particular ministry which he had neglected to inform; so the serving of the writ, coupled with his departure from the place, amply satisfied their craving for justice. Little did they think as they climbed the hill and saw the shabby haggard priest for the first time, that Mervent's only claim to fame, centuries later, would be its brief association with him.

The secular priest says that as many as a hundred pilgrims came every day "to help the hermit priest enlarge the cave so that it could hold the bed, the table, the stool, and the candlestick with which the prophet of Israel had been content." He says there was a running brook near the cave, which sang to Louis of his Lady. The cave was at Mervent, but in the "forest of Vouvant." He adds:

"One thing no power of man has ever been able to effect, and that is to prevent the cave of Mervent from being, from that day to this, a place of pilgrimage to all who love the memory of Blessed Louis Marie de Montfort. The water still flows from the rock into the basin and pilgrims, coming from far and wide, drink it, and attribute to it marvelous effects. On certain days they may be seen in large numbers kneeling before the cave and praying with exceeding fervor."

It was about this time that Louis met young Father René Mulot. He was at Vouvant, and Father Mulot asked him to preach a mission in his brother's parish, St. Pompain.

St. Louis shook his head from side to side. He was busy with the mission in Vouvant. But the young priest insisted.

St. Louis made a strange proposition to him.

"I will go to St. Pompain," he said, "if you will help me with this mission, and promise to work with me all the rest of your days."

That sounded crazy and outrageous to Father Mulot. The missionary was taking an undue advantage of him—asking his life in exchange for a week or two in St. Pompain. He refused to bargain—but on diplomatic grounds.

"Father," he said, "you're asking for a miracle. I am paralyzed on one side. I have a pressure on my chest. I suffer such terrible headaches I do not sleep, day or night. How can I be of any use to you, now or ever—to say nothing of 'all the rest of my life.' There aren't many days left me."

St. Louis said, in effect, "No life, no mission."

As Father Mulot was turning sadly away, he caught a note of affection, and a note of hope, in the saint's voice. He stopped, and listened.

"Don't bother about infirmities," Louis said. "I bid you follow me, if it be God's will. The moment you begin to work with me for souls, all your ailments will leave you."

Mulot believed. He walked with the priest to the confessionals. Almost immediately his chronic headache left him. Within a few days the paralysis disappeared. His chest was free of pressure. He felt bound for life to Louis—and happy to be so bound.

Louis had thus assured the continuance of his company of priests, which he had decided to call "The Company of Mary." Father Mulot would be his successor; and would become known in time, as the "second founder."

The miracle of his return to health and vigor has been authenticated by many witnesses.

During his missions in Brittany Louis performed many other marvels of healing—with witnesses to testify to them. But some astounding miracles have been attributed to him that have little or no basis in fact. The story about the cherries, for instance. The secular priest historian to keep it fresh for us wraps it in the waxed paper of respectable—but dead—narrators. He records it thus:

"Father Fonteneau related an interested story which was communicated to him by the Curé of Vouvant in 1887. He wrote it as follows: 'I gathered this fact from the lips of an old unmarried lady of the name of Poedevant, who died at least fifteen years ago, more than eighty years old, and who has left behind her at Fontenay the reputation of having been a woman of good sense. She herself had been told it by an old man of Vouvant, who also died an octogenarian.

"One winter evening—it was the month of December—Father de Montfort arrived at Vouvant and knocked at the door of a good old woman known as Mother Imbert. He was suffering from hunger, and asked his hostess to give him something to eat. When she made excuse, saying she had absolutely nothing to offer him, the man of God said to her, 'Go into your orchard and you will find some cherries.' The good woman thought Father de Montfort was jesting; but, as he insisted, she went.

"She came back quite joyous, and said she had seen one of her cherry trees in blossom. 'Go back again,' said the holy man, 'and you will find cherries on it.' At his words, Mother Imbert returned . . . gathered the cherries and carried them to the priest, who made his supper of them. Wishing to gather more after the holy missionary had left, she went to the orchard, but all had disappeared. She found neither blossom nor fruit."

This is an example of how some stories grow. Like coral islands, they begin in dark and unplumbed depths. They rise polyp by polyp, through the murky years, until they appear above the waters, then look like solid land.

Can anyone believe that such a man as Louis de Montfort hungered for a certain out-of-season fruit—just like an expectant mother? Can anyone believe he would drive a dear old lady twice out into the bitter cold night so that she might serve his selfish whim?

Couldn't he have blessed the tree, made it bear fruit, and picked the cherries all by himself?

Can anyone believe that he made a meal of these raw December cherries? Didn't he have the lady make a pie of them, or a cobbler?

Maybe he let her warm herself by the stove while she boiled them for him? (She must have been chattering and shivering when she finally came into her kitchen. She must have been grateful—if, in fact, the saint did let her approach the stove, or the fireplace, if she had a fireplace or a stove.)

The story doesn't say whether the cherries were red or black, whether they were ripe or under ripe—or over ripe. It doesn't tell us whether the old lady carried them into the house in her apron, in a white silk handkerchief which the saint had provided for her—out of nothing—or in her beautiful wrinkled old hands.

And we are left to feel that Louis wolfed those cherries down, every last one of them—and that he then "unblessed" the miraculous tree, to deny his hostess the saintly privilege of eating winter cherries.

All that story needs is an exact date. Suppose we make it Christmas eve! Then you can stick sleigh bells and angel choirs into it; put a nice red—or black—cherry in the toe of every little stocking; and wind up with the blessed news that "to this very day" the good housewives, in this most happy part of Brittany, always put cherries in their Christmas gin.

Undoubtedly some of the stories told about de Montfort are pietistic lies. But the story of the healing of Father Mulot is an attested fact. He lived to be sixty-six; and for nearly forty years after Louis' death, he governed both the Daughters of Wisdom and the Company of Mary, without a headache, without a twinge of paralysis, and without any serious pressure in his chest.

One miracle like this tells more about Louis Marie than a hundred thousand books.

25   His Last Pilgrimage

While still in the vicinity of Vouvant and St. Pompain, Louis Marie knew that the treasure chest of his time was emptying itself. But he squandered its golden hours as recklessly as though they were inexhaustible. He revealed this to a noble lady who had asked a favor of him. He would, he said, be dead before the year had ended.

And he squandered his wisdom as prodigally as his days and nights.

Wisdom, he let it be known, had come to him through Mary, the Seat of Wisdom, the treasurer of Wisdom, the dispenser of all the graces that Wisdom can bestow on men . . . that Divine Wisdom who loves to be with the children of men . . . that Wisdom Who chose the cross for His death bed.

Solomon had sung of Wisdom as something feminine—like a man who gives woman's traits to everything he loves or hates, such as ships, guns, hurricanes, bombing planes, tractors, trucks, tanks, the moon, the seas, the treacherous roily rivers. "She was with you in the beginning . . . she was your craftsman, the maker of all the things that have been made."

To St. John, Wisdom was masculine—the Word made flesh.

To St. Louis, Wisdom had no gender. It was a gift of God. It was infinitely more than a gift. Wisdom was Jesus Christ, the Son of God, the Son of Mary. And he wanted to share this Wisdom with all the world. Until his last breath he must not falter.

Twelve days before his death he wrote Sister Marie Louise . . . "I adore the just and loving Wisdom of God in His guidance of His little flock, which is but poorly lodged among men, that it may be well lodged in His Divine Heart, which has been pierced for this very end."

Marie Louise was having trouble in the little house in La Rochelle, and was afraid that the congregation of the Daughters of Wisdom might end before it had a chance to begin.

"How pleasant and snug is this sacred hiding place to a soul truly wise! Here she remains, hidden with Jesus Christ in God, more victorious than conquerors, more richly crowned than kings, more brilliant than the sun, and higher than heaven. If you are the disciple of Wisdom, one chosen from among a thousand, how sweet your abandonment must seem, how rich the contempt men show you. . . . With these you purchase Wisdom, freedom, and the Godhead of the heart of Jesus crucified. . . . I look for overthrows more terrible and grievous . . . in order to found the Community of Wisdom, on the Wisdom of the Cross of Calvary—not on the shifting sands of gold and silver, not on personalities, which, however powerful they may be, are but handfuls of straw . . ."

Perhaps the individual who gained most from the mission Louis gave at St. Pompain, was the parish priest of that village, the elder brother of Fr. Mulot. It was he who had invited the missionary to visit St. Pompain. This priest, according to one writer, was a "very strange character." He was, it appears, "irreproachable in doctrine and life . . . but rather given to amusement than to the ministry of a parish, fonder of parties than of study." He had two enemies among his parishioners, one of whom was the "squire," or the farmer general of the lord of the place.

De Montfort, knowing the circumstances, worked first on the squire, asking him to forgive his enemies. The squire was so touched that he gave a banquet in his home, and invited the priest and his other enemy. A general reconciliation followed. In St. Pompain, eventually, everybody forgave everybody else. And the priest changed his way of life. He tells his story this way:

"I called M. de Montfort to give a mission in my parish, and he brought forth admirable fruit. I alone was untouched by anything he said. Fifteen days passed and my heart was as hard as stone. I was present at the exercises, but it was less with a view to my own conversion than for the sake of the good example to my parishioners. Toward the middle of the mission he preached on mortal sin with a zeal as new as it was extraordinary. The hearts of my people were broken with sorrow, while my heart seemed to harden more and more. My conversion, however, was not far off, for, at the end of the sermon I heard, all of a sudden, a penetrating voice which seemed to come from the bottom of the church. It was the voice of Brother Jacques singing 'I have lost my God'!

This was one of St. Louis' most simple "cantiques."

Through my sins I have lost my God!
Ah, how my soul is stirred!

210

My heart, so cold and soiled,
Now seethes with a fierce remorse.

"For my poor heart," Fr. Mulot continues, "this was like the blow of a hammer. The more he sang, the more my heart was broken. Before he had ended—

My heart is choked with sorrow,
And I beg You, Lord, for peace.
And I make You a solemn promise,
Never to hurt You again.—

"Before he had ended, I had thrown myself, my eyes washed with tears, and no longer master of my sobs, at the feet of de Montfort who was gracious enough to hear my general confession."

As at every other mission, Louis raised up a number of Saintlings to continue his work in the parish. It was not enough to leave just a cross, or a Calvary. There must also be an association of some kind—such as the Soldiers of St. Michael, the Friends of the Cross, the Confraternity of the Rosary, the League of Virgins—to keep the memory of the mission alive and vigorous.

In St. Pompain, he fused thirty-three men into a group. They called themselves the Penitents. He arranged a special treat for them, a pilgrimage to the shrine of Our Lady of Ardilliers at Saumur. They were to ask God to send good missionaries to the Church, through the intercession of Mary—men who might walk "in the footsteps of the Apostles, by an abandonment to Divine Providence." These missionaries were to be placed, by the prayers of the Penitents under the protection of Our Lady. And they were to be endowed, by Wisdom, with virtues they must practice and not merely preach.

He gave the thirty-three a set of rules and regulations, going into minute details as to how they should act, and what they should do. They were to walk in a "religious silence" most of the way, but were also to pray aloud as well as silently; and they were advised to sing hymns. They were to carry Rosaries and crucifixes. They were to say the beads at certain hours, to be silent at certain hours, to rise at certain hours, to go to Mass at any hour set for it by priests along the way, to eat at certain hours, and to retire at certain hours in the various inns where they might stop.

They were to go fasting and on foot. Fifteen minutes before reaching the city of Saumur, they were to take off their shoes and walk ahead singing hymns to Mary. Two by two they were to enter the chapel, still singing—unless Mass was being offered. In that case they were to wait. All of them were to go to Confession in the chapel, and to Communion at the Mass.

They were to go in procession, two by two, through the city; and must not "trouble themselves" at anything ungodly people might do or say. On their return they were to give an account of all the crosses they had had to carry. Then a "special Mass of thanksgiving" would be said for them.

Louis sent his two disciples—his entire "Company of Mary"—with the Penitents.

"The penitents," says one chronicler, "and the two priests, kept faithfully to the rule and walked their twenty miles a day in the severe cold. One, who was old and sick, followed the others on horseback, but he dismounted from time to time and offered his mount to the weariest. Many people came out to meet them. At Thouars, on its river-encircled hill, the Curé of St. Jean received them at the door of his church and spoke to them of the penance of the Ninivites. After three days, they reached Saumur, where the inhabitants crowded to doors and windows to see them pass . . . The return journey to St. Pompain also took three days, and was closed by the Benediction of the Blessed Sacrament."

Throughout the week, Louis had been preparing to make this pilgrimage himself, his last pilgrimage—"the consecration, as it were, of his whole pilgrimage on earth."

"When he had first knelt before the picture of Our Lady with the body of her dead Son in her arms," says the Secular Priest, "the flush of health and youth and vigor was on his cheek, and he was going forth, under her banner, and with her blessing, to spend his life and to be spent in the service of her Son. When he knelt there after his return from Rome he was in the flower of manhood . . . Now the beauty of his manhood was faded and gone, and the vigor of his strong frame had passed away . . ."

It was still cold when Louis set out, with some of the Brothers, and there was deep snow on the road . . . a long white carpet to the home of his beloved!

He had walked this road many times before; but not in winter.

Once in a while he had been able to rest—and listen, perhaps, to a woodpecker tapping out a code message which his heart could easily read, because it beat in rhythm. "Thank You, God, for wing and claw

212

and belly and long hard bill, and for these delicious and enriching grubs I found in the rotting wood."

Sometimes a man could sit on a rock and watch a butterfly, and think of Christ coming out of the tomb, alive and resplendent, even as that worm had come alive and glorious out of his cocoon.

Sometimes a man could stop and regard the girth of a great tree, one that was old before he was born, and would be alive and vigorous when he was dead.

But now there was nothing to see but snow and ice; and sometimes the snow was blinding. But even as he prayed or sang, he could look at the snow that fell on his hands—the hands that held the crucifix—staff and the statue of Our Lady—and see, in the frosty filigree of each snow flake, the beauty and the love and the power and the tenderness of God, as he had in the Spring wild flowers, in the trees, the birds and the beasts, and in the people, as he plodded along in the dust, or the rain, in the sun, or beneath the blossoming stars.

"One last prayer he had come to offer through Mary. One last thing he had come to ask, not for himself, but for her . . . For the last time the burning words went up to the throne: 'Lord Jesus, be mindful to give your mother children, servants, slaves; otherwise I die. It is for her I ask. Be mindful of her womb and of her breasts, and do not refuse. Remember You are her Son, and hear me. Fulfill my prayers. Holy Spirit, beget and form children of God with Mary Your faithful spouse' . . . And now dismiss Your servant Lord, in peace; for my eyes have seen your salvation."

He had walked sixty miles and more—carrying how many little Crosses!—to show his Lady how much he loved her, how much he needed her. He would have to walk sixty-odd miles back, through snow and ice and bitter winds. But he didn't feel he should walk the few miles to the Abbey of Fontevrault, to see his sister. He wanted to see her. Indeed he did. Family ties were still strong in him. He wanted to talk to her about their father, who had died on Jan. 21st. But he must use the gold of his days, not for the family, but for God. He had promised to preach a mission at St. Laurent-sur-Sèvre, that was his Father's business; and he must be about it.

26   His Last Mission

Spring had come to St. Laurent-sur-Sèvre. The world that had been so dazzling white, had acquired a pale green look. The sky was an April blue, and the river that washed the foot of the hills was trying to look like the sky. The birds had come back. Wild flowers were scampering everywhere, joyous and unrestrained. Bees freighted with life-giving pollen, were visiting the maiden buds and seeds, trading their wares for honey and nectar and wax. And priests were everywhere, reversing the role of the bees, giving the honey of heaven to hordes of sinners.

The beggars were back too, lured by the memory of Father de Montfort's savory soup. Every day an enormous cauldron was prepared, and it was ladled out to them in the church. Thus they were given the privilege of hearing the saint preach while they waited in line for their bowls, and while they ate their dinner.

"Many beggars," says Father Bolger, "attended daily instructions, simply, at first, to obtain the soup . . . but they could not listen for long to the preaching of a saint without being in some way affected by it. Before long the people . . . began to notice a remarkable difference in the beggars; they no longer blasphemed. And great was the local astonishment when it became known that they had built themselves an oratory, where, every evening, they recited the Rosary."

The rains came and washed and dressed the city, "the holy city of La Vendée," and its valley and its hills. Beauty and joy and life came back to the world. And it was time for St. Louis Marie to die.

He arrived in the city on the first day of April, 1716, and chose a small inn for himself, the two Fathers Mulot, several other priests, and a few lay brothers. The inn was known as The Greek Oak, according to Fr. Wilfred Jukka, S.M.M.

It took its name from a remarkable oak tree that had been trained to grow alongside the house, much the same way that ivy grows. The inn

215

survives, as does the oak, though now with the extra girth that 250 years puts on oak trees. Separated from the inn by a small courtyard was a single-storey series of small rooms, perhaps eight in all, which were used to lodge those guests who wished to stay the night. Father de Montfort probably hired the whole small block for the duration of the mission, and he chose for himself the only room with a door onto the little side lane running alongside.

"It was important that people should have free access to his room, without having to go through the courtyard . . . The fact that it was also the smallest and most inconvenient room, may have been an added attraction for him. (In 1720, his spiritual daughters . . . bought a house almost opposite the place where their father died. In 1721, his spiritual sons bought the inn, including the room where the saint had died. In 1722, priests and nuns exchanged residences. Almost immediately the nuns began to build extensions. Fortunately they did not destroy either the inn or the adjacent rooms . . . In the course of time, they blocked the doorway giving access to the saint's room, though, by a happy chance, the work was done so badly that the outline of the door is clearly visible from the street . . . The Greek Oak became the nucleus of the mother house of the Montfort Sisters)."

While he was making preparations for the mission, Louis concerned himself with other missionary activities. He was especially interested in the future of his hospital at Nantes, and the characters of the women who would be chosen to take care of them. To the superior of this hospital, early in April, he wrote a long letter of instructions and advice. Those she chose to nurse the incurables might be intelligent or stupid. It didn't matter, so long as they had charity, so long as they trusted solely on the providence of God. It didn't matter how rich or poor they might be, so long as they faithfully obeyed the rules. It didn't matter how efficient or inefficient they might be, so long as they learned to suffer joyously "all kinds of crosses."

"This house," he wrote, "is the house of the cross . . . and the first thing to be done is to erect a cross in the house . . . in order to acquire the name and grace and glory of the cross for ever."

He realized how rare were the nurses he must have for these poor sufferers. "O my God, how few maidens there are, obedient, silent, prudent, crucified! Everyone is self-sufficient in her heart, or at least in her head."

He said that he might visit her, on May 5th, unless the Bishop of Nantes should forbid his venturing back into that diocese.

216

He would like to visit the city again, he said, if only to obtain a little rest after the completion of this mission. But he was afraid he would lose "the infinite treasure" of saying Mass every morning. He had written the bishop, asking for permission; but he seemed to be sure the bishop would again say "No."

But he reminded the director, if he didn't visit her, things would "go infinitely better."

When a house had been placed under the management of Mary, it had no need for him, he felt.

He had predicted he would die within the year, but evidently he expected to be alive—and able to walk to Nantes—on May 5th. In his letter to Sister Marie Louise, written a week later, however, one senses that he realized his end was very close. He sees the cross so clearly.

"It has been stained, the divine and adorable cross—it has been stained, empurpled by the blood of God. It has been chosen out of all created things, the sole spouse of His heart, the sole end of His labors, the sole weapon of His arm, the sole sceptre of His empire, the sole crown of His glory, and the sole companion of His judgment. And yet, O incomprehensible decree of God!, this cross was cast down with contempt and horror, and was hidden and forgotten in the earth for four hundred years!"

The mission, the last mission of his life, opened on Palm Sunday, April 5th. Louis, waiting in a side chapel until it would be time for him to preach, saw the procession coming to the church. As the leaders filed in for Mass, he stepped forward, took the heavy cross from the husky young man who bore it, put it on his shoulder, and carried it through the aisles to the altar.

It was, for him, a remarkably strange mission. Nobody insulted him. Nobody heckled him. And no bishop harassed him.

It may have been that mission that gave us the legend of the happy altar boy. The child has no name. He has no age. It is possible he existed only in some story-teller's fancy. But he lives "happily ever after" in the story of St. Louis.

The priest was late for Mass this particular morning, and the altar boy was concerned for him. The poor Father was so sick and so weak! Maybe he was too weak and too sick to celebrate mass. The lad went, therefore, to the wretched "Providence" where the priest lived. (Louis always called each temporary residence his Providence.) He looked through the window, or through the partly opened door. And he saw a beautiful and shining lady talking to the priest. He waited until the

217

heavenly conversation had ended, then accompanied the saint to the church and served his Mass. Afterwards he talked about the Lady.

Louis blessed him with a smile. "You are a happy boy," he said. "Only the pure of heart may see that Lady."

According to the legend, the boy lived only a short time after the event. Then, as one writer put it, "he went to live in Paradise with the angels and the innocents of God," and with the shining Lady.

The story may or may not have had some basis in fact. There were many people, men, women, and children, who claimed to have seen Louis talking to the Blessed Virgin—or to have seen his face lighted up as though he were talking to her.

Louis had established his group of Penitents and Virgins—women who consecrated themselves to Chastity for one year—and was planning a large Calvary—when he heard that his bishop, The Most Rev. M. de Champflour, was coming to bless the mission.

He was so excited about this joyous, and most unusual, occurrence that he over-exerted himself. He immediately organized a procession of welcome, which was to go into the town and bring the bishop to the church; and he intended to lead it. But he could hardly move. He had to lie down.

Within a few hours he knew that he was sick, and that he might die of that sickness. He had arranged for a reception and dinner for the bishop. He could attend neither affair. And he had arranged to preach that afternoon.

"But you mustn't get out of bed," young Father Mulot protested. "This looks like pleurisy. It would be madness to take the pulpit now. It might kill you, Father."

Life or death, Father de Montfort knew, was in the hands of God. But, it seemed to him, it was the will of God that he should preach this afternoon, in the bishop's presence. His enemies would take advantage of his illness. They would say he feigned the sudden attack because he was afraid of what the bishop would say about his preaching. They would spread the news, far and wide, that Father de Montfort was a heretic and a coward—a man who dared not let his own bishop hear his ideas about God, about Wisdom, and especially about the Blessed Virgin.

By sheer force of will he got out of bed, dressed, and dragged himself to the pulpit.

Rigault is the only one of all Louis Marie's biographers who portrays him as a preacher.

218

"Behold him in the pulpit," he writes. "A striking figure. One always felt oneself in the presence of an ascetic, even when the smiling lips were saying pleasant things. But from the pulpit he shines with dominating force. Those eyes, which look alternately at the tabernacle and the crowd, have an amazing brilliancy. The long face framed by flowing black hair, the wide mouth, the aquiline nose, the flaming glance, who has not seen such a face upon the battlefield?

"He was like Condé, with his powerful, irresistible ugliness. God seems to use the same mould for certain great men.

"But there was a gentleness in that eagle face, for the war which he was carrying on with such energy and strategy was to lead to true peace. He never terrified his audience; the only alarm for them was his departure, when he would order his volunteers to take the cross upon their shoulders. With him they came out of darkness into the light . . . M. Henri Brémond adds a singularly powerful commentary; 'This great missioner must have been one of the most irresistible orators the world has ever heard . . . Even today, he being dead yet speaketh, still touches us and almost takes away our breath!' "

On this April day Louis was still the eagle, but a dying eagle, and everybody in the church was aware of this; and hoped he would finish his sermon before he died. He spoke of the gentleness of Jesus, His tenderness even to Judas. And he spoke, of course, of Mary.

When he left the pulpit, he went directly back to his bed. Father Mulot had removed the straw, and the rock-pillow, and had placed a mattress for him. Louis thought this was a touch of luxury that should not be given him; but, since it came from the priest he had chosen as his confessor and spiritual guide, he could not refuse it.

He asked Father Mulot to give him the last rites of the Church. And he went happily to sleep when he was anointed. A few days later he made his will. He didn't have much to give away. A little furniture. A few books. His statues. A few banners. Some properties donated to his Daughters and his Sons. Whatever remained in "the common purse." He wanted to be buried in the church yard, and he wanted his heart to be placed "under the step of the altar of the Blessed Virgin."

He died the next day, April 28, 1716, peacefully, the indulgenced crucifix in his right hand, the statue of his Lady in the other—both of which he had kissed repeatedly during the last few days.

Young Father Mulot, who scarcely left his bedside, tried to "console" him. But Louis, needing no consolation, consoled Father Mulot —and instructed him in what he must do for the Company of Mary.

219

The boyish priest dwelt humbly on his weakness of body, his lack of wit, his inexperience, and his fears at all the responsibility Louis was thrusting on him.

"Don't worry," Louis assured him again and again. "I will pray for you. Have confidence in me."

It was a frightening experience for Father Mulot. A short time ago he had been a paralytic. He had had constant headaches. He had never had any great confidence in himself. Now he had none at all.

He could not preach. He had never tried to preach, had never even thought of being a preacher. Now he would not only have to preach; he would have to teach others, his superiors in mind and body, to do all the things missionaries must do. It was true that he had only one priest to teach right now, Father Vatel, but he was sure God would send many others.

The dying man's prayers assured him of that. He would be in charge of them! He would also be in full charge of the women, the nuns, the Daughters of Wisdom! God help him, what a mess he was going to make of everything!

Father M'Geoy, in his book, tells what happened to him.

"Like the hidden manuscript, 'True Devotion,' that lay for years concealed from the eyes of men until the time had come for its discovery . . . so the little Company of Mary and the Daughters of Wisdom were to live their lives hidden and unknown until it was God's will to reveal their destiny . . . Toward the end of Lent, 1718, the Curé of Loges invited Father Mulot and Vatel to come and labor in his parish. They were under the impression that the invitation extended only to the duty of hearing confessions, and they joyfully consented. To their great astonishment, when they arrived, they learned that the Curé had announced to his parishioners that a regular mission was to be opened by the successors of Father de Montfort!

"Filled with consternation at the prospect placed before them, they decided to decline the task. The Curé, however, insisted; they were forced to yield. They had made no preparations, were not trained in preaching, and had not the wealth of words that go to make up the orator, but with a humble and confident reliance on God, and the intercession of their late superior, they essayed their first attempt as missioners.

"The effect was startling in its success. It may be judged from the words of M. d'Hillerin, a dignitary of the Cathedral of La Rochelle;— 'There was nothing vehement in the tone or action of the preacher (Father Mulot). The truths of which he spoke were not always those which were striking in themselves. Even when he used most action there was not that arrangement or those touches of eloquence of which Christian orators make use to stir the human heart; and yet the effect upon his audience was almost marvelous. It was not simply sighs, accompanied by tears, but a terrible burst of cries and sobs, which rose from all sides, and which showed how strong was the impression made by the missionary on all alike, without distinction, who listened to him! After this significant event there was no longer any doubt that de Montfort's spirit was with them, and all united in regarding M. Mulot as his successor.' "

There are no reports that anyone saw Louis Marie talking to Our Lady while he lay there in the inn waiting to die. But no one can doubt that she was present. The room was alive with his prayers.

"Hail Mary full of Grace . . ."

Had he not written—"You never think of Mary without Mary's thinking of God. Mary lives only in relation to God, whose echo she is, the echo that says and repeats only 'God!' If you say 'Mary,' she says 'God.' St. Elizabeth praised Mary and called her blessed; and Mary, in answer, sang the Magnificat, 'My soul doth magnify the Lord.' "

Scores of people tried to elbow or shoulder their way into his dark little room on the last day; but the place was already full; and everyone was sobbing, even as they prayed. Every little while someone wailed and asked for a blessing; and Louis gestured with the crucifix. He tried to console them, but could not. He even sang them verses of hymns he had written:

> Let's go, dear friends, let's go.
> Let's go to Paradise.
> Whatever we've gained on earth—
> There's more in Paradise.

Sometimes he talked to the devil, not in his sleep, but wide awake, pitying him, deriding him, defying him. He once said he was between Mary and Jesus, and he was safe; he had finished his course and would never sin again.

> Be quiet, misleading earth,
> I trample your glory underfoot.
> Jesus, mighty conqueror,
> Sing victory over me.
>> Love!

Live in my heart, Jesus,
Live in my heart, Mary.
Let no one speak to me
Of other love than Love.

Love!

Jesus is my love
Night and day;
Mary is my love;
Night and day.

God alone.

In short, St. Louis Marie, who had happily suffered so many crosses in his life, enjoyed a happy death.

It might be said of him as it was said of his altar boy, "he went to live in Paradise with the angels and the innocents of God"—and the Shining Lady.

He did not go alone. St. John Bosco once said that a priest takes many with him, to heaven or to hell.

He left two extremely small religious Orders orphans. There were four Daughters of Wisdom, two priests in the Company of Mary, and six or seven lay brothers. But those Orders have expanded widely in the years that have gone by; surviving many crises, such as the French Revolution, during which 9 priests and two brothers were martyred. After the Terror had passed there were only five priests and two brothers left.

"The Lord," says the secular priest, "had shown Louis, in a vision, how the Daughters of Wisdom would multiply exceedingly . . . Had he shown him the 39 houses founded in poverty under the direction of his successor . . . before Sister Marie Louise of Jesus died . . . at the same hour, on the same day of the same month . . . to be laid by his side in the little chapel of St. Laurent? Had he shown him their cruel persecutions at the hands of those who had persecuted him . . . We do not know."

We do know that the Daughters of Wisdom have grown enormously in numbers; and that the Montfort Missionaries, as the Company of Mary is now called, are missionaries to all the world; and that a worldwide community of teaching Brothers, known as the Brothers of St. Gabriel, also claim St. Louis de Montfort for their Spiritual Father.

And we do know that St. Louis Marie de Montfort, Mary's slave of slaves, and Wisdom's fool of fools, could do for this generation and the next, and the next, what he did for the people of Brittany if we let him.

222

CHRONOLOGICAL OUTLINE OF DE MONTFORT'S LIFE

1673
January 31   His birth at Montfort-La-Cane
February 1   Baptism in church of Saint-Jean
1675-1685   At Bois-Marquer in Iffendic
1685-1693   Studies at College of St. Thomas a Becket, in
                  Rennes
1693 (autumn) Trip from Rennes to Paris
1693-1694   Resident at M. de la Barmondière
1694 (autumn) Resident at M. Boucher
1695-1700   Resident at the "Petit Seminaire" of St. Sulpice
1697   Becomes acquainted with Madam de Montespan
End of 1697
or beginning
of 1698   Ordained a Sub-Deacon
1699   Pilgrimage to Our Lady of Chartres
1700
June 5   Ordained to the Priesthood
October   Arrives at Nantes
Winter of 1700-
1701   Remains inactive at M. Lévêque's
1701
April 25-27   Trip from Nantes to Fontevrault
April 29-May 1   Trip from Fontevrault to Poitiers
June-Sept.   Missions at Grandchamps and surrounding areas
October   Trip from Nantes to Poitiers
End of Nov.   Becomes chaplain at General Hospital, there
                  meets Marie-Louise Trichet

1702
summer   Trip to Paris
Oct.-Easter
1703   Ministry at Hospital, Poitiers

223

Wisdom's Fool

1703	
February 2	Marie-Louise Trichet receives Religious Habit
spring	Trip to Paris. Ministry at la Salpêtrière. Visits with Poullard-des-Places
summer-autumn	At Rue du Pot-de-Fer
winter	Among the hermits of Mount-Valérien
1704	
March	Returns to Hospital at Poitiers
1705	Final break with Hospital. Missions at Montbernage, Saint-Savin and Calvaire Meets Mathurin Rangeard (Brother Mathurin)
1706	
Jan.-Feb.	Mission at Saint Saturnin
spring	Pilgrimage to Rome, via Loreto
June	Audience with Pope Clement XI
Aug. (end)	Returns to Poitiers
Sept. 29	Visits Mount St. Michel
Oct.	Stay at Rennes and visit to his home territory
end of year	Missions at Dinan, St. Suliac and Bécherel
1707	Member of M. Leuduger's Mission Band.
spring-summer	Missions in the dioceses of St. Malo and St. Brieuc.
July	Mission at Montfort-La-Cane
August	Mission at Moncontour Parts company with M. Leuduger
Sept.	Stay at the hermitage of St. Lazare
1708	
May	Missions and Retreats in the area
mid-year	Returns to the area of Nantes. Mission at St. Similien
end-of-summer	Mission at Valet
autumn	Missions at: La Renaudière, Landemont, La Chevrolière, Vertou
December	Mission at St. Fiacre
1709	
January	Retreat to Penitents (women)
Lent	Mission at Campbon
Apr.-May	Mission at Pontchâteau
summer	Missions in Grande-Brière region Begins construction on Calvary

224

November	Mission at Missillac
1710	
early part	Missions at Herbignac, Camoël
May-June	Mission at St. Donatien of Nantes
July	Mission at Bouguenais
Sept. 13	Interdict on blessing of Calvary
end of Sept.	Mission at St. Molf. Forbidden to exercise his ministry
Nov. 10	Joins 3rd Order of St. Dominic
1711	
early part	Leaves Nantes
Lent	Mission at La Garnache
May-Aug.	Missions at Lhoumeau and La Rochelle
winter of	
1711-12	Missions in the country places of the diocese of La Rochelle
1712	
Lent	Mission at the Island of Yeu
May	Mission at Sallertaine
June	Mission at St. Christophe-du-Ligneron
July	Second Mission at La Garnache
October	Mission at Thairé-d'Aunis
1712-13	Missions at St. Vivien, Esnandes, Courçon
1713	
spring	Missions at Beugnon, Bressuire, Argenton-Chateau
May-June	Mission at La Séguinière
July	Trip from La Rochelle to Paris
August	Visits Holy Ghost Seminary in Paris
Aug.-Sept.	Mission at Mauzé
winter (1713)	Second Mission at Courçon
1714	
spring	Missions in the diocese of Saintes
May	Mission at Roussay
June	Trip to Nantes
Aug. 15th	At Villedieu-les-Poêles, diocese of Avranches
Aug.-Sept.	Mission at St. Lô
mid-Sept.	Meeting with Canon Blain at Rouen
	Retreat to Sisters at Ernemont
October	Return to Nantes—Trip to Rennes

Wisdom's Fool

November	Return to La Rochelle
December	Missions at Loiré, Le Breuil-Magné, the Island of Aix, St. Laurent-de-la-Prée, Fouras
1715	
February	Meeting with M. Vatel
March-April	Mission at Taugon-la-Ronde
end of March	Arrival of Marie-Louise Trichet and Catherine Brunet at La Rochelle
April	Mission at St. Amand-sur-Sèvre
May-June	Mission at Mervent and his stay in the grotto
August-Sept.	Mission at Fontenay-le-Comte
Sept.-Oct.	At the grotto of Mervent
	Vocation of M. Mulot
autumn	Mission at Vouvant
Dec.-Jan. 1716	Mission at St. Pompain
1716	
February	Mission at Villiers-en-Plaine
March	Pilgrimage to Our Lady of Ardilliers of Saumur by the 33 "Penitents" of St. Pompain
April 1	Arrives at St. Laurent-sur-Sèvre
April 5	Opening of Mission at St. Laurent
April 28	Death of Father de Montfort
1838	Declared "Venerable" by Pope Gregory XVI
1869	
Sept. 29	Pius IX proclaimed his virtues heroic
1888	
Jan. 22	Beatified by Pope Leo XIII
1947	
July 20	Canonized by Pope Pius XII

WRITINGS OF ST. LOUIS-MARIE GRIGNION DE MONTFORT

Letters
The Love of Eternal Wisdom
Letter to the Friends of the Cross
The Admirable Secret of the Rosary
Various ways to recite the Rosary
The Secret of Mary
Treatise on True Devotion to Mary
Prayer for Missionaries
Rule for the missionary priests of the Company of Mary
Exhortation to the Members of the Company of Mary
The Wisdom Cross of Poitiers
Original rule for the Daughters of Wisdom
Maxims and lessons of Divine Wisdom
Letter to the townspeople of Montbernage
Rules for the Association of the "Forty-Four Virgins"
Rules for the Association of the "White Penitents"
The holy Pilgrimage of the Penitents to the shrine of Our Lady of
    Saumur to obtain from God good missionaries
Covenant with God (Renewal of Baptismal vows)
His Last Will and Testament
Little Crown of the Blessed Virgin (prayer)
Night Prayers
Hymns (24,000 verses)
Note books
Rules of the Voluntary Poverty of the Early Church
Summary of Four Meditations on Religious Life
Book of Sermons
Dispositions for a Happy Death

1987 Second printing

5000

Design: J. Harding